The
TECHNOLOGY COORDINATOR'S
HANDBOOK Fourth Edition

A Guide for Edtech Facilitators and Leaders

Max Frazier & Doug Hearrington

International Society for Technology in Education

ARLINGTON, VIRGINIA

The Technology Coordinator's Handbook, Fourth Edition
A Guide for Edtech Facilitators and Leaders
Max Frazier and Doug Hearrington

Director of Books and Journals: *Emily Reed*
Senior Acquisitions Editor: *Valerie Witte*
Copy Editor: *Courtney Burkholder*
Proofreader: *Emily Padgett*
Indexer: *Kento Ikeda*
Book Design and Production: *Kim McGovern*
Cover Design: *Eddie Ouellette*

Library of Congress Cataloging-in-Publication Data
Names: Frazier, Max, author. | Hearrington, Doug, author.
Title: The technology coordinator's handbook : a guide for edtech facilitators and leaders / Max Frazier and Doug Hearrington.
Description: Fourth edition. | Portland, Oregon ; Arlington, Virginia : International Society for Technology in Education, [2024] | Third edition: 2017. | Includes bibliographical references and index.
Identifiers: LCCN 2023049942 (print) | LCCN 2023049943 (ebook) | ISBN 9781564849830 (paperback) | ISBN 9781564849847 (epub) | ISBN 9781564849854 (pdf)
Subjects: LCSH: Educational technology—Handbooks, manuals, etc. | Technology consultants.
Classification: LCC LB1028.3.F725 2024 (print) | LCC LB1028.3 (ebook) | DDC 371.33—dc23/eng/20231115
LC record available at https://lccn.loc.gov/2023049942
LC ebook record available at https://lccn.loc.gov/2023049943

Fourth Edition
ISBN: 978-1-56484-983-0
Ebook version available

Printed in the United States of America

ISTE® is a registered trademark of the International Society for Technology in Education.

About ISTE

The International Society for Technology in Education (ISTE) is home to a passionate community of global educators who believe in the power of technology to transform teaching and learning, accelerate innovation and solve tough problems in education.

ISTE inspires the creation of solutions and connections that improve opportunities for all learners by delivering practical guidance, evidence-based professional learning, virtual networks, thought-provoking events and the ISTE Standards. ISTE is also the leading publisher of books focused on technology in education. For more information or to become an ISTE member, visit iste.org. Subscribe to ISTE's YouTube channel and connect with ISTE on social media.

About the Authors

Max Frazier spent a 44-year career in Kansas schools. Starting as a middle school classroom teacher in the late 1970s, he went on to positions as an educational technology specialist and a district technology coordinator. Originally trained as a secondary teacher at the University of Kansas, he later earned a doctorate in educational administration and leadership from Kansas State University. He finished his career in 2022 as director of teacher education in Wichita, Kansas. During his time in higher education, he helped to train nearly 100 secondary teachers who now work in schools across the Midwest. In retirement, he lives in Wichita with his wife Nancy and a little white dog named Belle.

Doug Hearrington spent more than a dozen years as a classroom teacher and technology coordinator in Las Vegas area schools, and more than 15 years working in faculty and administrative positions with responsible for online and blended learning and digital learning innovation with universities in three states. He is currently engaged in the leadership and development of professional learning and talent management as a civilian employee of the United States Army in Alabama. He earned his bachelor's degree from San Diego State University and his master's and doctoral degrees from the University of Nevada, Las Vegas. His doctoral areas of focus were educational technology and curriculum and instruction. While a faculty member, he helped educate over 1,000 undergraduate, graduate, and post-graduate students who now work in schools in the Southwest and Southeast. He lives with his wife Joy and daughter Kate near Huntsville, Alabama.

Acknowledgments

Max Frazier: This book would not have been possible without the willingness of the many dedicated and inspiring technology leaders from across the country who agreed to sit for interviews and answer all our questions. A sincere thank you to Anita McAnear, Lynne Schrum, Mark Gall, Leigh Zeitz, and Al Rogers, whose conversations helped me get to know Dave Moursund in preparation for writing the dedication for this book. Thanks always to my patient wife Nancy, whose support got me through another book project. This text would not have been possible without Emily Reed and the rest of the fine folks at ISTE, who have supported my work in so many ways since 2004. Special thanks to my good friends Tom, Gary, and Angelo, who inspired me with conversations about the joys and frustrations of writing and life.

Doug Hearrington: I am indebted to the many technology coordinators who provided needed input for this work. I thank Emily Reed and the entire ISTE publishing team who made this fourth edition possible. I must indirectly acknowledge the many mentors, colleagues, and co-workers who have contributed to my experience, knowledge, and skills over the years everywhere I have worked, with a special mention to my doctoral advisor, Dr. Neal Strudler. Most importantly, I am grateful for my supportive and patient wife Joy, and wonderful daughter Kate, who helped me in this effort. Finally, I would like to thank Dr. Max Frazier for inviting me, again, on this journey with him.

Dedication

The technology coordinator position has become a standard and vital part of the school district leadership team over the past four decades. The position first appeared in the 1980s, when schools began to install and use computers in day-to-day instruction. David Moursund, a professor at the University of Oregon, was the first to describe this important technology leadership position in detail in his 1992 book *The Technology Coordinator*. His text, an early ISTE publication, examined the need for the position and provided a description of the general and technical qualifications necessary for success. Moursund's work inspired the author's research and writing throughout our careers. Without his ideas and pioneering spirit, our work would not have been possible. This fourth edition of our text is dedicated to him.

David Moursund, founder of ISTE, was a pioneer and a visionary leader in the use of computer technology for education. Born and raised in Eugene, Oregon by two University of Oregon (UO) math professors, he earned an undergraduate degree in mathematics from the UO in 1958. His professional studies culminated with masters and PhD degrees in mathematics from the University of Wisconsin at Madison. Following a brief professorship at Michigan State University, Moursund returned to the UO as a professor until his retirement in 2002.

Together with a group of 47 educators, Moursund established the Oregon Council for Computers in Education (OCCE) in 1971. That organization expanded to become the International Council for Computers in Education (ICCE) in 1979. ICCE merged with the International Association for Computers in Education (IACE) in 1989 to form the International Society for Technology in Education (ISTE) with Moursund serving as the chief executive officer and editor-in-chief for ISTE publications. The UO campus building that for many years served as ISTE headquarters was the same building where Moursund attended kindergarten in the 1940s.

Although originally trained as a mathematics and computer science professor, Moursund's interest in using calculators to teach math led him to collaborate with faculty in the College of Education in establishing the nation's second master's degree in computers in education and the first PhD program in that field. During his career, he served on the dissertation committees of more than 75 students who earned doctoral degrees in computers in education. Moursund was also the principal investigator on a series of grants and related contracts with organizations such as the National Science Foundation and the U.S. Department of Education to support summer training institutes for teachers and other research and development activities. These activities attracted educators from around the world who wanted to study with Moursund. Articles written by his students about computer education often appeared in the ICCE/ISTE journal *The Computing Teacher*. One of the main goals for Moursund and his student's work was the development of new methods for helping teachers become comfortable and proficient with technology so they could make a positive impact on students' learning in the classroom.

Following a short illness, Moursund died on September 1, 2021, at the age of 84. His attitude about teaching can be summarized by his own words: "A hundred years from now, it will not matter what my bank account was, the sort of house I lived in, or the kind of car I drove. But the world may be different because I was important in the life of a child." Those interested in learning more about Moursund and his work can find additional resources at the Moursund AGATE Foundation website (moursundagatefoundation.org).

Dave Moursund at the ISTE conference in 2019.

Contents

INTRODUCTION

An Evolving Leadership Position

Technology coordinators have issues. This position, relatively new to school leadership teams, is often tasked with a growing list of responsibilities. The rapid infusion of technology along with the increased demands for technology training and support during the recent pandemic created new challenges for technology leaders. Interviews with technology leaders from across the country revealed that the rapid shift to online learning, quick implementation of one-to-one device programs for all grades, and inconsistent technology skill base of instructional and support staff created many new challenges. Technology leaders shared stories of a variety of challenges faced as they were forced to transition in a matter of weeks or months to an entirely new teaching model. We heard stories of rapid transitions and challenges with equipment, but we also heard about progress, growth, and the promise of better serving students when each of them has their own device to use. The list of issues for technology coordinators is often long, but they have come a long way since the first technology coordinator appeared in schools four decades ago.

As the number of computers in schools has rapidly increased and the use of technology has expanded in a wide variety of ways in the teaching and learning process, it became obvious to administrators that there was a real need for additional resources to manage the newly available educational technology. One of the first steps school districts took was to fund a technology coordinator position, and soon even more support roles were added. Those working in the technology coordinator role assist with the effective implementation of learning technologies in classrooms and administrative technology in school offices. School staff working in technology leadership positions now have a variety of titles, including director, specialist, manager, and others. For the purposes of this text, those who provide leadership in the area of educational technology will be referred to as *technology coordinators*.

The number of technology coordinator positions in school districts increased dramatically during the 1990s, concurrent with the dramatic growth of computer technology in K–12 curricula. Taie and Lewis reported in the NCES report "Characteristics of 2020–21 Public and Private K–12 Schools in the United States" that there were more technology specialists employed in K–12 schools (70,930) than librarians/library media specialists (70,460) (2022). Today almost every school organization has someone working in a technology support or leadership position, even if that person's title is not technology coordinator. As the number of computing devices and technology resources, along with the complexity of computer networking equipment, increased during the 1990s and 2000s, even small districts found it necessary to hire technology coordinators. These early coordinators were expected to provide technical and instructional assistance to teachers and students, plan for long-range integration and implementation of technology, supply professional development programs, prepare budgets, write grants, and even maintain the schools' equipment. More recently, the technology coordinator role went from someone "who blazes a trail for technology in the school or district and understands how all the hardware, software, policies, and procedures fit together in the big picture of the school's or district's technology implementation" to someone "who is able to address the student vision for learning through mobile, online, and digital learning" (Walker, 2015).

Although the number of technology coordinators has increased dramatically, there is often little consistency in titles, responsibilities, and preparation among the positions. This technology expert position is a relatively new addition to central administration. Unlike most school or district leadership positions, educational preparation for these positions varies; in many states, certifications are not a requirement. In a recent survey conducted among New Jersey School Technology coordinators regarding Google/Microsoft Certification/Trainer it was noted that 47% of respondents do not hold any such certification. The formal preparation for technology coordinator administrative positions varies by state and location (McGraw, 2019).

Inconsistencies in preparations and expectations often lead to considerable differences in the way technology coordinators approach their everyday work, provide support, set goals for the organization, and make decisions. Collum (2015) reports that "in 1992 a District Technology Coordinator's duties were approximately 80 percent technical; in 2013 the duties were only 20 percent technical and 80 percent leadership, vision and coordination of the educational environment with technology." There is a need for a clearly defined and commonly shared definition and description of this important leadership position. A better and more consistent understanding of the position by the board of education, administration, and staff will help technology coordinators make better policy and budgetary decisions and lead technology initiatives that are more reliable.

Although many school districts have added technology coordinator positions in recent years, the role of the technology coordinator sometimes lacks clear definition in the district decision-making hierarchy. Some technology coordinators are hired as staff and work on an hourly basis, others work under an extended teacher's contract, and still others are clearly hired as part of the administration and have a place in the district's organizational chart. The technology coordinator is expected to regularly guide technology implementation, yet technology staffers, principals, and district-level administrators often contribute to the decision-making process and influence choices.

Schools have invested billions of dollars in the past forty years to purchase, install, implement, and upgrade educational technology. The recession of 2008 forced school districts across the country to make budget cuts, resulting in a significant reduction in technology investment, as well as in leadership and support positions. Districts were forced to delay purchases, reduce support staff, and, in some cases, eliminate technology leadership positions. While these decisions were necessary to meet the near-term budget requirements, the elimination of technology leadership and support positions, as well as the increasing difficulty in making regular investment in equipment replacement and upgrades, made effective planning and support more difficult in the long term. The recent pandemic and the related influx of support dollars to public schools led to significant increases in technology. Schools had to shift to online learning in the spring of 2020, and this shift resulted in a massive acquisition of technology to support the new online learning focus. Bushweller reports that in March of 2020, in response to the pandemic, "the 55,000-student Boston public schools, for instance, purchased 20,000 new laptops in March to try to make sure that all students in the district had access to learning during the school building closures" (2020). During this period, schools made significant investment in technology resources. According to Cutts,"the 1:1 device to student movement has swept across the nation at a rapid pace, putting a Chromebook or similar device in the hands of every student not only during the school day, but at home as well" (2019). That trend has continued and intensified since the pandemic.

Even so, only a limited number of teacher training or educational leadership programs around the country focus specifically on preparing candidates to become school or district technology leaders. Currently, only a few states—examples exist in Pennsylvania, Wisconsin, Illinois, New York, and North Carolina—have established clear licensing requirements for the training of technology coordinators, and certification programs for those who aspire to work in this position. Some states are only now in the process of training and certifying technology coordinators planning to work at the district level. Other states have yet to develop and implement programs to certify those who aspire to serve in this increasingly important district leadership position. The recent pandemic-related influx of both technology and related hiring of staff to support those resources will likely influence training and licensing requirements.

ISTE has been instrumental in helping to establish standards at the national level for students, teachers, school administrators, and technology coaches. The most recent update to the student standards was released in 2016, and the teacher standards update was published in 2017. The ISTE technology standards for school administrators were refreshed in 2018, while the standards for technology coaches were released in 2019. Since they began publishing standards in 1998 with the initial release of the first student standards, ISTE has made a commitment to continually revise and refresh these standards to provide important leadership and support to the educational community. These standards are important guides for those who aspire to work as technology leaders and facilitators both at the school and the district level. More information about the standards documents for various audiences, along with useful tools and resources, can be found in the Standards section of the ISTE website (iste.org/standards).

This handbook was developed specifically to address the lack of resources about the technology coordinator position. We hope that this handbook will inform and guide the work of technology leaders and assist those interested in serving as a school or district technology coordinator with the information necessary to provide effective leadership and make good decisions. With the help of this handbook, all stakeholders can more clearly understand the differing roles, requirements, and unique demands of the technology coordinator position. Specifically, technology coordinators can use this handbook to become better prepared and have a more complete understanding of their position. In doing so, they can become more effective learners and leaders who are capable of assisting students, teachers, staff, and administration in the use of educational technology. Education leaders can also use this handbook to effect the institutional changes needed in order to make full use of the technology now available to K–12 schools.

Wearing Many Hats

To provide the necessary technology leadership for a school or district, a technology coordinator must be comfortable wearing many hats. First and foremost, a technology coordinator must establish and articulate a vision for the use of technology in a school or district and develop a plan for successfully carrying out that vision. This vision must encompass four areas: development and implementation of appropriate technology policies; acquisition, monitoring, and maintenance of technology; planning and conducting an effective professional development program; and providing technical support for all end users.

The technology coordinator must employ a variety of leadership skills to implement this vision. These skills include the ability to communicate effectively with various constituent groups, to work with diverse groups and interests to effectively solve different types of problems, and to deal with changing technical issues related to devices and other hardware.

An effective technology coordinator must have the skills to carry out a wide variety of tasks such as:

- Communicating the organization's vision for technology

- Designing and conducting effective professional development programs and other training sessions for various audiences

- Developing appropriate and effective policies and establishing plans for both the short and long term

- Working with teachers and students to model the effective use of technology in learning

- Guiding purchasing decisions

- Assisting teachers with the effective integration of technology in the classroom

- Planning for and working with a variety of network structures and services

- Fulfilling the data and reporting needs of administrators

- Coordinating end-user technical support

Teaching and learning are at the heart of all educational organizations and must be a primary focus of the technology coordinator. The coordinator must work with both teachers and administrators to provide appropriate instructional technology resources for use in the classroom, and then help teachers understand and use these new and exciting resources to enhance student learning. The coordinator will be responsible for collecting and sharing information with staff regarding current research and best practices. By effectively managing these instructional technology tools and resources for the school or district, the technology coordinator can help to create an effective technology vision, aligned with the district mission, that can have a direct and lasting impact on student learning.

Providing end users with timely and appropriate technical support is another important responsibility of the technology coordinator. Any organization that hopes to implement technology successfully must be prepared to provide users with technical support when equipment fails or there are other problems. To help minimize user frustration, the technology coordinator must establish effective procedures for providing timely assistance and must establish and maintain a system for reporting, documenting, and repairing equipment.

The technology coordinator is also responsible for ensuring that software licenses and application installations are current and problem-free. They must also ensure that appropriate network and device protection measures are in place to defend against viruses, spam, malware, and outside intrusion. The technology coordinator must work with school or district administrators to create appropriate and timely plans for the regular maintenance, upgrade, and replacement of existing technology resources as equipment becomes outdated or otherwise inadequate. By successfully addressing each of these issues, the coordinator can ensure that end users will be able to effectively make use of their school or district's technology resources with a minimum of frustration and difficulty.

The school or district network plays a vital part in connecting classrooms, offices, and support services for purposes of communication, data storage, and sharing of information. Consequently, the technology coordinator must play a role in planning, implementing, and supporting network operations to ensure that a school or district has the infrastructure necessary to achieve the goals of its technology plan. The technology coordinator works closely with network administrators to manage user accounts, maintain and support the district email system, provide internet access, protect users from electronic intrusions and attacks, and train users to utilize technology resources appropriately. By successfully carrying out these responsibilities, the technology coordinator can help ensure that the network operates smoothly and with a minimum amount of downtime, and that users will gain the maximum utility from available network resources.

Another major role for the technology coordinator is overseeing the administrative computing operations of a school or district. A successful school organization must be able to plan, implement, and manage a variety of application and database structures to support management of student information and processing of grades; storage and management of human resources information, purchasing, and inventory records; and other academic and business-related information. The technology coordinator should be prepared to assist with the management of a robust information processing system that is capable of handling current needs and that has the capability to grow and expand to meet the future needs of the organization. In addition to planning and implementation, the technology coordinator will be expected to train and assist users of these systems to ensure that district employees can carry out the many tasks necessary to manage the business functions of the organization.

To be successful in these important roles, it is essential that the technology coordinator be skilled in budgeting and planning. The technology coordinator typically has primary responsibility for developing and supervising the school or district's technology plan. They are also responsible for working with other district staff and administration to promote a shared vision for the use of technology. For these reasons, the technology coordinator must work with various constituent groups to develop the budgetary support for this shared vision and evaluate the success of the plan over time. The technology coordinator is also often expected to help identify and secure supplemental resources, such as grants and E-Rate funding. By helping to establish and implement an effective technology plan that includes working with executive administration and the board of education to ensure the necessary budgetary support, the technology coordinator can help in carrying out the most effective implementation of technology resources for teaching, learning, and business functions.

Organization of This Handbook

This handbook is organized around the Technology Coordinator Issues Model (TCIM). The model identifies seven areas of essential concern for schools and districts of all sizes that most technology coordinators must address (Figure 1.1).

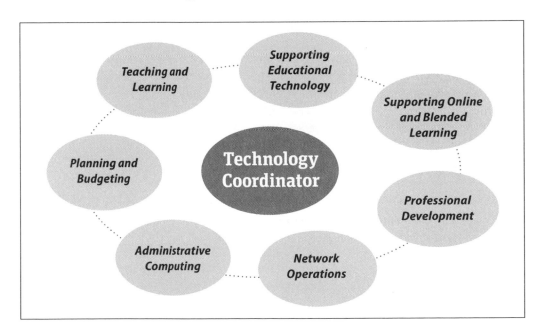

Figure 1.1. Technology Coordinator Issues Model.

The seven areas of essential concern identified in the model can be described as follows:

1. **Teaching and Learning:** The integration of technology into the classroom to enhance and enrich the learning process.

2. **Supporting Educational Technology:** The technical and instructional support required by users of classroom technology resources throughout the organization.

3. **Supporting Online and Blended Learning:** The technical and instructional support necessary to provide fully online learning experiences, along with experiences that pair traditional instruction with online learning.

4. **Professional Development:** Providing the training and instructional support necessary for teachers, staff, and students to maximize the successful use of technology in teaching, learning, and other school functions.

5. **Network Operations:** The infrastructure and equipment that make electronic communication and access to the internet possible through local- and wide-area networks and other telecommunication services.

6. **Administrative Computing:** The devices and software programs that support the administrative and business functions of the organization.

7. **Planning and Budgeting:** The financial planning and decision making required to carry out and support the school or district's technology objectives.

Within each of these general areas, the technology coordinator must understand and address specific issues. In the chapters that follow, these issues are discussed in detail, and their importance to the technology coordinator's overall responsibilities is explained.

Additional Resources

In addition to the main text, each chapter contains a variety of resources that will prove useful to technology leaders, helping them make effective decisions. Sections appearing in every chapter include:

Essential Questions. Located at the start of each chapter, these essential questions are designed to help readers fully understand an issue and reach the best solution to a problem.

Answers to Essential Questions. These answers appear toward the end of each chapter and summarize the information discussed.

Tech Leader Profiles. These profiles introduce the reader to a series of established technology leaders from across the U.S. who work in a variety of positions and school organizations. These profiles provide snapshots of the leaders' backgrounds, their school or district, challenges they face in the position, and tips they have for others in similar leadership positions.

Toolbox Tips. Toolbox Tips are concrete recommendations for dealing with specific issues or situations. These techniques are currently used by technology coordinators in the field or are derived from the relevant scholarship.

Professional Development Spotlight. Professional Development Spotlights describe professional development opportunities for technology coordinators or others in the district interested in leadership. These features provide basic information about each opportunity and where to find more information.

Resources. Online Resources include websites, downloadable documents, and other information found online. These resources can help you accomplish important tasks and stay abreast of new developments and techniques in the field of educational technology.

References. The books, journal articles, blogs and other resources used in developing this handbook can help deepen a technology coordinator's understanding in the field.

Appendix A provides sample job descriptions. This handbook also provides a **Glossary** of key terms.

A Guide and a Reference

This handbook is designed to be used as a guide for understanding essential questions and as a model for identifying the wide variety of tasks and responsibilities faced by technology coordinators. It can be read from beginning to end or used as a reference tool to find information on a particular area of interest. Skimming the entire handbook should provide an overview of the issues and responsibilities that make up the technology coordinator position. In-depth reading of a single chapter should provide sufficient background on a particular area of responsibility, such as computer support.

The handbook should also be useful in helping district administrators and board of education members understand the wide range of technology issues and questions that must be addressed to successfully integrate technology into the learning process and other school district operations. Those who do not face the challenge of providing technological support and leadership on a daily basis may lack an in-depth understanding of the technology coordinator's role. The figures, examples, references, and resources of this handbook are intended to be useful in helping anyone understand and address the complex issues of technology implementation and support.

One goal of this handbook is to help focus the discussion in the U.S. regarding licensure standards for the technology coordinator. Although this handbook cannot be viewed as a comprehensive document that addresses all issues faced by technology coordinators, it nonetheless provides an important and useful description of the work performed by the technology coordinator, and serves as a functional reference for those who aspire to, or currently serve in, this important technology leadership position. This handbook is intended to serve as a point of departure in the discussion of important issues and how they should be addressed, in order to provide effective technology leadership for a school organization.

Chapter 1

QUALIFICATIONS AND EXPECTATIONS

Essential Questions

1. What are the major responsibilities the technology coordinator will be expected to assume?

2. What skills, abilities, and attributes will be needed to succeed in the position?

3. What day-to-day operational tasks will the technology coordinator most likely face?

4. How can my school or district select the best candidate for the position of technology coordinator?

Major Responsibilities

As illustrated throughout this book, the technology coordinator plays a major role in the successful use of educational technology in a school or district. These days technology is critical for teaching, learning, communications, record keeping, and most other aspects of the administration of any educational enterprise. The Technology Coordinator Issues Model (TCIM), revised from earlier versions of this work, illustrates the essential areas of concern for any technology coordinator. The model serves to organize the complexity of this critical leadership position while calling attention to its components. These components, or issues, have importance individually and as a part of the larger, integrated model.

The successful technology coordinator must possess a wide range of skills and abilities. The technology coordinator must support and facilitate the integration of technology in teaching and learning, offer professional development, offer technical support for devices and systems, and manage or coordinate with others to ensure effective uses and functionality of digital tools (Strudler & Hearrington, 2009). Technology leaders, including technology coordinators, must help an organization along a path of continuous improvement while keeping the focus on effective instructions, quality curriculum design, and shared decision making. Building on the work of Sugar & Holloman (2009), Walker (2015) describes the nine technology leadership characteristics needed by technology coordinators as "1) Corporate Vision, 2) Development of Others, 3) Facilitating, 4) Servant Leadership, 5) Problem-Solving, 6) Resource Management, 7) School Communications, 8) Student Centeredness, and 9) Systems Thinking." (p. 11). This extensive list provides a glimpse into the complexity of the technology coordinator position. Dexter (2018) is helpful by identifying critical elements of the position and making their commonalities and interactions more apparent by illustrating three broad leadership areas that are key to the work of the technology coordinator:

- Providing leadership to set the direction
- Providing leadership to develop people
- Providing leadership to make the organization work

Webster (2010) also clearly describe the functions of the technology coordinator by distilling their work into three important areas (based in part on the work of McLeod 2003):

- **Technology Support:** Providing access to functional and useful technologies along with the necessary problem-solving assistance for end users

- **Training:** Providing successful professional development based on research-based instructional processes and practices

- **Administration:** Implementing the decision making and strategies to ensure timely technical and instructional support, staffing with full- and part-time dedicated people, and the development of communities of teachers, staff, and students within schools dedicated to helping one other

As illustrated by the two bulleted lists above, the technology coordinator position is a specialized blend of the roles played by teachers, curriculum leaders, administrators, professional developers, and technicians. Additionally, in order to set the direction for the organization, the technology coordinator must know the trends in educational technology in particular and in information technology in general. Additionally, setting the direction requires leadership skills, strategic planning, and interpersonal skills. Setting the direction is an ongoing process, and the uses of technology in schools are in constant flux. Once a direction is set, an effective leader must ensure that functional and useful technologies are available to meet the established goals while providing professional development to all stakeholders according to their need and uses for the technologies. An array of support must be in place to address inevitable unexpected technical issues and to provide ongoing pedagogical training for the use of the technologies. The technology coordinator must be supported by building administrators along with the central office leadership team to assist them in setting the conditions for success of technology coordinators and the technology resources they are asked to support.

Position Description

The position description included here synthesizes information from more than twenty posted job descriptions for technology coordinators responsible for all aspects of technology in a district. For further reference, a collection of sample job descriptions from across the country is included in Appendix A. The position title for these leadership roles may be specialist, coordinator, manager, director, or assistant/associate superintendent, depending on the size of the organization served and the placement of the position in the organizational chart. In some school districts, the technology coordinator leads an instructional technology group within the information technology division. In other organizations, you will find information technology as a subordinate division of instructional technology. In still other school districts, there is a single technology coordinator responsible for both instructional and information technologies. Regardless of the job title or position in the school district's organization, the technology coordinator is usually expected to perform a range of duties more or less like the sample position description provided.

Sample Position Description

POSITION TITLE

District Technology Coordinator

DESCRIPTION

Reporting to the superintendent, the technology coordinator provides leadership in the development, implementation, articulation, evaluation, and communication of the district's technology program. Additionally, the technology coordinator supervises a team of technicians, network administrators, a teacher on special assignment who provides professional development and works with schools on pedagogical issues, and an administrative assistant.

ESSENTIAL DUTIES AND RESPONSIBILITIES

- Works closely with district administrators and stakeholders to develop a shared vision for meaningful and effective use of technology and the steps needed to meet the board's strategic plan.

- Develops and maintains a technology budget, both annually and long range. Works with school technology committees, principals, and the superintendent to create the budget. Solicits and develops budget recommendations and oversees purchases and installation/implementation.

- Leads the process of infusion of innovative technologies into the curriculum, instruction, and assessment. Promotes and leads the implementation of best and next practice methodologies, tools, and programs in support of technology for teaching and learning.

- Develops and implements professional learning opportunities for staff that integrate technology into curriculum, instruction, and professional duties in coordination with the director of curriculum and the director of instruction.

- Ensures that a sequential program of studies with supporting curriculum documentation is in place for teaching students the use of computers and educational technology.

- Develops, monitors, evaluates, and reports on the district's technology plan.

- Maintains a working inventory of computer-related equipment and software. Sets standards for the evaluation, selection, and procurement of all hardware and software with input from appropriate stakeholders.

- Designs bid specifications for equipment, hardware, software, and furniture; evaluates bids and selects vendors.

- Creates and implements a preventative maintenance and upgrade plan and program for all hardware and software.

- Plans and oversees all tasks related to technical systems, network infrastructure, and device management.

- Chairs the district technology committee and attends/supports the building technology and library media specialist committees.

- Supervises and evaluates technology staff per district policies and procedures.

- Applies, coordinates, and manages the district's E-Rate program.

- Supervises the implementation and maintenance of the student information system, financial and payroll system, instructional media collection software, food service software, transportation software, and emergency communication system.

- Directs, coordinates, and maintains the district's website, email and productivity applications, help ticket system, subscription web tools, Voice Over IP (VoIP) communication system, and other forms of communication.

- Works as the district liaison for all telecommunication issues.

- Plans for and provides security and protection for all technology equipment and data; develops and maintains a plan for disaster recovery and continuity planning.

- Oversees the necessary online security for compliance with the Child Internet Protection Act (CIPA) and leads the management of the district's acceptable use policy (AUP).

- Designs and distributes periodic communication for all staff members containing examples of technology use throughout the district; prepares and provides updates on the technology plan and technology issues for the board of education.

- Performs other duties as assigned.

Continued

REQUIRED QUALIFICATIONS

- Earned bachelor's degree from a regionally-accredited college or university.

- Teaching license from the State Department of Public Instruction. (This is a common but not universal requirement.)

- Knowledge of relevant laws and programs to include CIPA, FERPA, and E-Rate.

- Advanced degree or training in computer science, computer information systems, instructional technology, or educational technology with an emphasis on the integration of educational technology into teaching and learning. (This is also a common but not universal requirement.)

- Five or more years of successful experience in a public-school setting using educational technology for teaching and learning. (This is important if a certified/licensed position, but less important when considering technical-background candidates.)

- Ability to collaborate, lead, and problem solve with others.

- Commitment to high professional standards and ethics.

- Knowledge, technical skills, and experience related to computer hardware, software, networks, and computer use in education.

- Demonstrated ability to interact effectively with others in person, by phone, and in writing.

- Good communication and leadership skills.

- Ability to develop and manage budgets.

- Ability to supervise people.

PREFERRED QUALIFICATIONS

- An earned master's degree or above.

- Prior successful experience as a technology coordinator.

Salary ranges will typically vary depending on the location of the district, where the position falls in the organizational chart, and the size of the school or district. Many states have laws requiring disclosure of the salaries of public employees. Searching a database of available public salaries during a job search may reveal the salary of the current or previous technology coordinator for reference.

The Technology Coordinator Issues Model

Technology coordinators serve in leadership positions that include a wide variety of duties and responsibilities and may fall in multiple locations within the organizational structure. Whereas some technology coordinators are hired and work under an administrative contract, other technology coordinators may not actually hold an administrative position, even though they have a title and a position of responsibility. Some school districts prefer to keep the technology coordinator as a member of the teaching staff, even though the coordinator undertakes largely administrative responsibilities and works with adults rather than with children. In some cases, at the school level, a person assigned to the role of school library-media specialist may be able to provide building level technology leadership and support.

Teaching and Learning	*Supporting Educational Technology*	*Supporting Online Learning*
• Standards • Delivery modes • Professional development • Purchasing processes • Digital safety and citizenship	• Lifecycle management • Security and protection • Systems support • Policy considerations • Technology-supported innovations • Professional development and diffusion	• Key concepts • Standards and guidelines • Accessibility and online content • Tools for online learning • Supporting teachers • Supporting students

● ● ●   TECHNOLOGY COORDINATOR ISSUES MODEL, VERSION 4   ● ● ●

Network Operations	*Administrative Computing*	*Planning and Budgeting*
• Network infrastructure • Wireless and voice over IP • User account management • Backup and disaster recovery • Data privacy • Cybersecurity • Remote management	• Processing grades and records • Student information systems • Data-driven decision making • Human resources • Business operations • Document imaging	• Technology planning • Budgeting • Evaluation • Software licensing • Equipment maintenance • Recycling and disposal • IT staffing • Grants • E-Rate applications

Figure 1.2. Technology Coordinator Issues Model (TCIM 4.0).

Regardless of title or position in the organizational structure, the technology coordinator must be a combination of "someone who has a global understanding of the how the hardware, software, policies, and procedures fit together in the big picture of district's technology plan along with being able to address the student vision for learning through mobile, online, and digital learning" (Walker, 2015). The TCIM in Figure 1.2 provides an overview of the various areas of responsibility and identifies some specific issues that focus the work of the technology coordinator. As the TCIM shows, six major areas of leadership and responsibility are shared, to varying degrees, by all technology coordinators. Additionally, the TCIM illustrates how the technology coordinator performs in an environment of changing conditions and technologies, laws and policies, interpersonal and organizational dynamics, and standards and expectations. This position is a complex and multifaceted job that requires negotiating a complex environment in which many issues and challenges will arise and various types of change must be successfully managed.

Hiring a Technology Coordinator

Because the role of a technology coordinator is so complex, even at the school level, it can be challenging to find and select the best candidate for this position. One popular approach to hiring a technology coordinator is to start by selecting a search committee to screen, rank, and recommend the best candidates for the job to those who are responsible for the hiring. Often the hiring authority rests with the person to whom the technology coordinator will report. If a suitable description has not already been established for the position, or if the position description is out of date and should be revised, the search committee may be asked to write or update the description before beginning their work.

Beginning the hiring process by developing a clearly written and up-to-date position description is always a good first step for a hiring committee. The committee will also want to review appropriate hiring policies and procedures. Establishing standardized interview procedures, pre-selecting lists of interview questions, and establishing scoring and ranking guides for evaluating and ranking candidates can be very helpful in making the hiring of a quality candidate successful. Useful information about the process of hiring candidates using structured interviews is available online from the excellent guide prepared by the United States Office of Personnel Management (USOPM) (2008).

Interview Questions

The USOPM recommends using a structured interview process in which all candidates are asked the same questions in the same order, and in which all candidates are evaluated using a common rating scale. Structured interviews have higher levels of reliability (consistency among interviewers) and validity (extent to which potential job performance is measured) than unstructured interviews (USOPM, 2008).

Based on a job analysis, the search committee should begin by determining the competencies to be assessed by the interview, choose the appropriate interview format, and then develop questions. When determining the competencies, it may be helpful to choose at least one from each of the five areas of the TCIM, and at least one from the surrounding environmental factors in which the TCIM is situated. It will be helpful to use the position description to select other key competencies to address in interview questions. Allow adequate time during the interview for the candidate to address each question, so the time devoted to each interview may help determine the number of questions to ask. Asking twelve questions during a typical sixty-minute interview allows five minutes to address each question. The committee may choose to use a behavioral interview format if they plan to focus on the candidates' past behavior. A situational interview, by contrast, uses questions focused on hypothetical behavior. A combination of the two types of questions may be used (USOPM, 2008). The USOPM recommends that all interview questions be reflective of realistic competencies of the job, be open-ended, and be clearly worded and easily understood. Each question should focus on a single job competency.

Scoring Guides

The USOPM recommends the development and use of a common rating scale for all candidates, based on a pre-established proficiency range. Table 1.1 shows a sample interview question and scoring guide, and Table 1.2 shows a five-level scoring scale.

The committee should develop rating scales and scoring guides to use with their situational interview questions. The guide produced by USOPM is an excellent resource for this purpose. Once the interview questions and scales are completed, it is often useful to pilot test the interview procedures and process by doing a trial run with volunteers simulating the role of the applicant.

Table 1.1. Sample Interview Question and Rating Scale

COMPETENCY: Interpersonal Skills

DEFINITION: Shows understanding, friendliness, courtesy, tact, empathy, concern, and politeness to others; develops and maintains effective relationships with others; may include effectively dealing with individuals who are difficult, hostile, or distressed; relates well to people from varied backgrounds and different situations; is sensitive to cultural diversity, race, gender, disabilities, and other individual differences.

QUESTION: Describe a situation in which you had to deal with individuals who were difficult, hostile, or distressed. Who was involved? What specific actions did you take, and what was the result?

PROFICIENCY LEVEL	DEFINITION	QUESTION-SPECIFIC BEHAVIORAL EXAMPLES
Level 5 *Expert*	• Applies the competency in exceptionally difficult situations. • Serves as a key resource and advises others.	• Presents shortcomings of a newly installed HR automation system in a tactful manner to irate senior management officials. • Explains the benefits of controversial policy changes to a group of upset individuals at a public hearing. • Diffuses an emotionally charged meeting with external stakeholders by expressing empathy for their concerns.
Level 4 *Advanced*	• Applies the competency in considerably difficult situations. • Generally requires little or no guidance.	• Facilitates an open forum to discuss employee concerns about a new compensation system. • Builds on the ideas of others to foster cooperation during bargaining agreement negotiations. • Identifies and emphasizes common goals to promote cooperation between HR and line staff. • Identifies and alleviates sources of stress among a team developing a new automated HR system.
Level 3 *Intermediate*	• Applies the competency in difficult situations. • Requires occasional guidance.	• Restores a working relationship between angry coworkers who have opposing views. • Remains courteous and tactful when confronted by an employee who is frustrated by a payroll problem. • Establishes cooperative working relationships with managers, so they are comfortable asking for advice on HR issues.
Level 2 *Basic*	• Applies the competency in somewhat difficult situations. • Requires frequent guidance.	• Offers to assist employees in resolving problems with their benefits election. • Works with other HR staff on a cross-functional team to improve coordination of activities. • Works with others to minimize disruptions to an employee working under tight deadlines.

PROFICIENCY LEVEL	DEFINITION	QUESTION-SPECIFIC BEHAVIORAL EXAMPLES
Level 1 *Awareness*	• Applies the competency in the simplest situations. • Requires close and extensive guidance.	• Refers employees to the appropriate staff member to resolve their issues. • Works with others in the HR office to organize information for employee intervention sessions on controversial issues. • Works with others to obtain employee concerns about controversial policy changes.

Source: United States Office of Personnel Management (2008).

Table 1.2. Scoring Scale for Candidate Proficiency

PROFICIENCY LEVEL	GENERAL COMPETENCIES	TECHNICAL COMPETENCIES
Level 5 *Expert*	• Applies the competency in exceptionally difficult situations. • Serves as a key resource and advises others.	• Applies the competency in exceptionally difficult situations. • Serves as a key resource and advises others. • Demonstrates comprehensive, expert understanding of concepts and processes.
Level 4 *Advanced*	• Applies the competency in considerably difficult situations. • Generally requires little or no guidance.	• Applies the competency in considerably difficult situations. • Generally requires little or no guidance. • Demonstrates broad understanding of concepts and processes.
Level 3 *Intermediate*	• Applies the competency in difficult situations. • Requires occasional guidance.	• Applies the competency in difficult situations. • Requires occasional guidance. • Demonstrates understanding of concepts and processes.
Level 2 *Basic*	• Applies the competency in somewhat difficult situations. • Requires frequent guidance.	• Applies the competency in somewhat difficult situations. • Requires frequent guidance. • Demonstrates familiarity with concepts and processes.
Level 1 *Awareness*	• Applies the competency in the simplest situations. • Requires close and extensive guidance.	• Applies the competency in the simplest situations. • Requires close and extensive guidance. • Demonstrates awareness of concepts and processes.

Source: United States Office of Personnel Management (2008).

Interviewer's Guide

After finalizing the questions and rating tools, the next step is creating an interviewer's guide. This guide should provide general instructions about the interview process, including instructions for the interviewers and for the candidates. The guide should include all questions with related scoring guides and rating scales, and any sample prompts the search committee might want to offer in case the candidate does not address a portion of an interview question.

CANDIDATE NAME:

INTERVIEW DATE:

INSTRUCTIONS: Transfer each interviewer's competency ratings onto this form. A consensus discussion must occur with each panel member justifying his or her rating. Any changes to the individual ratings during consensus discussion should be initialed by the panel members. A final group consensus rating must be entered for each competency.

COMPETENCY	COMMITTEE INDIVIDUAL RATINGS				CONSENSUS GROUP RATING
	(1)	(2)	(3)	(4)	
Writing					
Oral Communication					
Problem Solving					
Interpersonal Skills					

COMMENTS:

ACTION: ☐ Highly Recommended; ☐ Recommended; ☐ Not Recommended

Name of Committee Chairperson #1:

Name of Committee Member #2:

Name of Committee Member #3:

Name of Committee Member #4:

Figure 1.3. Sample candidate rating form.

Final Candidate Rating Form

Following the interview, each member of the search committee should individually rate the candidate on the competencies identified for the job using a rating form like the example shown in Figure 1.3. Following the final interview, the ratings can be aggregated for all candidates on a form to summarize and compare the candidates.

Hiring the best candidate for an important position like technology coordinator is a challenge for any organization. Making sure there is a current and accurate position description will ensure that both candidates and the hiring committee have a clear picture of the ideal candidate, along with their qualifications. Implementing effective hiring procedures, including the use of structured interview questions and rating forms for use in evaluating candidates, will help ensure that the candidate selected is fully capable of addressing all the job qualifications. The TCIM can be helpful in understanding and identifying important areas of responsibility and expertise and assuring that these areas will be successfully addressed.

Answers to Essential Questions

1. **What are the major responsibilities the technology coordinator will be expected to assume?**

    Working in a dynamic environment, the technology coordinator is expected to provide vision, leadership, and supervision in five areas: teaching and learning, computer support for teaching and learning, network operations, planning and budgeting, and administrative computing. See the TCIM earlier in this chapter for a graphic overview of these responsibilities.

2. **What skills, abilities, and attributes will be needed to succeed in the position?**

    To be successful in this position, the technology coordinator will need a combination of strong interpersonal skills, effective problem-solving skills, leadership and planning skills, and technical skills.

3. **What day-to-day operational tasks will the technology coordinator most likely face?**

    The technology coordinator will conduct professional development training sessions, work with users to solve problems and answer questions, communicate with vendors, meet with district administrators to do planning or develop policy, and speak to community groups about district technology initiatives. The technology coordinator is often responsible for the management of other technology personnel, such as network administrators, computer technicians, help desk operators, and building-level technology specialists.

4. **How can my school or district select the best candidate for the position of technology coordinator?**

    Hiring someone to fill such a complex position is an important responsibility. Do an audit of the position to determine required competencies. Create a rating scale and scoring guide for each competency. Select applicants to interview based on the rating scale. Write questions for the interview that address the most important competencies of the position. Score the interviewed candidates individually using the scoring guide. Aggregate the scores of the individual committee members on a standardized form, and make a recommendation for each final candidate to the hiring authority. Of course, follow your district's hiring policies and procedures.

Chapter 2

TEACHING AND LEARNING WITH TECHNOLOGY

Essential Questions

1. What are the instructional delivery modes a technology coordinator may be called on to support?

2. What should the technology coordinator know about designing instruction to support effective teaching and learning with technology?

4. How can the technology coordinator promote digital citizenship and safe uses of technology?

5. What are some key theories and frameworks that a technology coordinator should be familiar with that can be helpful in guiding decisions, plans, and professional development related to teaching and learning with technology?

Technology coordinators are key players in fostering, supporting, and sustaining the use of technology for teaching and learning. All purchases of technology in schools are ultimately in support of teaching and learning, from internet access to school network infrastructure, to the hardware and software in the hands of teachers and students. The technology coordinator is often called upon to advocate for technology in support of teaching and learning in budget discussions, to provide professional development in support of meaningful uses of technology for teaching and learning, and to provide support for the technologies and systems that are necessary to enable the use of technology for teaching and learning. In this chapter we answer five essential questions for technology coordinators regarding their work in supporting teaching and learning. These questions are based on five essential issues related to teaching and learning, as depicted in Figure 2.1.

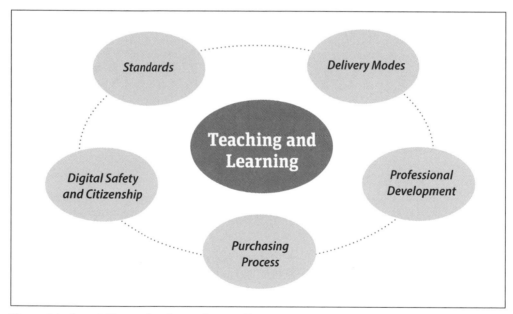

Figure 2.1. Essential issues related to teaching and learning.

ISTE Standards

When it comes to teaching and learning with technology, it is important to know what is expected of K–12 students and the standards for their learning about and with technology. The International Society for Technology in Education (ISTE) has created a set of standards to answer these questions. As a technology coordinator, making sure that teachers are aware of these standards and are incorporating them in their planning, teaching, and evaluation processes is very important.

The student section of the ISTE Standards is designed to empower student voice and ensure that learning is a student-driven process. The seven overarching standards for students are:

1. Empowered Learner

2. Digital Citizen

3. Knowledge Constructor

4. Innovative Designer

5. Computational Thinker

6. Creative Communicator

7. Global Collaborator

The full set of ISTE Standards and their performance indicators can be accessed at iste.org/standards. The ISTE website also offers explanatory videos, guidance on adopting the standards, downloadable posters, and more.

One strategy for addressing these standards with teachers is to showcase the work of teachers who are implementing one or more of these standards well. Another is to weave them into professional development activities. A third might be to have students explain what they did on video to play back to teachers during professional development time.

 The various ISTE Standards are very useful for technology coordinators to know and leverage. Later in this chapter we address how the ISTE Standards for educators are useful for professional development planning and assessment, just as the student standards are when working with students.

Delivery Modes

The most common method of instructional delivery mode in K–12 education takes place in the traditional classroom, where teacher-directed, face-to-face instruction is the norm. This is especially true in K–3 classrooms, where the students may not have significant technological literacy or skills like keyboarding. However, a spectrum of instructional delivery modes is emerging, as some states, for example Florida and Virginia, now require high school students to take at least one class online to graduate, and many states offer fully online instruction in publicly funded online schools ranging from upper elementary grades to high school. Additionally, public charter schools offering online learning for upper elementary to high school students seem to be growing in popularity. In the spring of 2020, during the COVID pandemic, the U.S. Census Bureau's Pulse Survey found that nearly 93% of people in households with school-age children reported their children engaged in some form of "distance learning" from home. Due to the pandemic, many more children now have experience with online learning than ever before.

Tech Leader Profile

Travis True, Curriculum Technology Specialist

Travis True is a curriculum technology specialist for the Topeka Public Schools. His is an urban district serving a diverse population of about 14,000 students across 31 schools in the Kansas capital city; over 70% of these students qualify for free or reduced lunches. Travis joined the Topeka schools in 2004 and became a curriculum technology specialist in 2012. While more than thirty people work in the technology department for the Topeka Public Schools, Travis is one of three curriculum technology specialists who are all assigned to the Teaching and Learning Department. Originally trained as an educator and with twelve years of classroom experience, Travis holds master's degrees in Instructional Design and in Educational Administration, along with being a Google Certified trainer. His main job responsibilities include technology support and integration training, and he is responsible for researching new hardware, software, and technology trends in education. One of the main challenges Travis faces every day is providing accurate information and answers to teachers while not being officially part of the technology department. He is proud of the fact that his district provides more technology resources to teachers and students than other districts in the area. Travis would encourage other technology leaders to "be flexible and open to change, as this field changes rapidly. You must know your stuff so you can successfully train people and explain how the technology will improve student achievement." He believes that change is a constant and that if you are not willing to adapt, your job will only become more difficult. You can follow his work here: @travistrue.

A middle ground on the spectrum between fully face-to-face and fully online modes of teaching and learning has been emerging over the last few years with the increasing popularity of hybrid learning initiatives. Building on the success of one laptop or tablet per student initiatives, these hybrid programs make use of student laptops and tablets to supplement and enhance the face-to-face learning process. In addition to traditional classroom activities to engage students and allow them to work with other students, teachers are also able to integrate these devices into their instruction, giving students ready access to the internet and to a variety of applications, ranging from traditional productivity tools such as word processors, spreadsheets, and presentation tools to multimedia creation tools and web-based applications.

Toolbox Tip

Using a Gameboard for New Teacher Orientation

New teacher orientation for the Francis Howell School District (FHSD) in O'Fallon, Missouri, is a week-long boot camp of all things curriculum, instruction, and technology for teachers new to the district. Like most organizations, they use a variety of online applications ranging from instructional resources to online benefits managers. The annual challenge is making sure all new teachers are correctly added as application users, and providing a quick overview of each application. For years, April Burton, FHSD instructional technology content leader, assigned reading of a five-page packet containing this information. She recently developed a more attractive and efficient way to provide an overview of essential online resources. New teachers now receive a copy of the tech applications gameboard (shown in Figure 2.2) with their district laptop, prior to orientation. Using a shortened URL or QR code Burton includes on the gameboard, they can click through the hyperlinks to access information about each program.

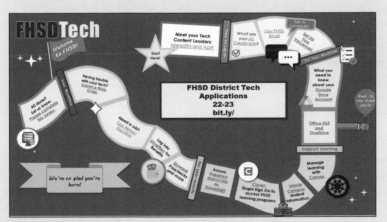

Figure 2.2. FHSD District technology application gameboard. Reproduced with permission.

The scope of delivery modes is growing even more diverse as an increasing number of schools are implementing the use of learning management systems (LMSs). Some have chosen to adopt free, open-source solutions like Moodle, which have limited budgetary impact, but other school districts are providing full-blown commercial LMSs to their teachers. In doing so, these organizations hope to leverage the school-provided technology already in the classrooms for instruction and for learning assignments using their LMS. Innovative teachers in schools without an official LMS have increasingly been using free tools such as Google Classroom, Edmodo, and Schoology. This trend has led to the creation of a range of delivery methods and has contributed to the growing popularity of the flipped classroom model of instruction, a blended delivery method. In the flipped classroom model, teachers offload some activity normally conducted in the classroom for students to do at home, aided by internet resources or an LMS. For example, the teacher may ask students to watch selected TeacherTube or YouTube videos, engage in an online discussion (helping to ensure that all students participate, not just those who usually speak up in class), or create and upload their own materials from home as homework. Classroom time then emphasizes activities, projects, and opportunities to check for understanding and correct any misunderstandings. Of course, the flipped classroom is less feasible in situations where students do not have necessary access to technology resources and dependable internet access at home.

The spectrum of instructional delivery modes is clear, with fully face-to-face instruction on one end of the continuum, a variety of blended instructional methods in the middle, and fully online instructional modes on the other end. The technology coordinator must be aware of issues involved in supporting all areas of the continuum. This support should include teacher professional development as well as support for teaching using this entire range of modes. One very useful model of the types of blended learning is offered by Heather Staker of the Innosight Institute (2011). Staker's six models of blended learning are briefly described in Table 2.1.

Table 2.1. Models of Blended Learning

MODEL 1 **Face-to-Face** **Driver**	The programs that fit in the face-to-face-driver category all retain face-to-face teachers to deliver most of their curricula. The physical teacher deploys online learning on a case-by-case basis to supplement or remediate, often in the back of the classroom or in a technology lab.
MODEL 2 **Rotation**	The defining feature in the rotation model is that, within a given course, students rotate on a fixed schedule between learning online in a one-to-one, self-paced environment, and sitting in a classroom with a traditional, face-to-face teacher. It is the model most in between the traditional face-to-face classroom and online learning, because it involves a split between the two and, in some cases, between remote and onsite. The face-to-face teacher usually oversees the online work.

MODEL 3 Flex	Programs fitting into the flex model feature an online platform that delivers most of the curricula. Teachers provide on-site support on a flexible and adaptive as-needed basis through in-person tutoring sessions and small group sessions. Many dropout-recovery and credit-recovery blended programs fit into this model.
MODEL 4 Online Lab	The online-lab model encompasses programs that rely on an online platform to deliver the entire course, but in a brick-and-mortar lab environment. Usually these programs provide online teachers. Paraprofessionals supervise, but offer little content expertise. Often students that participate in an online-lab program also take traditional courses and have typical block schedules.
MODEL 5 Self-Blend	The nearly ubiquitous version of blended learning among American high school students is the self-blend model, which encompasses any time students choose to take one or more courses online to supplement their traditional school's catalog. The online learning is always remote, which distinguishes it from the online-lab model, but the traditional learning is in a brick-and-mortar school. All supplemental online schools that offer *a la carte* courses to individual students facilitate self-blending.
MODEL 6 Online Driver	The online-driver model involves an online platform and teacher that deliver all curricula. Students work remotely for the most part. Face-to-face check-ins are sometimes optional and other times required. Some of these programs offer brick-and mortar components as well, such as extracurricular activities.

Purchasing Process

Long before any software or hardware is selected, make sure you are knowledgeable about your district purchasing regulations and procedures, because each school district has unique policies to guide purchasing without school board approval, approval of contracts, when formal price quotations are required and how many must be obtained, request for proposal procedures, details on the awarding of contracts; payment policies, and timelines for purchasing.

For larger purchases, the technology coordinator is usually responsible for the specifications of the goods to be purchased, and perhaps for preparing and submitting a resolution to the school board for permission to bid. Before preparing the specifications, it is usual to convene a hardware/software/service evaluation committee to identify needed features, help prepare the specifications documentation, and ensure that the identified needs are met. It is also common for the technology coordinator to prepare purchasing specifications for someone in the district's purchasing office, who will then prepare a request for proposals (RFP). The RFP will be reviewed by the district's legal department before the purchasing office publishes the RFP and vendors can submit bids. Typically, before the bids are due, the purchasing office holds a pre-bid conference to answer any questions that potential bidders may have. Following the submission of bids by vendors, the technology coordinator and someone in purchasing will select a provider for the hardware, software, or service being purchased. Ideally, hardware and software will be made available for evaluation before the final decision is made.

For smaller purchases, those under the district's threshold dollar amount for the bidding process, the technology coordinator typically has to get a certain number of bids for what is needed. If only one provider of a product or service exists, each district will likely have special procedures to follow as well. Regardless of the process, the input of a hardware/software/services evaluation committee is indispensable. Before the purchase is made, ensure that the evaluation committee has had a fair chance to try each vendor's product. This process is important because the technology coordinator will likely have to explain why the hardware, software, or service was selected and why it is the best value for purchase.

A technology coordinator representing an entire district may often get the best possible value on tools for digital teaching and learning if they can join together with several other school districts and form a purchasing consortium. If several school districts are going to purchase a common piece of software, chances are a consortium of those districts will be able to negotiate a much better price than could one district alone.

Digital Citizenship

Given the ubiquity of technology, the responsibility to teach students how to use technology safely and be good digital citizens often falls to schools. ISTE has taken a leading role in developing resources for that purpose. Most of ISTE's standards documents address digital citizenship in significant ways. For students, standard 2 is about digital citizenship; for educators, standard 2 concerns the citizen; for education leaders, standard 1 addresses being an equity and citizenship advocate, and for coaches, standard 7 involves being a digital citizen advocate. One of the roles of the technology coordinator is to make sure teachers and other educational professionals in schools are familiar with and are implementing the ISTE Standards. The most current student standard addressing digital citizenship reads, "Students recognize the rights, responsibilities and opportunities of living, learning and working in an interconnected digital world, and they act and model in ways that are safe, legal, and ethical" (International Society for Technology in Education, 2016).

In a keynote address at the ISTELive 2019 conference in Philadelphia, CEO Richard Culatta described digital citizenship instruction as "Far too often, digital citizenship is taught in a negative way—here's the list of all the stuff you should not do online. And while I appreciate the intent behind anti-cyberbullying campaigns, we don't teach other things as "anti-" in schools. I mean, we don't have anti-illiteracy campaigns—we teach kids to love to read. Digital Citizenship shouldn't be a list of don'ts, but a list of do's." During this address, Culatta announced that ISTE was joining several partner organizations to create the DigCit Coalition where the members would be working together to redefine digital citizenship. In his ISTELive address, Culatta identified five competencies for digital citizenship: inclusive, informed, engaged, balance, and alert.

An overview of digital citizenship compiled from Culatta's ISTELive presentation, along with additional definitions of the five digital citizenship competencies along with related examples is presented in Table 2.2.

Table 2.2. Digital citizenship competencies and examples

DIGITAL CITIZENSHIP COMPETENCIES	A GOOD CITIZEN...	A GOOD DIGITAL CITIZEN...
1. INCLUSIVE **Definition:** Is open to hearing and respectfully recognizing multiple viewpoints, and engages with others online with respect and empathy	Advocates for equal human rights for all	Engages others online in a respectful way and shows empathy to others
2. INFORMED **Definition:** Evaluates the accuracy, perspective, and validity of digital media and social posts	Actively pursues an education and develops habits for lifelong learning	Evaluates digital information accurately to insure validity and perspective
3. ENGAGED **Definition:** Uses technology and digital channels for civic engagement, to solve problems and be a force for good in both physical and virtual communities	Is actively involved with the community, interacts with others, and shows a sense of community responsibility	Uses digital resources in positive ways for civic engagement and problem solving
4. BALANCED **Definition:** Makes informed decisions about how to prioritize time and activities online and off	Participates in a way that makes the most of the time involved	Uses time wisely for both online and offline activities
5. ALERT **Definition:** Is aware of online actions and knows how to be safe and create safe spaces for others online	Pays attention to what is happening in the community to maintain safety and security	Ensures that online actions will maintain safety and security for self and others

Sources: Infographic: I'm a Digital Citizen, International Society for Technology in Education (2022) and The 5 competencies of digital citizenship, International Society for Technology in Education (2021).

ISTE offers a variety of publications addressing digital citizenship. The most recent offering, *Deepening Digital Citizenship: A Guide to Systemwide Policy and Practice* (Rogers-Whitehead & Monterosa 2023), provides models, case studies, and a variety of additional information for those seeking resources.

Theories and Frameworks

The technology coordinator must be aware of various theories and frameworks that can help to guide decisions in the areas of learning, motivation, instructional design, assessment of implementation of technologies for teaching and learning, and assessment of professional development.

Assessment of Implementation

Several common questions posed to technology coordinators are:

- How much of the technology we are buying is actually being used?
- Is it being used broadly across our school or schools?
- Is it being used in meaningful ways?
- Is it making a difference in student achievement or some other measurable student outcome, such as attendance rates?
- How well did the latest faculty development program work?

To answer these sorts of questions, technology coordinators are commonly expected to assess the implementation of these sorts of initiatives. Depending on the people and other resources available, assessment can be a time-consuming and detailed endeavor. For a technology coordinator without a staff, assessment can be a significant burden. It is important to consider that good assessment of what is going on in your school or district need not be entirely the task of the technology coordinator. Almost any college or university with a department, school, or college of education will typically have at least one faculty member interested in this area. Such help may even be available for free, although permission to publish anonymous results may be requested in return for assistance. It is best to ask for assistance early, so that all steps of the process will benefit from the expertise of the evaluation specialist.

We recommend the following six steps in program planning, including assessment:

1. **Assess Needs:** What do the students, teachers, staff, or community need as part of the hardware, software, teaching methodology, or professional development program to be implemented? Employing an advisory group is a great idea. Set priorities.

2. **Plan:** Use a logic model (see below). Include evaluation in your plan. Make a timeline. Plan for assessment and to collect the data.

3. **Develop the program:** Include people, places, schedule, assessments, and materials. Make stakeholders aware of plan and schedule.

4. **Deliver:** Implement the professional development, use of technology, teaching method. Gather assessment data. If possible, have an external evaluator observe events and collect data.

5. **Evaluate:** Collect remaining data. Analyze and interpret data. Involve the advisory group or other advisors in this stage as well. Compile a written report.

6. **Disseminate results:** Share the written report with all stakeholders.

Toolbox Tip

Technology Integration Assessment Rubric

Harris, Grandgenett, and Hofer (2010) have developed and tested a rubric based on the TPACK (technology, pedagogy, and content knowledge) framework for assessing the quality of technology integration. This "pedagogically inclusive" instrument is designed to reflect key TPACK concepts and, based on their research, has proven to be both reliable and valid in two rounds of testing using these categories of assessment:

- **Curriculum Goals & Technologies:** curriculum-based technology use

- **Instructional Strategies and Technologies:** using technology in teaching/learning

- **Technology Selection(s):** compatibility with curriculum goals and instructional strategies

- **Fit:** content, pedagogy, and technology together

 The rubric, which contains a creative commons license, can be accessed by scanning the QR code or by visiting the URL bit.ly/3PGERLv.

Tech Leader Profile

Joan McGettigan, Director of Instructional Technology

Dr. Joan McGettigan has served as the director of instructional technology for Darien Public Schools in Connecticut since 2019. Prior to that, she was director of educational and information technology at North Broward Preparator, an Apple Distinguished School. Originally trained as an elementary classroom teacher, she has master's degrees in Elementary Education and in Educational Technology, as well as a doctorate in Instructional Leadership. Joan is also recognized as an ISTE Certified Educator, an Apple Distinguished Educator, and an Apple Learning Coach. Her responsibilities include overseeing Technology Education and Libraries (a total of fourteen people), conducting professional development, and providing curricular support. She reports directly to the assistant superintendent for curriculum and instruction. Darien schools are in the suburbs outside New York City. The district serves around 4,500 students and is ranked as one of the top 5% of school districts in the state. Joan describes her biggest challenge on any day as how best to serve the multiple diverse needs of teachers and students in her district. Dr. McGettigan thinks the best part of her job is helping others learn new ways to teach in innovative and creative ways using technology. She points out that "all districts need someone to speak up for the teaching and learning side and advocate for the goals the instructional side of the house is trying to achieve. The one-two punch of the pandemic and the advance of artificial intelligence present challenges to learning we are just beginning to understand." For those aspiring to a position like hers, she offers this advice: "listen carefully, be empathetic, advocate for students and teachers, and be willing to shape the path for any needed change." You can follow her work at: @drmcgettigan.

Developing a Logic Model

An effective logic model is often helpful with planning both the implementation and the assessment portions of your implementation. Sometimes called a "theory of change" or a "program theory," logic models typically contain five parts and are often arranged into columns. The first two columns represent planned actions, and the last three represent intended results. Logic models, like the one shown in Table 2.3, are often linear, but they may take on other forms. A logic model is usually expected to be included in a grant proposal, and they are taken seriously by funders. A guide to reading a logic model is shown in Figure 2.3.

Table 2.3. Logic model for mathematics achievement.

INPUTS ▶	ACTIVITIES ▶	OUTPUTS ▶	OUTCOMES ▶	IMPACTS ▶
Hardware, software, & infrastructure.	SMBW is deployed on classroom computers.	Teachers gain an understanding of how SMBW can enhance math learning.	Student scores on basic math operations increase by 20%.	Reduced student math anxiety.
Trainers and PD planned bi-weekly.	Teachers, principals, and coaches receive training on SMBW implementation.		Student scores on word problems increase by 15%.	Increased student math self-efficacy.
Administrative expectation to use SMBW at least 30 minutes each day.	Teachers implement SMBW with fidelity for at least 30 minutes each day.	Teachers can integrate SMBW at least five ways into mathematics instruction with fidelity at least 30 minutes per day.	Student scores on fractions, ratios, and percentage problems increase by 15%.	Increased student engagement in mathematics.
Scheduled weekly teacher team planning and discussion of SMBW implementation.	Teachers meet weekly for a structured SMBW discussion as a team led by a coach.	Teachers' comfort level integrating SMBW in the five ways increases.	Student scores on pre-algebra problems increase by 15%.	Increased student enjoyment of mathematics.
Weekly SMBW coaching per teacher.	Teachers meet individually each week with assigned SMBW coach.	Teacher lessons show increasing sophistication with SMBW integration.	Student scores on mathematics vocabulary increase by 20%.	Reduced student retention rate. Increased average daily attendance.
Assessment Data to Collect				
Deployment schedules. PD schedules. Memo from principals to teachers. Meeting schedules. Baseline math test scores.	SMBW utilization rates from central management software. Records of meetings such as notes, agendas, and teacher reflections. Pre-implementation (baseline) student math anxiety, self-efficacy, engagement, and enjoyment scores.	Teacher reports and coaches' observations of teaching practice. Teacher comfort measurement results. Collected teacher lesson plans.	Student test scores.	Post-implementation student math anxiety, self-efficacy, engagement, and enjoyment scores. Retention rates. Daily attendance rates.

Table 2.3 shows a sample logic model for the implementation of a fictitious software program called "Super Mathematics Brainiac Wizard" (SMBW), designed to increase elementary school mathematics achievement. Across the bottom of the logic model is a section indicating the data to be collected at each stage of the program so the success of the program can be assessed and so impact on student learning can be measured. A guide to reading a logic model is shown in Figure 2.3.

As illustrated in the table, a good plan includes the data that should be collected in all stages of the program, including pre- and post-test data when appropriate. Assessing teaching and learning with technology usually includes implementation of the technology, as well as student outcomes such as learning. Theoretically, implementation of technology in ways that are faithful to the plan and best uses of the technology (implementation fidelity) should result in improvements in learning.

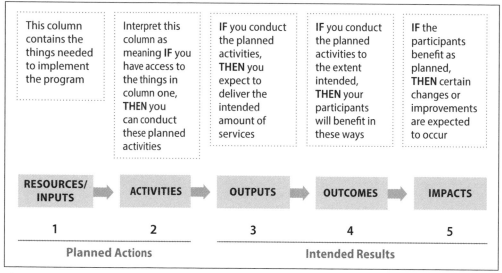

Figure 2.3. Guide to reading a logic model.

Concerns-Based Adoption Model

A well-researched and useful set of tools for assessing innovation adoption, such as a new use of technology for teaching or learning, is the Concerns-Based Adoption Model or C-BAM (Hall & Hord, 2015). This model is easy to implement and contains three diagnostic dimensions: 1. An Innovation Configuration Map to provide both an exemplar to guide efforts and a measurement of implementation, 2. A Stages of Concern measurement in questionnaire form to enable the attitudes, beliefs, and related concerns about a new program or innovation to be addressed, and 3. A Levels of Use structured interview tool to determine how well individuals and groups are implementing a program. Additionally, the C-BAM model offers suggestions to help improve attitudes and beliefs of individuals and groups in order to move from slow adoption to levels that are conducive to effective implementation.

Professional Development Spotlight

Online Training Opportunities from ISTE

Both teachers and technology leaders can benefit from ongoing professional development opportunities. One source for these opportunities might be the offerings from ISTE U. This program offers a variety of options ranging from self-paced courses, to summer learning academies, to instructor-led courses. These learning opportunities allow individuals or groups to choose from a variety of time commitments and costs. The self-paced courses offer topics such as "Assessing Learning in Online Environments" and "Creating Communities in Online Classrooms" with a time commitment of two hours. The instructor-led courses have set time commitments of approximately eight weeks and focus more in depth on topics such as "Digital Citizenship in Action" or "Understanding Learning Differences." These courses may count for graduate credit. The Summer Learning Academies combine online courses with webinars, virtual coaches, and online learning communities for participants. All of these would be useful professional development experiences for teachers, technology coordinators, tech coaches, or librarians who are looking to enhance their knowledge or skills. Group rates may be available.

ISTE also offers educators the opportunity to be certified with demonstrated mastery of the ISTE Standards for Educators. After participating in forty hours of professional learning focused on pedagogy and educational practice over fourteen weeks, those seeking certification will spend about six months developing a portfolio that demonstrates their mastery of the standards and will earn four units of graduate credit as part of the process. Those who earn certification are recognized for knowledge and technology leadership skills. There is a significant registration cost for those seeking certification.

More information about all ISTE professional development opportunities can be found by following the Professional Development link on the ISTE home page: www.iste.org.

Answers to Essential Questions

1. **What are the instructional delivery modes a technology coordinator may be called on to support?**

    There are many possible modes of delivering instruction, but direct instruction is ubiquitous and should be thoroughly understood. It is also important to be knowledgeable about Staker's six models of blended learning.

2. **What should the technology coordinator know about designing instruction to support effective teaching and learning with technology?**

    There are a variety of strategies that can be used to plan an instructional development project, and it would be useful for the technology coordinator to become familiar and comfortable with several models that might be shared with teachers to improve the teaching and learning process.

3. **How can the technology coordinator promote digital citizenship?**

    The technology coordinator should make use of the ideas of the Digital Citizenship Coalition and partner organizations to help prepare students to stay safe, solve problems, and become a force for good by acting as alert and engaged online citizens.

4. **What are some key theories and frameworks that a technology coordinator needs to be familiar with that can be helpful in guiding decisions, plans, and professional development related to teaching and learning with technology?**

    The technology coordinator must be aware of theories and frameworks useful in guiding thoughts, decisions, and actions about various aspects of learning, instruction, and assessment. There are many useful theories and frameworks out there. We chose to highlight the logic model, which is useful when designing professional development, learning experiences, or programs. When assessing programs, the Concerns-Based Adoption Model is useful and easy to implement.

Resources

Digital Citizenship Coalition (digcitcommit.org) is the website for the organization focused on teaching digital citizenship by preparing students to stay safe, solve problems, and become a force for good.

Ignitecast (ignitecast.com) is a video sharing tool also enabling the creation of interactive video.

iRubric (www.rcampus.com/indexrubric.cfm) allows for the creation of rubrics, evaluating student artifacts, or simply printing out a rubric.

PaperRater (www.paperrater.com) will allow users to upload a paper or copy and paste the text into the tool to check for grammar, spelling, and style issues.

RubiStar (rubistar.4teachers.org) allows for creating and saving rubrics online.

Socrative (socrative.com) is an online quiz tool that works like a student response system. It is very easy to use and works on any device that can connect to the internet.

Storyboard That (storyboardthat.com) will help with writing screen plays, skits, or movies.

UtellStory (www.utellstory) is similar to VoiceThread but has a simpler interface.

VoiceThread (voicethread.com) facilitates the creation of presentations and also functions as a multimedia collaboration and discussion tool.

Chapter 3

SUPPORTING ONLINE AND BLENDED LEARNING

Essential Questions

1. What are the potential benefits of online and blended learning for schools, teachers, and students?

2. Why is accessible content important in online and blended learning, and how can the technology coordinator support the use of accessible content?

Online and blended learning have become an integral part of K–12 education. Between 2020 and 2022 the COVID pandemic forced many schools to close their buildings temporarily, and during this time, online learning became the primary mode of teaching and learning. Teaching, leading, and coordinating online learning in K–12 education have become critical skills for teachers, administrators, and technology coordinators.

Online learning involves students accessing educational content and interacting with teachers and peers through a digital platform, while blended learning combines online learning with traditional classroom instruction. These approaches allow students to work at their own pace and engage with material in a way that suits their individual learning styles.

In this chapter we provide essential information and discuss important issues for technology coordinators as they support online learning. These issues are illustrated in Figure 3.1.

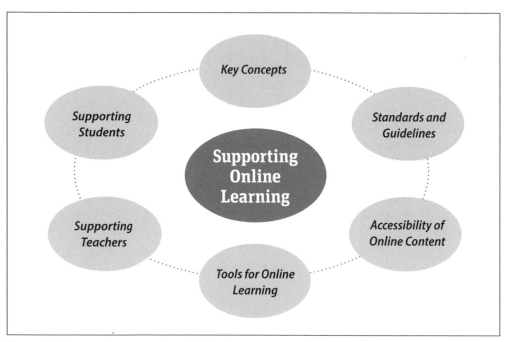

Figure 3.1. Issues when supporting online learning.

The recent shift to remote and hybrid learning models has highlighted the benefits of online and blended learning, including increased accessibility, personalized learning opportunities, and the ability to engage with students outside of traditional classroom hours. However, it has also raised concerns around issues such as equity, access to technology, and the need for adequate teacher training and support.

Post-COVID, some schools are planning to use hybrid learning as a standard model of teaching and learning. In March of 2023, the North College Hill City School District in Ohio (1400 students K–12, and 150 teachers) announced that in the 2023–4 school year it will move to a four-day school week for the entire year for all grade levels. On Mondays students and teachers will remain home, with students participating in self-directed asynchronous activities. Face-to-face instruction will take place Tuesdays through Fridays at school. The district hopes the plan will alleviate stress faced by students and staff and increase teacher retention. The plan will open opportunities for teachers to attend doctor's appointments without using a sick day and will eliminate the need for substitute teachers on Mondays. The district is working to solve issues of childcare and food options for students on Mondays. The Independence School District near Kansas City, Missouri, adopted a four-day school week in 2023 (Reilly, 2023).

Overall, online and blended learning have the potential to transform K–12 education and provide students with a more flexible and personalized learning experience. As technology continues to advance and more schools adopt these models, it will be important to address the challenges and maximize the benefits of this approach to education.

Key Concepts

Online learning refers to a mode of delivering educational content and instruction through the internet or other digital means. It typically involves students accessing course materials, such as lectures, readings, and assessments, through an online platform, often at their own pace and on their own schedule. Online learning may also incorporate synchronous components, such as live video conferences or chat sessions with instructors or peers. This mode of learning is often used in distance education, where students and instructors are geographically separated, or in blended learning, where it is combined with face-to-face instruction. Online learning can provide flexibility and accessibility to students, enabling them to access educational resources from anywhere at any time.

Blended Learning

Blended learning refers to a mode of instruction that combines traditional face-to-face classroom instruction with online learning activities (Garrison & Vaughan, 2008). This mode of learning is becoming increasingly popular due to its potential to enhance student engagement, motivation, and achievement, as well as to provide flexibility and personalized learning opportunities (Vaughan, Cleveland-Innes, & Garrison, 2013).

There are several models of blended learning that have been implemented in K–12 education, each with its unique characteristics and benefits (Horn & Staker, 2015). One model of blended learning is the rotation model, in which students rotate between online and offline learning activities in small groups or individually (Horn & Staker, 2015). For example, in the station-rotation model, students move between stations in the classroom, each with a different activity or task, such as online research, hands-on experiments, or peer discussions (Brame, 2016). In the lab-rotation model, students spend a portion of their class time in a computer lab, completing online assignments or assessments (Horn & Staker, 2015).

Another model of blended learning is the flex model, in which students have more control over the pace, path, and place of their learning (Horn & Staker, 2015). In this model, students can choose to complete online modules or activities at home, and then attend face-to-face sessions with the teacher for support, feedback, and enrichment (Brame, 2016). The flex model can also involve project-based or inquiry-based learning, in which students work on authentic, self-directed projects and receive guidance and feedback from the teacher and peers (Horn & Staker, 2015).

The flipped classroom model is another popular model of blended learning, in which students watch video lectures or complete online activities before class, and then engage in hands-on activities, discussions, or assessments during class (Bishop & Verleger, 2013). The flipped classroom model can provide more time for active learning and collaboration, as well as for individualized instruction and feedback (Talbert, 2017).

To support students in blended learning, teachers can use a range of technology tools, such as learning management systems, interactive multimedia, and online assessments (Graham et al., 2013). They can also use data analytics and adaptive learning systems to monitor student progress and provide targeted interventions (Van Laer, Elan, & Clarebout, 2017). Furthermore, teachers can foster collaboration and social interaction among students, both online and offline, to promote higher order thinking and peer learning (Vaughan et al., 2013).

Blended learning can offer several benefits to students, such as increased flexibility, access to a variety of resources and experts, and opportunities for personalized learning and feedback (Means et al., 2013). However, it also poses some challenges, such as the need for teachers to be proficient in technology integration, to provide clear instructions and support, and to ensure equity and accessibility for all students (Graham, Woodfield, & Harrison, 2013).

Asynchronous Online Learning

Asynchronous online learning is a mode of instruction where students access learning materials and complete assignments at their own pace, without real-time interaction with their teachers or peers (Ferdig et al., 2020). This mode of learning is gaining popularity due to its flexibility, convenience, and potential to enhance student engagement and learning outcomes (Cavanaugh, Barbour, & Clark, 2020).

Asynchronous online learning can take various forms, including video lectures, online readings, discussion forums, and multimedia resources (Li & Pitts, 2020). To support students in this mode of learning, teachers can provide clear instructions, feedback, and opportunities for self-assessment (Ferdig et al., 2020). They can also use technology tools such as learning management systems, video conferencing, and digital portfolios to facilitate communication and collaboration (Li & Pitts, 2020).

Asynchronous online learning also poses some challenges, such as the need for students to be self-motivated, disciplined, and technologically proficient (Cavanaugh et al., 2020). Additionally, it may exacerbate inequalities in access to technology and support, especially for disadvantaged students (Ferdig et al., 2020). To address these challenges, teachers can provide scaffolding and support, such as online tutorials, peer mentoring, and virtual office hours (Li & Pitts, 2020).

Asynchronous online learning is a promising mode of instruction in K–12 education that can provide flexibility, convenience, and opportunities for student-centered learning. However, it requires careful planning, design, and implementation, as well as ongoing support and assessment to ensure its effectiveness and equity.

Synchronous Online Learning

Synchronous online learning is a mode of instruction where students and teachers interact in real-time through video conferencing, chat rooms, or other online communication tools (Cavanaugh et al., 2020). This mode of learning is gaining popularity due to its potential to provide interactive, engaging, and social learning experiences, as well as to support continuity of learning during disruptions such as pandemics (Ferdig et al., 2020).

Synchronous online learning can take various forms, such as live video lectures, online discussions, virtual labs, and collaborative projects (Hew & Cheung, 2013). To support students in this mode of learning, teachers can provide clear instructions, feedback, and opportunities for active participation and reflection (Garrison & Cleveland-Innes, 2005). They can also use technology tools such as virtual whiteboards, screen sharing, and breakout rooms to facilitate group work and peer learning (Hew & Cheung, 2013).

Synchronous online learning also poses some challenges, such as the need for reliable and high-speed internet access, and for students to be available at specific times and locations (Cavanaugh et al., 2020). Additionally, it may require teachers to adapt their pedagogical strategies and communication skills to the online environment (Garrison & Cleveland-Innes, 2005).

To address these challenges, teachers can provide alternative modes of participation and assessment, such as recorded lectures, asynchronous discussions, and online quizzes (Hew & Cheung, 2013). They can also use a variety of communication modes, such as audio, video, and text, to accommodate different learning preferences and needs (Garrison & Cleveland-Innes, 2005).

Synchronous online learning is a promising mode of instruction in K–12 education that can provide interactive, engaging, and social learning experiences. However, its effectiveness and equity depend on support, careful planning, design, and implementation, as well as ongoing evaluation and improvement.

Tech Leader Profile

Jennifer Freedman, Coordinator of Instructional Technology and Library Media Specialists

Jennifer Freedman joined the Lindenhurst Union Free School District in New York as a middle school library media specialist in 2013 and began coordinating technology and libraries in 2021. Her path to this position has been winding—she began her career as a computer programmer, became a librarian, and later transitioned to a technology director position. Jennifer was an undergraduate English major who went on to earn a Master of Science in library science and graduate certification and licensure in both building and district leadership. She also has earned an extensive list of other certifications, including ISTE Certified Educator, Google Certified Educator, and Certified Microsoft Innovative

Educator. Her main responsibilities in her current position include communication with administrators, faculty, students, and parents, coordinating innovation in teaching and technology, and providing equitable technology access for all. Her department is made up of nine other people; most of them are supervised by Jennifer. She reports directly to a deputy superintendent. The Lindenhurst district is made up of nine schools serving approximately 5500 students in a suburban district that is diverse in both ethnicity and socioeconomic status and is located approximately forty miles east of New York City on the south shore of Long Island. Jennifer's biggest daily struggle is providing quality customer service to all the administrators and teachers. She does this by having easy-to-book office hours, regularly visiting classrooms, and communicating in a timely matter via email and text. For those who aspire to a similar position, Jennifer reminds us that district leaders must "view this as a customer service position. Avoid saying no; when there is no other solution, find a different way." You can follow Jennifer's work here: @jlf74.

Learning Management Systems

A learning management system (LMS) is a software platform that enables the delivery, management, and tracking of online learning experiences (Ally, 2004). An LMS can provide a variety of tools and features, such as course management; content creation and sharing; communication and collaboration; and assessment and evaluation (Picciano, 2017).

The main purpose of an LMS is to support and enhance teaching and learning in various settings, such as K–12 education, higher education, and corporate training (Ally, 2004). An LMS can offer several benefits to learners and instructors, such as flexibility, convenience, access to a variety of resources, and opportunities for personalized and collaborative learning (Picciano, 2017).

To use an LMS effectively, teachers need to have a clear understanding of its features and functionalities and should attempt to design and deliver online learning experiences that are engaging, interactive, and aligned with learning goals (Song & Singleton, 2018). Learners also need to have the necessary digital literacy and self-regulation skills to navigate and succeed in the online learning environment (Picciano, 2017).

Many LMS platforms are available, both proprietary and open source, each with its unique features, strengths, and limitations (Huang et al., 2017). Choosing the right LMS platform depends on various factors, such as the school or district's needs, budget, infrastructure, and pedagogical goals (Picciano, 2017).

An LMS can provide various tools and features to support and enhance teaching and learning in different contexts, but its effectiveness and impact depend on careful planning, design, support, and implementation, as well as ongoing evaluation and improvement.

Some of the most popular LMS platforms in K–12 education include Google Classroom, Schoology, Canvas, and Edmodo (Cavanaugh et al., 2020; Tucker, 2021). In addition to these popular LMS platforms, other emerging platforms are gaining popularity in K–12 education, such as Nearpod, Seesaw, and Flipgrid, which offer interactive and multimedia-rich learning experiences, as well as opportunities for student creativity and voice (Tucker, 2021).

Learning management systems (LMS) are not only used in online and blended learning environments but also in face-to-face teaching in K–12 education. An LMS can be used in face-to-face teaching to enhance communication, collaboration, and engagement among students and teachers, as well as to provide access to resources and feedback (Huang & Liang, 2021; Wu et al., 2020).

One way that an LMS can be used in face-to-face teaching is to provide access to course materials and resources, such as syllabi, readings, and multimedia content, that can be accessed by students anytime and anywhere (Huang & Liang, 2021). This access helps support student learning and provides flexibility and convenience for students who may miss classes due to illness or other reasons.

Another way that an LMS can be used in face-to-face teaching is to facilitate communication and collaboration among students and teachers. For example, LMS platforms can provide discussion forums, chat rooms, and messaging tools that enable students to ask questions, share ideas, and receive feedback from teachers and peers (Wu et al., 2020). LMS platforms can also enable students to work on group projects, share files, and co-create content, which can help to promote social interaction, teamwork, and creativity (Huang & Liang, 2021).

In addition, an LMS can be used in face-to-face teaching to support assessment and evaluation. For example, LMS platforms can provide online quizzes, surveys, and assignments that can be used for formative and summative assessment (Wu et al., 2020). An LMS can also provide automated grading, feedback, and analytics that can help teachers monitor student progress and identify areas for improvement (Huang & Liang, 2021).

Each LMS has its unique features and benefits. The choice of an LMS platform depends on various factors, such as the school or district's needs, budget, infrastructure, support, and pedagogical goals.

Web-Conferencing Platforms

Web-conferencing software platforms enable real-time communication and collaboration between learners and teachers. They are used in education at all levels for video and audio conferencing, screen sharing, chat features, virtual breakout rooms, document sharing, collaborative authoring, and virtual whiteboards.

Some of the most popular web-conferencing software platforms in K–12 education include Zoom, Google Meet, Microsoft Teams, and Webex (Cavanaugh et al., 2020; Tucker, 2021). In addition to these popular web-conferencing platforms, other emerging platforms are gaining popularity in K–12 education, such as BigBlueButton, Jitsi, and Adobe Connect, which offer similar features and benefits (Tucker, 2021).

As with other software tools, the choice of a web-conferencing platform depends on many factors, including the needs and pedagogical goals of the school or district, budget, infrastructure, and support. The technology coordinator will likely be expected to help teachers and students learn how to make the best use of web-conferencing and other online and blended-learning software tools.

Toolbox Tip

Grant Writing

Often, school districts find it challenging to function effectively when limited to the financial support received from local, state, and federal funds. Applying for a grant that will provide financial support for a project is time-consuming and requires concentrated effort, commitment, and persistence. Solomon (2001) provides some very useful pointers on things to do before beginning to write a grant:

- Have a solid idea and plenty of supporting details.

- Read the guidelines carefully, and make sure the grant fits your needs.

- Involve others to build commitment to the project so that there is plenty of support to carry out the project, if funded.

- Make sure the funding will be sufficient for the project; look for matching funds from other sources if necessary.

- Make sure you have the commitment from administration to carry out the project.

- Read all the directions and follow them carefully.

Standards and Guidelines for Online Learning

The rapid growth of online and blended learning in K–12 education has resulted in an increasing need for well-defined standards and guidelines to ensure quality learning experiences. Following is an overview of the key standards and guidelines that have been developed to promote best practices in online and blended learning. These standards and guidelines have been developed by organizations to guide the design, implementation, and evaluation of online and blended learning in K–12 education. These organizations include the International Society for Technology in Education (ISTE), the Aurora Institute, and the Quality Matters (QM) program.

ISTE Standards

The ISTE Standards provide a framework for effectively integrating technology into teaching and learning. They emphasize the importance of digital citizenship, collaboration, communication, critical thinking, and creativity (ISTE, 2018).

The student section of the ISTE Standards provides a framework for using technology to enhance learning experiences in K–12 education. These standards were developed to help students develop digital literacy skills and to promote effective use of technology in the classroom. The Standards are divided into six categories, each addressing a different aspect of technology integration in education.

The ISTE Standards are designed to be flexible and adaptable to the needs of different schools and districts. They are also aligned with other national and international standards and frameworks for technology integration in education, such as the Aurora Institute Standards and the Common Core State Standards.

Research has shown that the ISTE Standards can have a positive impact on student learning outcomes. A study conducted by ISTE in 2016 found that schools that implemented the ISTE Standards reported improvements in student engagement, critical thinking skills, and digital literacy skills (ISTE, 2016).

The educator section of the ISTE Standards provides a framework for using technology to enhance teaching and learning experiences in K–12 education. These standards are particularly relevant in online and blended learning environments, where technology plays a central role in facilitating learning experiences.

The standards in the educator section are organized into six categories, each addressing a different aspect of technology integration in education. The standards are relevant to online and blended learning in K–12 education because they emphasize the importance of using technology to create engaging, student-centered learning experiences. In online and blended learning environments, teachers must use technology to facilitate collaboration, provide individualized feedback, and support student engagement and motivation (Watson & Kalmon, 2018). By using the ISTE Standards as a framework for technology integration, educators can ensure that online and blended learning experiences are effective, engaging, and accessible for all learners.

To see all of the ISTE Standards and learn more about using them, visit iste.org/standards.

Aurora Institute Standards

The Aurora Institute Standards for Quality Online and Blended Learning in K–12 Education, formerly known as the iNACOL Standards, were developed by the Aurora Institute to provide a comprehensive framework for ensuring high-quality learning experiences in online and blended environments. These standards are designed to address the unique challenges and opportunities associated with online and blended learning, and they cover a wide range of topics, including curriculum and instruction, student support, professional learning, and evaluation and assessment.

The Aurora Institute Standards are organized into seven categories, each addressing a different aspect of quality online and blended learning. The categories are:

1. Vision and Planning
2. Curriculum and Instruction
3. Instructional Resources
4. Student Support
5. Professional Learning
6. Evaluation and Assessment
7. Leadership

The Aurora Institute Standards are intended to be flexible and adaptable to the needs of different schools and districts, as well as to different grade levels and subject areas. They are also aligned with other national and international standards and frameworks for quality online and blended learning, including the ISTE Standards for Students and the Quality Matters Rubric.

Implementing the Aurora Institute Standards can have a positive impact on the quality of online and blended learning experiences for students. A study conducted by the Aurora Institute in 2018 found that schools and districts that implemented the Aurora Institute Standards reported improvements in student engagement, academic achievement, and teacher effectiveness (Alderman et al., 2019).

Quality Matters Standards

The Quality Matters (QM) program is a widely recognized, research-based, faculty-centered approach to designing, developing, and delivering online and blended courses. The QM program was originally designed for higher education but has since been adapted for K–12 education. The QM K–12 Secondary Rubric is a set of standards designed to evaluate the quality of online and blended courses in K–12 education.

The QM K–12 Secondary Rubric consists of eight general standards:

1. Course Overview and Introduction
2. Learning Objectives
3. Assessment and Measurement
4. Instructional Materials
5. Course Activities and Learner Interaction
6. Course Technology
7. Learner Support
8. Accessibility and Usability

The QM K–12 Secondary Rubric can help to ensure that online and blended courses in K–12 education are designed with clear learning objectives, appropriate assessments, and effective instructional materials. Research shows that online and blended learning can be just as effective as traditional classroom instruction when designed and implemented well (Zawacki-Richter et al., 2020). By using the QM K–12 Secondary Rubric to design and evaluate courses, K–12 educators can ensure that their online and blended courses are effective and engaging for learners.

Incorporating accessibility and usability criteria into course design is critical to ensuring that all learners, including those with disabilities, have equal access to course content and activities (Burgstahler, 2015). The QM K–12 Secondary Rubric includes specific criteria related to accessibility and usability, ensuring that course content and activities are available in multiple formats and are easily navigable.

The QM K–12 Secondary Rubric includes comprehensive standards that promote best practices in course design, development, and delivery. By using the QM K–12 Secondary Rubric to evaluate and improve online and blended courses, K–12 educators can help to ensure that all learners have access to high-quality education.

Other Research-Based Guidelines for Online Learning

Effective implementation of quality online and blended learning requires a comprehensive approach that encompasses curriculum design, alignment, teacher development, and ongoing support.

Curriculum Design

Curriculum design should be guided by a clear understanding of learning objectives, appropriate instructional strategies, and assessments that align with desired outcomes (Darling-Hammond et al., 2020). Additionally, Rose et al. (2018) emphasized the importance of Universal Design for Learning (UDL) principles in ensuring accessibility and meeting the diverse needs of all learners. UDL is a research-based framework that focuses on designing instructional materials and activities in a flexible and inclusive manner, allowing all students, including those with disabilities, to access and engage with the curriculum effectively. By incorporating UDL principles, educators can create learning environments that are adaptable to individual learning styles, preferences, and needs, ultimately promoting success for all students (Rose et al., 2018).

Alignment

Alignment is a fundamental concept in the design of online and blended courses, referring to the coherent and intentional connections between learning objectives, instructional strategies, and assessment methods (Anderson, 2018). In well-aligned courses, the learning objectives clearly state what students are expected to know or be able to do upon completing the course, while instructional strategies and activities facilitate the achievement of these objectives. Assessment methods are designed to evaluate whether students have met the objectives, providing evidence of learning outcomes (Darling-Hammond et al., 2020).

The importance of alignment in online and blended courses lies in its ability to create a cohesive and effective learning experience. When courses are aligned, students can better understand the purpose of instructional activities and assessments, as they are directly related to the learning objectives (Anderson, 2018). This clarity enables students to focus their efforts on achieving the desired outcomes, ultimately improving their learning experiences and academic performance (Darling-Hammond et al., 2020).

Additionally, alignment plays a crucial role in ensuring that online and blended courses meet high-quality standards and adhere to relevant state and national content standards, such as Quality Matters. By designing aligned courses, educators can ensure that their instruction is rigorous, relevant, and engaging, while also promoting accountability and continuous improvement in online and blended learning environments (Anderson, 2018).

Teacher Development

Effective online and blended learning requires teachers who are skilled in both pedagogy and technology. Professional development should address the unique challenges of online and blended learning environments, as well as the effective use of digital tools to support student learning (Cavanaugh et al., 2019).

Ongoing Support

Tucker (2020) highlighted the importance of ongoing support for the successful implementation of quality online and blended learning programs. This support includes providing resources for technical support, fostering a community of practice among educators, and using data-driven decision making to inform continuous improvement efforts. Tucker emphasized that establishing a strong support system is crucial for ensuring the sustainability and effectiveness of online and blended learning programs, ultimately promoting student achievement and positive learning experiences.

Standards and guidelines for online and blended learning in K–12 education provide a framework for designing, implementing, and evaluating quality educational experiences. By adhering to these best practices, educators can create learning environments that effectively leverage technology to support achievement for all students.

Accessibility of Online Content

The importance and legality of accessibility for online content and teaching materials in K–12 education cannot be overstated. Ensuring equal access to education for all students, including those with disabilities, is not only a moral obligation but also a legal requirement (IDEA, 2004; Rehabilitation Act, 1973; ADA, 1990). Accessible online content enables students with disabilities to actively participate in their education, fostering social inclusion and academic success (CAST, 2018).

The IDEA is a law well-known for ensuring children receive a free, appropriate, public education in the least restrictive environment, but it also governs assistive technologies, and the spirit and intention of IDEA is that educational resources, including digital materials, be accessible to all students, including those with disabilities.

Section 504 plays a more significant role in the accessibility of digital content and tools than does the IDEA for any school that receives federal financial assistance. Section 504 requires that individuals with disabilities be provided with equal access to programs and activities. It specifies that information presented digitally must be as comprehensible to those with disabilities as to those without. Schools covered by Section 504 are required to provide appropriate auxiliary aids and services to individuals with disabilities, such as captioning for videos, screen reader-compatible documents and digital content, and accessible digital formats or tools. Section 504 prohibits discrimination based on disability. Digital content and tools provided by schools receiving federal funds cannot be discriminatory in their accessibility features. Finally, Section 504 requires schools receiving federal funding to have grievance procedures in place to address complaints of disability discrimination, which includes digital content or tools that are not accessible. While Section 504 sets foundational requirements for digital accessibility, specific standards for what constitutes accessible digital content often come from other sources, such as the Web Content Accessibility Guidelines (WCAG). The ADA requires effective communication to individuals with disabilities, including digital communication in the form of websites, apps, online learning platforms, digital notifications for students, parents, or guardians with disabilities. This includes closed captioning for videos, accessible design for online assignments, and compatibility with screen readers or other assistive technologies.

For K–12 schools, compliance with the Americans with Disabilities Act (ADA) of 1990 in the realm of digital accessibly is both a legal mandate and a step toward inclusive education. Title II of the ADA applies to public entities, such as schools, and schools are required to ensure that programs, activities, and services are accessible to individuals with disabilities. This includes digital programs, services, and activities such as online learning platforms, electronic resources, and school websites.

Creating accessible educational content means considering the needs of diverse learners, such as those with visual, auditory, cognitive, or motor impairments, and implementing universal design principles (Burgstahler, 2015). Web content and teaching materials should follow the Web Content Accessibility Guidelines (WCAG) 2.1 (World Wide

Web Consortium [W3C], 2018) to ensure usability for all students. Inaccessible content hinders learning and may result in legal consequences for educational institutions that do not comply with accessibility laws (ADA, 1990; Section 504, 1973).

The Web Content Accessibility Guidelines (WCAG) are a set of guidelines developed by the World Wide Web Consortium (W3C) with the aim of ensuring that web content is accessible to people with disabilities (World Wide Web Consortium [W3C], 2018). The guidelines provide a framework for making web content more accessible across a range of disabilities, such as visual, auditory, cognitive, and mobility impairments. The WCAG are organized under four principles known by the acronym POUR (W3C, 2018):

1. **Perceivable:** Information and user interface components must be presented in ways that all users can perceive. This includes providing text alternatives for non-text content, creating adaptable content that can be presented in various ways without losing information, using distinguishable methods to make it easier to see and hear content, and more.

2. **Operable:** Users must be able to operate the interface and navigate the content. This encompasses making all functionality available from a keyboard, providing users enough time to read and use content, not designing content in a way that is known to cause seizures, and providing ways to help users navigate and find content.

3. **Understandable:** Information and operation of the user interface must be understandable. This means text is readable and understandable, web pages operate predictably, and users are assisted in avoiding and correcting mistakes.

4. **Robust:** Content must be robust enough to be reliably interpreted by a wide variety of user agents, including assistive technologies. This involves ensuring compatibility and adaptability with current and future technologies.

Each principle has a set of guidelines associated with it, and each guideline has testable success criteria at three levels: A (basic), AA (intermediate), and AAA (advanced). Most legal requirements and recommendations reference Level AA as the standard to achieve.

The WCAG has at least six implications for K–12 schools:

1. **Legal Implications:** WCAG serves as the standard in many legal contexts related to web accessibility. For K–12 schools, WCAG compliance can assist in meeting the ADA or Section 504 requirements, which mandate accessibility for individuals with disabilities (U.S. Department of Justice, 2015).

2. **Inclusive Learning:** Accessible digital environments support the broader educational aim of inclusivity, ensuring equal learning opportunities for all students.

3. **Parent and Guardian Access:** Parents and guardians often use school digital resources. WCAG-compliance ensures all parents, including those with disabilities, can participate in their child's education.

4. **Future-Proofing:** Adhering to WCAG's robust principle ensures long-term accessibility as technology evolves (W3C, 2018).

5. **Digital Tools and Resources:** K–12 schools frequently employ third-party digital tools. The accessibility of these platforms should be a key consideration.

6. **Training and Awareness:** Implementing WCAG-compliant changes can lead to an inclusive environment, reducing legal risks and enhancing usability for everyone.

Providing accessible online content and teaching materials in K–12 education is essential for supporting the learning of students with disabilities and meeting legal requirements. By adhering to accessibility guidelines, educators and educational institutions can foster an inclusive learning environment that promotes academic success for all students.

In this section we will provide an overview of Universal Design for Learning (UDL), as well as how to make Microsoft Word and PowerPoint files, webpages, and PDF documents accessible.

Universal Design for Learning

UDL is an educational framework that seeks to create inclusive learning environments that cater to the diverse needs of all learners, including those with disabilities (CAST, 2018). UDL is rooted in the understanding that there is no "one-size-fits-all" approach to teaching and learning, as each individual has unique learning styles, preferences, and needs. The framework is built around three main principles (CAST, 2018):

1. Multiple Means of Representation

2. Multiple Means of Action and Expression

3. Multiple Means of Engagement

The principles of UDL aim to create equitable and inclusive educational experiences by catering to the diverse needs and preferences of all learners. By implementing UDL principles in teaching practices and learning environments, educators can better support the academic success and social inclusion of all students, including those with disabilities.

Microsoft Word

To create accessible Microsoft Word documents in compliance with UDL principles, several key considerations must be addressed.

First, use appropriate headings and styles to create a clear structure within the document. This allows screen readers to easily navigate the content and facilitates comprehension for all users (Microsoft, 2021). Apply headings by selecting the desired text and choosing a predefined style from the "Styles" pane.

Next, provide alternative text for images, charts, and other non-text elements to ensure that visually impaired users can access the information conveyed by these elements (Microsoft, 2021). To add alternative text, right-click the object, choose "Edit Alt Text," and enter a concise description of the object's content and function.

Another important consideration is the use of accessible tables. Tables should have a simple structure, with row and column headers clearly identified. Avoid merging or splitting cells, as this can create confusion for screen reader users (Microsoft, 2021).

Color contrast is crucial for users with visual impairments or color blindness. Ensure sufficient contrast between text and background colors by using high-contrast color schemes or checking the contrast ratio using online tools (WebAIM, 2021).

Additionally, use clear and concise language to improve readability. Select an easily readable font type and size and use bulleted or numbered lists to organize information (CAST, 2018).

By following these guidelines, educators can create accessible Microsoft Word documents that align with UDL principles, promoting inclusive learning experiences for all students.

Webpages

Creating accessible webpages that adhere to the principles of Universal Design for Learning (UDL) is essential to ensure that all learners, including those with disabilities, can effectively access and engage with online content (CAST, 2018). To achieve this, web designers must first focus on accessibility, followed by incorporating UDL principles.

Accessibility begins with adhering to the WCAG 2.1, which provide a comprehensive set of recommendations for creating accessible web content (W3C, 2018). These guidelines are organized around four key principles: perceivable, operable, understandable, and robust.

Providing multiple means of action and expression allows learners to interact with content and demonstrate their understanding in different ways, such as through text, audio, video, or interactive exercises (CAST, 2018).

By focusing on accessibility and incorporating UDL principles, web designers can create inclusive webpages that accommodate diverse learners and promote equitable educational experiences.

PDF Documents

When applied to digital documents like PDFs, UDL's principles ensure content is accessible to everyone, including those with disabilities (CAST, 2018). Here's an expanded guide on creating a UDL-compliant PDF document.

Structured Use of Headings *(UDL Principle: Representation)*
Headings are the backbone of document organization. They not only help in categorizing information but also assist assistive technology in navigating content.
> *How:* In popular word processors, like Microsoft Word or OpenOffice, utilize the preset heading styles. Once these documents transition to PDF, such styles enable better navigation.

Comprehensive Alternative Text for Images *(UDL Principle: Representation)*
Images often convey critical information. Alternative text descriptions ensure this content is not lost for those relying on screen readers.
> *How:* Tools like Adobe Acrobat and PDF-XChange Editor offer functionalities to add alt text. It's essential to ensure descriptions are both concise and informative.

Readable Font Size and Inclusive Styles *(UDL Principle: Representation)*
Ensuring readability means using discernible fonts and maintaining adequate size. Certain fonts, such as Arial and Calibri, are universally recognized as readable. However, considering fonts like OpenDyslexic can be crucial for dyslexic readers.
> *How:* Maintain a text size of 12 to 14 points for body text. For headings, the size can vary, but hierarchy should be evident.

Prioritizing High Contrast Colors *(UDL Principle: Engagement)*
High contrast ensures the text is discernible for everyone, including those with color blindness or vision challenges.

How: Popular combinations include black text on a white background or white text on a deep blue or black background. Tools like Color Contrast Checker by WebAIM can be invaluable in assessing appropriateness.

Text-based Equivalents for Audio and Video *(UDL Principle: Representation)*
All multimedia elements must be accompanied by text-based alternatives, such as transcripts or captions, to cater to those who are deaf or hard of hearing.
How: If embedding transcripts within the PDF isn't feasible, ensure an accessible link to the transcript is provided.

Meaningful Hyperlinks *(UDL Principle: Engagement)*
Hyperlinks should be self-explanatory, eliminating ambiguity regarding their destination.
How: Instead of generic directives like "click here", be specific. e.g., "Read more about UDL on the CAST website."

Keyboard Navigability *(UDL Principle: Action & Expression)*
Every PDF element should be accessible using keyboards or similar devices. This caters to individuals with motor disabilities who might rely on such tools.
How: Periodically test your document. Ensure forms, links, and interactive segments can be accessed solely using a keyboard. If using Adobe Acrobat, utilize the built-in accessibility checker.

Clarity in Language *(UDL Principle: Engagement)*
Adopting clear and uncomplicated language widens the range of readers who can access your content.
How: Eschew jargon where possible. If unavoidable, furnish definitions or explanations.

In the digital age, ensuring all readers, regardless of their abilities or disabilities, can access and engage with content is paramount. Embracing the principles of UDL when creating PDFs is a significant stride towards this inclusivity.

Tech Leader Profile

Brian Seymour, Assistant Superintendent of Academics and Innovation

After spending the first two decades of his career with the Pickerington, Ohio, schools, Brian Seymour became the assistant superintendent for academics and innovation for the Whitehall schools in 2022. Pickerington and Whitehall are both eastern suburbs of Columbus, the state capital and largest city in Ohio. Originally trained as a science teacher,

Brian spent his first eleven years teaching secondary science. His path to school leadership included positions as an instructional coach, curriculum advisor, and instructional technology director. Brian earned master's degrees in geosciences and in educational leadership. He also earned Google Educator certifications for Levels 1 & 2, is an ISTE Certified Educator, and is a CoSN Certified Education Technology Leader. While Brian is still learning a new job and a new organization, his major responsibilities include developing systems, processes, and procedures for his new district; establishing innovative practices for curriculum and instruction; and increasing the capacity of building level leaders throughout the organization. In his new job, he reports directly to the superintendent. Whitehall is made up of five schools (three elementary, one middle, and one high school) and serves around 3,500 students. One of the biggest challenges he faces in his position is time—the time needed to design and provide professional learning for educators or technology staff, address all the technology trouble tickets, or research the next effective technology tool. Brian's job satisfaction comes from spending time at the schools and seeing the technology being used in powerful ways to open doors and give so many students learning opportunities. He advises those who aspire to a technology leadership position to remember "a leader must be able to see the big picture and remember: your decisions will make an impact that will be felt for numerous years." You can follow his work here: @SeymourEducate.

Tools for Online Learning

Learning Management Systems (LMS) serve as central platforms in K–12 education for creating, organizing, and managing digital learning content while facilitating communication and collaboration among students and teachers (Watson, Watson, & Reigeluth, 2015). Content authoring tools enable educators to create interactive, multimedia-rich learning materials without extensive programming knowledge (Bower, 2016) that can be integrated into an LMS. Video conferencing tools are widely utilized to support real-time communication and collaboration in online and blended learning environments (Trust, 2020) to offer features such as screen sharing, breakout rooms, and whiteboarding to facilitate interaction and engagement. Online collaborative tools allow students and teachers to work together on documents, spreadsheets, and presentations in real time (Granić & Marangunić, 2019), allowing communication, file sharing, and project management, fostering collaboration and organization in the learning process. Virtual reality and augmented reality (VR/AR) technologies can enhance the online and blended learning experience by creating immersive and interactive learning environments (Radianti et al., 2020) to allow exploration, engage with complex concepts, and to foster creativity. Sometimes these technologies are called Mixed Reality (MR) when there is a blend of digital content and the physical world, or Extended Reality (XR) as an umbrella term for all immersive technologies. Adaptive learning platforms use artificial intelligence and data analytics to tailor learning experiences based on individual students' needs and preferences (Pane, Steiner, Baird, & Hamilton, 2015). Finally, a technology tool gaining popularity is the Virtual Desktop Environment (VDE). A VDE allows a student, teacher, or other school employee to interact with a desktop environment hosted on a remote server instead of on a local computer. VDEs are very useful as tools to support online learning because they allow for centralized management of multiple individual computers, cost efficiency because older or less powerful computers can be used, security because data is stored on a centralized server, and accessibility because the VDE can be accessed from any location if the end user has internet access. VDEs can generally support any of the technology tools mentioned in this section if those tools run on the operating system of the end-user's device. Table 3.1 shares technology tools often used in K–12 online education for quick reference.

Table 3.1. Technology tools for online education.

TOOL CATEGORY	REPRESENTATIVE TOOLS
Learning Management Systems	Canvas, Schoology, Google Classroom, Moodle
Content Authoring Tools	Articulate Storyline, Adobe Captivate, H5P
Video Conferencing Tools	Zoom, Microsoft Teams, Google Meet
Online Collaborative Tools	Google Workspace for Education, Microsoft Office 365
Virtual and Augmented Reality	Google Expeditions, CoSpaces Edu, MERGE Cube, SecondLife, The Sims
Adaptive Learning Platforms	DreamBox Learning for math, Lexia Core5 Reading for literacy, Smart Sparrow
Virtual Desktop Environments	VMware Horizon, Azure Virtual Desktop, Citrix Virtual Apps and Desktops, Google Cloud Compute Engine, Amazon Workspaces

Supporting Teachers

To enable effective online and blended learning, K–12 teachers require various types of support, including interpersonal, technical, administrative, and pedagogical (Hixon, Barbour, & Decker, 2020).

In today's rapidly evolving educational landscape, K–12 teachers are increasingly called upon to adapt to new online and blended learning environments. Providing interpersonal support to these educators is crucial for their success and effectiveness in these non-traditional settings. Of course, direct contact between the technology coordinator and individual teachers/groups of teachers is important and necessary for interpersonal support. But to provide even better interpersonal support, consider creating a Professional Learning Community (PLC). While a Professional Learning Network (PLN) is an informal, self-directed network of educators and experts who connect through various online channels, a PLC is a more structured, collaborative group of educators within a school or district who work together to improve their teaching practice and student outcomes (DuFour et al., 2006). Based on my own experience and the professional literature (DuFour et al., 2006), it helps to have a meeting of all teachers interested in being a part of such a community. In that meeting, define the purpose, objectives, and desired outcomes of the PLC to guide its development and activities. Emphasize the collaborative nature of the PLC, and continually reinforce open communication, sharing of ideas and resources, constructive feedback, and mutual support, so individuals will benefit from and contribute to the PLC. For example, teachers can use a PLC to focus on specific team or school goals, sharing curriculum or co-developing curriculum, and even data-driven decision making. Monitor the teachers who participate in the PLC and those who do not. Continue to encourage those who do not participate to voluntarily join and contribute to the group. Regularly share the testimony and experiences from participants who are successfully participating in, contributing to, and benefitting from the PLC to increase membership and participation.

In the early stages, hold regular meetings to highlight the successes of the PLC and discuss how to increase participation and sharing. Such meetings can be held in person but can also be held using the online tools of the PLC if that is the best way to bring the most people together. Create custom PLC groups for people teaching specific subjects and for people teaching different grade levels. Allow people to enroll themselves in the PLC groups that are of interest to them. For example, a middle school teacher may choose to join a PLC group focusing on teaching math and another focused on online and blended teaching. Promote ongoing reflection on teaching practices, student outcomes, and the PLC's goals and activities, adjusting strategies and approaches as needed (Hord, 2009). Guskey (2014) has many useful suggestions for fostering the success of PLC groups, such as regularly assessing the effectiveness of the PLC by collecting feedback from members, tracking engagement and contributions, evaluating progress towards goals, and scheduling regular meeting times. Be sure to provide necessary resources, such as technology, materials, and professional development opportunities, to support the PLC's activities. Monitor the teachers who participate in the PLC and those who do not. Continue to encourage those who do not participate to voluntarily join and contribute to the group. Regularly share the testimony and experiences from participants who are successfully participating in, contributing to, and benefitting from the PLC to increase membership and participation.

A popular set of tools to use for PLCs are Google Groups to support threaded discussions, Google Documents to share and co-create curriculum materials, and Google Meet to support synchronous virtual PLC meetings. Schoology has become a popular online and blended learning tool and Zoom plus Schoology can also be used to support PLC groups. Websites like Pinterest, Diigo, and Scoop.it can help teachers discover, organize, and share resources.

Technical support is also essential for teachers to effectively use digital tools and platforms in online and blended learning environments (Cavanaugh, Barbour, & Clark, 2009). Key strategies for technical support include providing helpdesk services for teachers, students, and parents. Providing on-demand video tutorials is another successful strategy. Most digital tools and platforms already offer on-demand video tutorials, but for those that do not, one strategy to create on-demand videos is to form a small committee of advanced users of those tools and ask them to create the needed videos and place them online in an organized viewing platform, such as YouTube, for easy access. Another highly successful strategy is to use dedicated technology coaches who can assist with troubleshooting and offer guidance in using various digital tools effectively (Siko & Hess, 2014). Technical support personnel are perhaps best suited for troubleshooting, but knowledgeable and tech-savvy teachers are also often able to assist peers in using digital tools successfully. If there is not a budget available to fund teachers to provide regular and frequent support of this type, consider offering before- or after-school support for helping teachers use digital tools. Having a "technology Tuesday" meeting led by a tech-savvy teacher after school is one such strategy that can provide peer support.

Administrative support plays a crucial role in creating an effective environment for online and blended learning, and this support must be purposefully aligned with the work of the technology coordinator. Indeed, without administrative support, the work of the technology coordinator is made far more difficult. School administrators can support teachers in providing online and blended learning through various strategies, including offering professional development opportunities, allocating resources, creating a supportive culture, and establishing clear expectations and guidelines. In addition to the administrative support offered by technology coordinators described elsewhere in this chapter, there are some specific ways principals and other administrators can help. A key role for administrators is providing access to resources and necessary technology, such as computers, software, and high-speed internet, to support online and blended learning (Tucker, 2013). Additionally, administrators can help ensure that teachers are aware of and trained in using various digital tools and platforms that can enhance their online instruction. Administrators can support the efforts of PLCs by encouraging teachers to share their experiences, challenges, and successes through regular meetings and through the PLCs themselves (Bergmann & Sams, 2012). Establishing clear expectations and guidelines for online and blended learning, including guidelines for participation in PLCs, is another way administrators can encourage collaboration, communication, assessment, and sharing of best practices. Because many teachers may be afraid to try new things in online and blended learning, administrators can provide teachers with permission to be flexible to experiment with different instructional strategies and tools, allowing teachers to customize their teaching approaches to meet the needs of their students. Finally, administrators can implement regular evaluation and feedback processes to assess the effectiveness of online and blended learning initiatives, and then use this data to inform future decision making and professional development opportunities, and to encourage continued best practices, experimentation, and customization of teaching approaches (Means et al., 2013).

Toolbox Tip

Developing a District Online Learning Guide

While serving as the executive director of instructional technology and innovation for the Pickerington Local School District in Pickerington, Ohio, Brian Seymour helped the district to develop an online resource called the Tradigital Learning Guide. The district developed the guide after they transitioned to a 1:1 device program and their curriculum plans and resources had been adapted to digital content. With versions for teachers, students, and parents, the learning guide helped the district to organize and provide easy access to resources and information. Following is a partial list of the resources included in the online guide, which can be accessed here: bit.ly/3sleEcn.

- District Innovation Conference information
- Digital content resources for elementary, middle level, and high school
- Digital content selection process
- Tradigital learning model information
- IT support and helpdesk information
- 1:1 device process and procedure
- Technology plan
- Professional learning resource
- Links to a variety of other resources

Pedagogical support is a separate but interrelated category of support that involves training teachers in designing curriculum and learning experiences that cater to online and blended learning environments (Darling-Hammond, Hyler, & Gardner, 2017). Key methods of providing pedagogical support include offering training sessions, workshops, and other professional development opportunities focused on the pedagogical aspects of online and blended learning, covering topics such as instructional design, assessment strategies, digital tools, and fostering student engagement in virtual environments. Such professional development should include presentations by experienced and successful peers who can assist other teachers in integrating technology into the curriculum by collaborating on lesson plans, providing resources, and demonstrating how digital tools can support and enhance instruction. Another good professional development practice is to hold "Tool Time" sessions where teachers share with their peers' recommended tools or uses of tools to support online and blended teaching. Similarly, teachers can share or model effective lessons, communication strategies, examples of student-centered learning, or formative assessment techniques that have worked in online and blended learning. Finally, pairing up teachers who are experienced and successful with tools, teaching techniques, or technology-integrated lesson planning with less experienced peers is an excellent strategy for pedagogical support.

Supporting Students

Supporting effective learning for K–12 students in online and blended education requires a combination of academic, emotional, social, and technological support tailored to the unique demands of these learning environments (Greer, Rice, & Dykman, 2014). All such support is dependent on clear channels of communication with students and families, providing regular updates on progress, assignments, and expectations.

Academic support in online and blended learning is like that provided in face-to-face, in-person, teaching, but with a few differences. First, students must be taught how to use the tools and environments their teachers or school will be using. Ideally, this should be done in person and supplemented by tutorial videos available online. It is best not to send students home to learn online, or to learn in a hybrid mode, without being ready. Unprepared students will likely become frustrated, unsure of themselves, unproductive, and less effective learners. Students and parents who can access video content to support their use of the tools and environments will fare far better. Students should also be taught time management and study skills to foster success, including skills such as setting goals, creating a schedule, and using self-regulation strategies

(Zimmerman, 2002). Support may include providing virtual tutoring services, scaffolding learning activities, and using adaptive learning technologies to personalize instruction based on individual needs and performance (Walkington, 2013).

Academic tutoring can be done via videoconferencing tools and by sharing documents or screens based on student/parent request or performance on assessments. Tutoring can also be provided by tutoring services through contracts. Teachers can create videos showing examples of how to solve problems or examples of excellent answers or solutions. Such videos can be used by students regardless of instructional delivery mode and can be watched repeatedly to help with understanding. Peer-to-peer tutoring or reciprocal teaching can be accomplished using these same videoconferencing and document-sharing tools. Adaptive or branching technologies, such as the Kahn Academy, can be used to scaffold and personalize student learning regardless of time or location.

Emotional support is essential for students' well-being and engagement in online and blended learning settings. Schools should ensure that students have access to counseling and mental health services, even when learning remotely, to address stress, anxiety, and other emotional challenges.

Social support involves facilitating opportunities for students to build connections and collaborate with their peers, which is particularly important in online and blended learning environments where students may feel isolated (Borup, West, & Graham, 2012). Teachers can foster a sense of belonging by incorporating discussion boards, group projects, and other collaborative activities into the curriculum (Rovai, 2002).

Technological support for students includes ensuring access to appropriate devices, reliable internet connections, and digital learning tools necessary for online and blended education (Cavanaugh, Barbour, & Clark, 2009). Schools should also provide technical assistance and resources to help students troubleshoot issues and navigate digital platforms effectively (Siko & Hess, 2014).

Finally, empower and engage parents and caregivers in supporting their child's online and blended learning by providing resources, guidance, and opportunities for communication with teachers and school staff (Hornby & Lafaele, 2011). Encourage teachers to hold optional meetings with parents and caregivers on a frequent basis, especially during times of extended online learning. Create office hours or provide access to a scheduling system such as doodle.com to enable telephone calls between teachers and parents or caregivers. This will promote a sense of teamwork between teachers and parents/caregivers that will promote understanding and transparency and will also benefit students and contribute to learning.

In this chapter we laid the groundwork for technology coordinators to understand the key concepts in online and blended learning, provided basic information about some of the primary standards for quality in online and blended learning, and offered a primer on accessibility of content for common document types used in online and blended learning. Finally, we provided technology coordinators with the information needed to support teachers and students to be successful teaching and learning in these modes.

Professional Development Spotlight

Connect with Other Tech Leaders through ISTE Loop

A great resource for technology leaders can be connections with others who have similar responsibilities and challenges. Locating people to connect with and establishing those connections can be time consuming and complicated. ISTE is working to solve those challenges for members with the ISTE Loop program. The program uses a proprietary algorithm to match participants based on a profile that is created in only a few minutes. Each week, you will have an opportunity to connect with someone whom you likely would not have an opportunity to connect with otherwise. Connections are arranged by email, and you can opt out if time does not permit a connection that week. Loop matches participants based on common interests to ensure a productive conversation, which is normally held in a videoconference meeting of thirty minutes. These meetings offer participants a chance to discuss interests, share best practices, and provide help and assistance with challenges from their own work. The program provides community guidelines and a code of conduct for meeting interactions to help with the process. The program is open to interested ISTE members. More information and details about participation can be found here: iste.org/companies-and-partners/iste-loop.

Answers to Essential Questions

1. **What are the potential benefits of online and blended learning for schools, teachers, and students?**

    Online and blended learning can benefit schools, teachers, and students by enabling instruction at any time and place; facilitating personalized learning experiences and assessment; and allowing for greater flexibility in scheduling, accommodating the needs of diverse learners and extracurricular commitments. Well-designed learning experiences can increase student engagement, allow for data-driven instruction, and even expand course offerings. Teachers can engage in continuous professional development through online resources, workshops, and collaboration with peers through PLCs.

2. **Why is accessible content important in online and blended learning, and how can the technology coordinator support the use of accessible content?**

    Accessible content is crucial in online and blended learning as it ensures that all students, including those with disabilities, can effectively access, engage with, and benefit from educational materials. By providing accessible content, educators promote equity and inclusivity, enabling every student to participate and achieve their full potential. Technology coordinators can support the use of accessible content through professional development; providing tools and platforms that facilitate the creation of accessible content, such as text-to-speech, adjustable font sizes, and closed captioning; and curating a repository of accessible instructional materials and multimedia content.

Chapter 4

PROFESSIONAL DEVELOPMENT

Essential Questions

1. What does the technology coordinator find in the literature regarding the elements of effective teacher professional development?

2. How does the technology coordinator design and evaluate a professional development program?

Any organization that wants to ensure a significant impact from technology in the classroom will need to provide quality professional development to teachers, staff, and administration. The technology coordinator is often responsible for the planning, implementation, and delivery of technology professional development for school and district personnel. Ensuring that there are quality professional development opportunities, provided at a variety of times to meet the needs of a diverse audience, and offered continuously throughout the academic year and when school is not in session will help to ensure that an organization can transform learning through technology.

Technology Transformation and Professional Development

Professional development is crucial in K–12 education for several reasons. One primary reason is the necessity for teachers to adapt to the continuously evolving landscape of education, which includes changes in pedagogy, learning strategies, and technology. Teachers play a vital role in shaping students' learning experiences and outcomes, and their ability to adapt to these changes directly impacts the quality of education provided.

First, professional development helps foster changes and improvements in pedagogy and learning. As research evolves, new strategies and methods for effective teaching and learning emerge. For example, research might reveal that certain teaching strategies, such as project-based learning or collaborative learning, are more effective in promoting student engagement and understanding than traditional lecture-based methods (Darling-Hammond, Hyler, & Gardner, 2017). Professional development provides teachers with the opportunity to learn about these new strategies and methods, practice them, and then implement them in their classrooms. This not only improves their teaching practices but also enhances the students' learning experiences.

Second, professional development is essential in assisting teachers in making effective use of technology. The integration of technology in education has become increasingly important in recent years, and the COVID-19 pandemic has accelerated this trend (Hodges, Moore, Lockee, Trust, & Bond, 2020). Teachers need to be proficient in using various digital tools and platforms, not only to deliver content but also to facilitate interaction, assess student performance, and provide feedback. Professional development can help teachers develop these skills and competencies, enabling them to leverage technology effectively to enhance teaching and learning.

Moreover, professional development is essential for fostering a growth mindset among teachers. A growth mindset, which is the belief that abilities and intelligence can be developed through effort and practice, is associated with a greater willingness to take on challenges, higher levels of persistence, and better performance (Dweck, 2006). By engaging in professional development, teachers demonstrate a commitment to continuous improvement and a willingness to adapt to new challenges. This not only benefits their own professional growth but also serves as a positive model for their students.

School administration has also been transformed by technology. Digital tools and platforms enable schools to manage various administrative tasks, such as attendance, scheduling, and record-keeping, more efficiently and effectively (Anderson, 2020). Additionally, technology can facilitate communication and collaboration among staff, leading to more coordinated efforts and better outcomes for students. Professional development is essential to ensure that school administrators and staff have the necessary skills and knowledge to use these tools effectively.

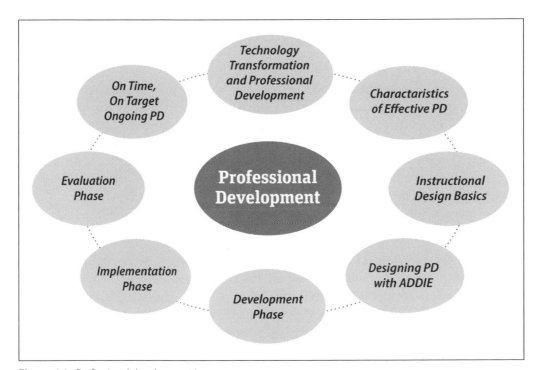

Figure 4.1. Professional development issues.

Parent communication is another area where technology has had a significant impact. Digital communication platforms enable schools to keep parents informed about their children's progress, upcoming events, and any issues that may arise (Murray, 2015). These platforms also provide parents with an opportunity to communicate with teachers and school administrators. Professional development can help teachers and school administrators to use these platforms effectively, ensuring clear and constructive communication with parents. Figure 4.1 identifies the various issues that technology leaders will encounter when delivering professional development to an educational organization.

Professional Development as a Change Management Tool

Effective change management is crucial in K–12 education as it helps schools and education systems adapt to new challenges and continuously improve. Teacher professional development plays a critical role in effective change management initiatives for several reasons.

First, teachers are at the forefront of implementing changes in the classroom. Whether the change involves new teaching methods, curriculum, or technology, teachers are the ones who must put these changes into practice. Professional development helps to equip teachers with the necessary knowledge, skills, and attitudes to implement changes effectively (Darling-Hammond et al., 2017). For example, a school might decide to implement a new curriculum that emphasizes critical thinking and problem-solving. Professional development can help teachers understand the rationale behind this change, learn new teaching strategies that align with the new curriculum, and develop the skills necessary to assess students' progress effectively.

Second, teacher professional development can help to create a positive culture of change within a school or education system. Change can often be met with resistance, and teachers may feel anxious or overwhelmed by new expectations or requirements (Fullan, 2007). Professional development can help to address these concerns by providing teachers with the necessary support, resources, and training to adapt to new challenges. This not only helps to reduce anxiety and resistance but also fosters a positive culture of continuous improvement.

Third, teacher professional development is essential for ensuring that changes are implemented consistently and effectively across a school or education system. Without adequate training and support, there is a risk that changes may be implemented inconsistently or superficially, leading to suboptimal outcomes for students (Desimone, 2009). Professional development helps to ensure that all teachers have a clear understanding of the changes being implemented, the rationale behind them, and the skills and knowledge necessary to implement them effectively.

Seven Characteristics of Effective PD

Darling-Hammond, Hyler, and Gardner (2017) outlined seven characteristics of effective teacher professional development programs. According to their study, effective professional development programs incorporate the following key features:

1. **Content Focus:** Effective professional development is deeply focused on the subject content and how students learn that content. It helps teachers gain knowledge in the subjects they teach and provides them with the ability to organize and apply that knowledge in ways that promote student learning.

2. **Active Learning:** Effective professional development provides teachers with opportunities to get involved in the process of learning in a meaningful way. This may include opportunities for teachers to engage in activities such as observing expert teaching, receiving feedback on their teaching, analyzing student work, or participating in structured discussions with colleagues.

3. **Collaborative:** Effective professional development promotes collaboration among teachers. This may include opportunities for teachers to work together in planning, observing each other's classrooms, or engaging in shared analysis of student work or teaching practice.

4. **Models of Effective Practice:** Effective professional development provides teachers with models of effective practice through the observation of teaching, videos of classroom practice, or well-defined case studies. It allows teachers to see and analyze the application of new knowledge and skills in a practical context.

5. **Coaching and Expert Support:** Effective professional development provides support from coaching and expert mentoring. This support helps teachers to analyze their practice, set goals, and apply what they have learned in their classroom teaching.

6. **Feedback and Reflection:** Effective professional development provides built-in time for teachers to think about, receive input on, and make changes to their practice by facilitating reflection and soliciting feedback.

7. **Sustained Duration:** Effective professional development is spread out over time rather than being a one-off event. It includes multiple sessions that are spread out over weeks or months, providing a total of at least 20 hours, and preferably 50 or more hours, of contact time.

Darling-Hammond, L., Hyler, M. E., & Gardner, M. (2017) noted that these features often interact, and therefore, professional development that incorporates multiple features is likely to be most effective. For instance, a professional development program that involves active learning, collaboration, and expert support, sustained over a period, is more likely to have a positive impact on teacher practice and student achievement.

Using a Logic Model to Plan a Teacher PD Program

In K–12 education, teachers continually strive to enhance their pedagogical skills to improve the learning environment for students. To achieve this, structured and effective professional development (PD) is paramount. The logic model is a valuable tool, providing a systematic framework to visualize and articulate the relationships between resources, activities, and desired outcomes in PD initiatives.

What Is a Logic Model?

A logic model serves as a visual and systematic representation of the resources, actions, and results tied to a program or project (W.K. Kellogg Foundation, 2004). It acts both as a planning and an evaluation instrument, detailing the flow from a program's inception to its end goals. The model consists of:

- **Resources/Inputs:** These are what's invested in the PD initiative. For teacher PD, inputs could be budgets allocated to training, available expertise (whether it's a renowned educator or skilled internal mentor), training materials, venues for workshops, or platforms for online sessions.

- **Activities:** With the defined resources, PD activities are then planned using the ADDIE model, explained below. In the context of teacher development, these could range from hands-on workshops about new educational technology tools, seminars on innovative teaching methodologies, collaborative group sessions for lesson planning, to mentoring sessions for early-career teachers.

- **Outputs:** These are tangible results stemming from the activities. For instance, if a school holds a seminar on inclusive education, outputs could include the number of teachers trained, materials distributed, and hours of training conducted.

- **Outcomes:** The anticipated short-term and intermediate benefits or changes due to the PD. In a teaching context, an immediate outcome might be heightened teacher confidence in a novel strategy, while an intermediate one might be the consistent application of this strategy in classrooms.

- **Impact:** The long-term effect or change attributed to the PD. For instance, over the years, there might be discernible improvement in student engagement, performance, or holistic development due to the enhanced teaching methodologies imparted during PD.

Applying the Logic Model to Teacher Professional Development

Incorporating the logic model into teacher PD involves:

1. **Defining Resources/Inputs:** Recognize and list available resources, such as budgets, experts, and training platforms, before commencing a PD initiative.

2. **Designing Activities:** Tailor PD activities to the needs of the teachers based on the available inputs. Use ADDIE, explained below, to design the PD activities.

3. **Anticipating Outputs:** Establish measurable targets, like the number of training sessions, participants, or total training hours. Examples include the number of teachers who completed the PD or the number who earned certificates; completion and submission of new lesson plans; or teacher attendance and participation statistics (e.g., 90% attendance rate) for the PD.

4. **Forecasting Outcomes:** Determine the short-term and intermediate changes or benefits anticipated from the PD, ensuring alignment with broader educational objectives. Examples of outcomes include enhanced pedagogical skills, increased proficiency in technology integration, and improved classroom management techniques.

5. **Assessing Impact:** Over an extended period, evaluate the long-term effects of the PD. This could involve tracking enhanced student outcomes or lasting changes in teaching methodologies. Additional examples of impacts include, improved student achievement, improved graduation rates, greater teacher retention rates, and a positive shift in school culture.

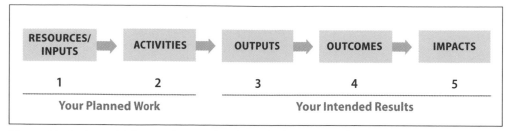

Figure 4.2. Logic model diagram showing the relationship between the five elements of a logic model.

The five-step logic model provides a comprehensive roadmap for planning, executing, and evaluating teacher PD initiatives. By clearly mapping the journey from resources to long-term impact, this model ensures that PD initiatives are not only well-organized but also lead to sustainable and meaningful transformations in the educational landscape.

Applying the Principles of Andragogy to Teacher PD

Before we move on to designing a professional development session or program, it is important to understand Andragogy, how adults learn. Andragogy should be another set of guiding principles kept in mind during all phases of the ADDIE Model you will soon learn more about.

Andragogy refers to the methods and principles used in adult education. It is based on the idea that adults learn differently than children and therefore require different approaches to learning. The concept of andragogy was popularized by Malcolm Knowles, who identified several key principles of adult learning (Knowles, Holton, Swanson, & Robinson, 2020):

1. **Self-concept:** As adults mature, they increasingly see themselves as self-directed. Professional development should allow teachers to take more responsibility for their own learning.

2. **Experience:** Adults have rich experiences that they bring to the learning environment. Professional development should leverage these experiences as a learning resource.

3. **Readiness to learn:** Adults are ready to learn things they feel are relevant to their lives. Professional development should be immediately applicable to teachers' current challenges and goals.

4.   **Orientation to learning:** Adults are motivated to learn to the extent that they perceive it will help them solve problems or improve their situation. Professional development should be problem-centered rather than content-centered.

5.   **Motivation:** While adults respond to external motivators, they are mostly driven by internal factors. Professional development should tap into intrinsic motivators such as the desire to improve as a teacher or to enhance students' learning experiences.

Applying these principles to teacher professional development for effective use of technology in K–12 schools involves the following:

1.   **Make it Relevant:** Ensure that the content of the professional development is directly related to the challenges that teachers face in integrating technology into their teaching practices. This addresses the *readiness to learn* and *orientation to learning* principles.

2.   **Leverage Experience:** Encourage teachers to share their experiences, challenges, and successes with technology integration. This can be done through discussions, case studies, or group activities. This addresses the *experience* principle.

3.   **Self-Directed Learning:** Provide opportunities for teachers to take control of their learning, for example, by choosing topics of interest or setting their own learning goals. This addresses the *self-concept* principle.

4.   **Problem-Centered Approach:** Focus on solving real-life problems that teachers face in their classrooms rather than just imparting theoretical knowledge. This can be done through activities such as scenario analysis, role-playing, or project-based learning. This addresses the *orientation to learning* principle.

5.   **Intrinsic Motivation:** Highlight the benefits of technology integration for both teachers and students, such as increased efficiency, improved student engagement, and better learning outcomes. This addresses the *motivation* principle.

By applying these principles of andragogy and the seven characteristics of effective PD identified earlier in the chapter, teacher professional development can be designed to be more effective and engaging for teachers, ultimately leading to more meaningful use of technology in K–12 schools.

Designing Professional Development with ADDIE

The next logical question is how to design individual professional development events or even a series of events in a professional development program. One widely used and easy to understand model to apply is called ADDIE.

The ADDIE model is a systematic instructional design framework used by educators and instructional designers to create effective educational experiences. It consists of five key stages: Analysis, Design, Development, Implementation, and Evaluation.

1. **Analysis:** This is the first phase where the instructional problem is clarified, the instructional goals and objectives are established, and the learning environment and learner's existing knowledge and skills are identified. For teacher professional development, this might involve identifying the specific areas where teachers need improvement, the goals for the professional development program, and the existing skills and knowledge of the teachers. An analysis of the student population would be informative in this stage as well. After professional development is implemented, participant feedback, participant learning, impact on teaching practice (gathered months after the PD), and impact on student learning (gathered months after the PD) should be analyzed to inform future professional development.

2. **Design:** In this phase, learning objectives, content, assessments, and instructional strategies are determined. For teacher professional development, this might involve deciding on the content of the program, the teaching methods to be used, and how the effectiveness of the program will be assessed (see the evaluation phase for more). This phase should take into consideration the seven features of effective professional development already mentioned, the ISTE Standards for Students, Educators, and Education Leaders if applicable. Finally, if the professional development program involves coaching (note Effective Professional Development Characteristic five), the ISTE Standards for Coaches would be informative during the analysis stage as well. Finally, if the professional development program is focused on teachers of computer science, consult the ISTE Standards for Computer Science Educators as well.

3. **Development:** This phase involves the creation of the instructional materials. For teacher professional development, this might involve creating presentations, handouts, activities, and assessment tools.

4. **Implementation:** This phase involves delivering the instructional materials. For teacher professional development, this might involve conducting workshops, online training sessions, or one-on-one coaching sessions. At the end of a professional development session or program, participant reaction and participant learning data are gathered.

5. **Evaluation:** This phase involves both formative and summative evaluation. Formative evaluation occurs throughout the entire ADDIE process, while summative evaluation occurs at the end of the implementation phase. For teacher professional development, formative evaluation might involve gathering feedback from teachers throughout the program to make ongoing improvements, while summative evaluation might involve assessing the overall effectiveness of the program in improving teacher knowledge and skills.

The ADDIE model can be applied to K–12 teacher professional development by using it as a framework to guide the design, development, implementation, and evaluation of professional development programs. This can help ensure that the programs are well-structured, relevant to the needs of the teachers, and effective in achieving the desired long-term impacts (Gustafson & Branch, 2002).

For example, a school district might use the ADDIE model to design a professional development program for teachers on implementing technology in the classroom. In the analysis phase, they might survey teachers to identify their current knowledge and skills related to technology and their learning needs. In the design phase, they might develop the learning objectives for the program, decide on the content to be covered, and the teaching methods to be used. In the development phase, they might create the instructional materials, such as presentations, handouts, and activities. In the implementation phase, they might conduct the professional development sessions, either online or in-person. Finally, in the evaluation phase, they might gather feedback from the teachers, assess their learning, and evaluate the overall effectiveness of the program.

Despite the ADDIE acronym seeming to represent a linear process, it is an iterative one. As depicted in Figure 4.3, ADDIE is a circular process, with evaluation at its core. Evaluation takes place during each of the phases of the process and evaluation can cause the revision of professional development design aspects from earlier phases as well as whichever phase is currently being worked on. Up until the implementation phase, designers of professional development can stop the process and return to an earlier phase as needed before moving forward again.

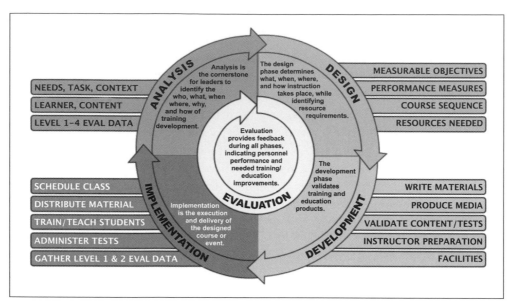

Figure 4.3. ADDIE graphic. Adapted from "TRADOC Pamphlet 350-70-1," by the United States Army Training and Doctrine Command, 2019, p. 13. Copyright 2019 by the U.S. Army. Available at bit.ly/3FKS1Bg.

Tech Leader Profile

Anthony Amitrano, Instructional Technology Specialist

Anthony Amitrano has been an instructional technology specialist with the Northridge Public Schools in Whitinsville, Massachusetts since 2019. His district is in a suburban area south and east of the city of Worcester in a town of roughly 16,000. Three schools make up the district and serve almost 2,000 students in grades K–12. District students come from rural and suburban homes with a largely white population of mixed socioeconomic status, and a sizable number identified as high-needs and low-income students in the district profile. Anthony spent the first seven years of his career as a music teacher before transitioning to a position as an assistant principal and director of technology integration. He earned master's degrees in both music education and educational administration. Anthony is also recognized as a Google Certified Educator Levels 1 and 2, and a Google Certified Trainer. His responsibilities include collaborating with teachers, staff, and administration; creating support materials and job-aids for using the available technology tools and developing professional development opportunities for the district. In his current position, he works in a technology department with four other people. Anthony reports directly to the director of educational technology. Some of Anthony's biggest challenges include staying on top of updates to tools used frequently by teachers, being aware of the newest tools that excite teachers, and helping administration appreciate the value of classroom technology integration. His satisfaction comes from helping teachers leverage technology with students to make their teaching more effective and their jobs easier and more efficient. Anthony advises those who aspire to technology leadership roles to remember that leaders must meet the people they work with at their level and provide information and support with the realization the patrons may not know as much as you, so you must tailor your approach to meet their needs. You can follow his work at: edupowertools.teachable.com.

The Design Phase

Note the key deliverables at each phase of the model shown in Figure 4.3. In the design phase, the outcomes, performance measures, sequence of events, and needed resources are identified. It is strongly recommended that performance objectives for the teachers be written and made clear to the participants of the program. In the same way teachers are expected to use Bloom's Taxonomy when writing measurable objectives for their students, the professional development should also use measurable objectives and the appropriate taxonomy for teacher professional development.

Bloom's Taxonomy of the Cognitive Domain categorizes cognitive learning objectives into six levels of complexity: Knowledge, Comprehension, Application, Analysis, Synthesis, and Evaluation. Here are examples of teacher professional development measurable performance objectives at each level of Bloom's Taxonomy, focusing on the effective use of technology by K–12 teachers, and explanations of each element:

1. **Knowledge**
    Objective: List five different types of technology tools that can be used to enhance classroom instruction.

    Explanation: This is a basic level objective that requires teachers to recall and list different types of technology tools that can be used to enhance instruction. The measurable aspect is the listing of five different technology tools, which demonstrates the teacher's ability to recall fundamental knowledge about technology in the classroom.

2. **Comprehension**
    Objective: Describe the educational benefits of each of the five technology tools listed.

Explanation: This objective requires teachers to demonstrate their understanding of the technology tools by describing the educational benefits of each one. The measure of success is the teacher's ability to describe the educational benefits accurately and clearly, demonstrating comprehension of the material.

3. **Application**
    Objective: Develop a lesson plan that incorporates at least three of the listed technology tools to enhance student learning.

    Explanation: This objective requires teachers to apply their knowledge and understanding of the technology tools by developing a lesson plan that incorporates them. The measurable aspect is the creation of a lesson plan that includes at least three of the technology tools listed and explained in the previous objectives.

4. **Analysis**
    Objective: Analyze the feedback from students and colleagues on the effectiveness of the lesson plan that incorporated technology tools and identify areas for improvement.

    Explanation: This objective requires teachers to analyze feedback on the lesson plan they developed and implemented. They must assess its effectiveness and identify any areas that could be improved. The measurable aspect is the completion of an analysis that includes both an assessment of effectiveness and identification of areas for improvement.

5. **Synthesis**
    Objective: Revise the lesson plan based on the feedback and analysis and create a guide for other teachers to implement the revised plan in their classrooms.

    Explanation: This objective requires teachers to synthesize the information from the feedback and analysis and use it to revise their lesson plan. They must then create a guide for other teachers to implement the revised plan in their own classrooms. The measurable aspect is the completion of a revised lesson plan and the creation of a guide for other teachers.

6. **Evaluation**
    Objective: Evaluate the effectiveness of the revised lesson plan after one month of implementation and make recommendations for further improvements.

    Explanation: This objective requires teachers to evaluate the revised lesson plan after implementing it for one month. They must assess its effectiveness and make recommendations for further improvements. The measurable aspect is the completion of an evaluation that includes an assessment of the plan's effectiveness and recommendations for further improvements.

Resource Requirements During the Design Phase

During the design phase of the ADDIE process, it is crucial to outline all the resource requirements to conduct the professional development program successfully. For a K–12 Teacher Professional Development program aimed at improving the effective use of technology for teaching and learning, resource requirements may include:

- **Technological Tools:** Teachers will need access to the specific technological tools that the professional development program is designed to address. This could include interactive whiteboards, tablets, laptops, specific software applications, or online platforms.

- **Trainers:** Qualified trainers who are knowledgeable about the technology tools and their applications in a classroom setting. These trainers may be internal staff who have expertise in technology integration or external consultants.

- **Training Materials:** Comprehensive training materials that provide detailed information, exercises, and examples of how to effectively use the technology tools for teaching and learning. This may include user manuals, tutorial videos, online modules, and sample lesson plans incorporating the technology.

- **Venue:** A suitable venue equipped with the necessary technology infrastructure (e.g., reliable internet connection, projectors, and computers) for conducting the training sessions. For online training, a virtual meeting platform with screen sharing and interactive capabilities is needed.

- **Assessment Tools:** Tools to assess the teachers' knowledge and skills before, during, and after the training. This may include pre-and post-training surveys, quizzes, and practical exercises.

- **Feedback Mechanism:** A system for collecting feedback from the participants during and after the training sessions. This may include online surveys, feedback forms, or interactive discussions.

- **Support System:** Ongoing support for teachers after the training sessions are completed. This may include access to a helpdesk, online resources, or a community of practice where teachers can share their experiences and seek advice. (Garet, M.S., Porter, A.C., Desimone, L., Birman, B.F., & Yoon, K.S., 2001)

During the design phase, the delivery mode of the professional development must be planned. Most are familiar with the traditional in-person delivery mode in which an instructor/facilitator presents and guides the teachers through the planned presentations, activities, and materials. Because of the recent COVID-19 pandemic, most schools and districts utilized an online delivery mode for professional development. And in some places, as the threat of COVID-19 faded away, a hybrid delivery was often employed that was a mixture of in-person and online delivery. But there is another way of scheduling professional development that is embedded in the regular teacher workday.

Embedded Professional Development

Embedded professional development, also known as job-embedded professional development, refers to learning opportunities that are grounded in the day-to-day teaching practice and are designed to enhance teachers' content-specific instructional practices with the intent of improving student learning (Hirsh, 2009). It is a form of professional development that occurs in the workplace during the regular school day.

Following are ways to schedule and structure embedded professional development:

1. **Coaching or Mentoring:** Experienced teachers or instructional coaches work one-on-one with teachers to provide feedback on their teaching, help them reflect on their practice, and offer suggestions for improvement (Knight, 2009).

2. **Lesson Study:** A group of teachers collaboratively plans, teaches, observes, and analyzes lessons. The process involves planning a lesson together, one teacher teaching the lesson while others observe, and then the group coming together to analyze and reflect on the lesson (Lewis, Perry, & Hurd, 2009).

3. **Professional Learning Communities (PLCs):** Groups of teachers meet regularly to discuss their practice, share ideas, and analyze student work and data. PLCs provide a supportive environment for teachers to learn from and with each other (DuFour, DuFour, Eaker, & Many, 2010).

4. **Action Research:** Teachers identify a problem or area of interest in their classroom, conduct research, implement a strategy or intervention, and then analyze the results to improve their practice (Mertler, 2016).

5. **Peer Observation:** Teachers observe each other's classes and then provide feedback and reflect on what they have learned from the observation (Zepeda, 2012).

Characteristics of effective embedded professional development are:

1. **Contextual:** Professional development should be closely connected to teachers' daily work and should be applicable to their specific teaching context and student needs (Darling-Hammond, Hyler, & Gardner, 2017).

2. **Collaborative:** Teachers should have the opportunity to work together, share ideas, and learn from each other (Hord, 2009).

3. **Ongoing:** Effective professional development is not a one-time event but a continuous process that provides teachers with multiple opportunities to learn, practice, and reflect on their teaching (Desimone, 2009).

4. **Focused on Content:** Professional development should be focused on the content that teachers teach, and it should help them deepen their understanding of that content and how to teach it effectively (Garet, Porter, Desimone, Birman, & Yoon, 2001).

Toolbox Tip

Creating a Professional Development Instructor Checklist

A comprehensive professional development checklist is essential for instructors to ensure they are well-prepared to deliver effective training. Follow the QR code or visit bit.ly/3QkKJJf for a sample checklist that a professional develop-

ment instructor could use prior to instruction, particularly focusing on technology integration in K–12 education.

Note that this checklist can be modified and adapted based on the specific needs and requirements of the training session. Additionally, the checklist is a guide for the instructor to ensure that they have considered all necessary aspects of the training, from preparation to follow-up. It is important for the instructor to continuously reflect on and improve their practice to ensure effective professional development (Darling-Hammond, Hyler, & Gardner, 2017).

5. **Incorporates Active Learning:** Teachers should have the opportunity to actively engage in the learning process, rather than being passive recipients of information (Desimone, 2009).

6. **Uses Data:** Effective professional development should use data to inform instruction and decision-making (Boudett, City, & Murnane, 2005).

Professional development embedded in the workday can be an effective approach because it allows for continuous learning and improvement without requiring teachers to dedicate additional time outside their regular working hours. This can include activities conducted before school, after school, or during preparation periods.

- **Before School:** Professional development activities can be scheduled before the school day starts. This can include meetings or workshops focused on a particular topic, collaborative planning sessions, or peer observations followed by feedback and reflection. For example, teachers could meet in the morning once a week to participate in a book study or discuss and analyze student data.

- **After School:** Similar activities can be conducted after school. This is a common time for professional learning communities (PLCs) to meet, for teachers to participate in workshops or trainings, or for staff meetings that include a professional development component. For instance, teachers could meet after school to collaboratively plan lessons, share teaching strategies, or discuss challenges they are facing and brainstorm solutions.

- **During Preparation Periods:** Preparation periods during the school day can also be used for professional development. Teachers can use this time to observe each other's classes, meet with a mentor or coach, engage in online professional development, or work on action research projects. For example, a teacher could use one preparation period a week to observe a colleague's class and then meet with that colleague to discuss observations and share feedback.

Incorporating professional development into the workday in these ways has several benefits:

- **Relevance:** By embedding professional development into the workday, the learning is immediately applicable to teachers' current context and can be integrated into their teaching practice right away (Darling-Hammond et al., 2017).

- **Sustainability:** Regular, ongoing professional development is more likely to lead to sustained changes in teaching practice (Desimone, 2009).

- **Convenience:** Embedding professional development into the workday makes it more accessible for teachers and reduces the need for them to dedicate additional time outside of their regular working hours (Hirsh, 2009).

- **Collaboration:** Embedding professional development into the workday provides opportunities for teachers to collaborate with their colleagues, share ideas, and learn from each other (Hord, 2009).

However, it is important to note that while embedding professional development into the workday has many benefits, it also presents challenges. For example, it may be difficult to find a time that is convenient for all teachers, and there may be logistical challenges related to finding substitute teachers or arranging for classroom coverage during preparation periods. Additionally, it is important to ensure that the professional development activities are meaningful and relevant to the teachers' needs and not just added to the workday for the sake of convenience (Darling-Hammond et al., 2017).

Development Phase

During the development phase, lesson plans and instructional media are developed for the presenters of the professional development. Validation of these materials is crucial to ensure that they are accurate, effective, and appropriate for the target audience. For K–12 teacher professional development materials, this validation can be done in several ways:

- **Expert Review:** Subject matter experts, experienced teachers, and instructional designers can review the materials to ensure that they are accurate, relevant, and aligned with the learning objectives. They can provide feedback on the content, instructional strategies, and assessment tools.

- **Pilot Testing:** Conduct a pilot test of the materials with a small group of teachers who are representative of the target audience. This will provide an opportunity to see how the materials work in a real-world setting and identify any issues or areas for improvement. After the pilot test, feedback from the participants can be used to make necessary revisions to the materials (Guskey, 2002).

- **Peer Review:** Have the materials reviewed by peers, such as other teachers or instructional designers, who can provide feedback on the clarity, organization, and effectiveness of the materials.

Toolbox Tip

Designing an Instructor's Guide

An instructor's guide is crucial for structuring the professional development training and ensuring its effectiveness. Follow the QR code or visit bit.ly/3StfPkD an example of an instructor's guide designed for a professional development training focused on improving teaching and learning with technology in a K–12 setting.

- **Alignment with Standards:** Ensure that the materials are aligned with relevant standards, such as the ISTE Standards previously mentioned or the Common Core State Standards. This will help ensure that the materials are of high quality and relevant to the teachers' needs.

- **Usability Testing:** Conduct usability testing to ensure that the materials are user-friendly and accessible. This may include testing the materials on different devices, checking for broken links or technical issues, and ensuring that the materials are accessible to individuals with disabilities (Zepeda, 2015).

During this phase of the ADDIE model, materials for both the instructor and the participants are created. For a Teacher Professional Development program, instructor materials may include:

- **Instructor Guide:** A comprehensive guide that includes an overview of the program, learning objectives, a detailed agenda, instructions for facilitating each session, discussion questions, and tips for engaging participants (Zepeda, 2015).

- **Presentation Slides:** Visual aids that the instructor will use to present the content. These may include slides with text, images, videos, and links to online resources.

- **Activity Instructions:** Detailed instructions for facilitating activities during the program. This may include group discussions, hands-on exercises, case studies, and role-playing scenarios.

- **Assessment Tools:** Tools for assessing the participants' knowledge and skills during the program. This may include quizzes, surveys, observation checklists, or other means of checking for participant understanding.

- **Supplemental Resources:** Additional resources that the instructor can use to supplement the training. This may include articles, videos, websites, and examples of lesson plans that incorporate technology.

- **Technology Setup Guide:** A guide that includes instructions for setting up the technology needed for the program. This may include instructions for setting up projectors, computers, and online platforms (Guskey, 2002).

- **Feedback Forms:** Forms that the instructor can use to collect feedback from the participants during and after the program.

Implementation Phase

The implementation phase is perhaps the most intuitive and easy to understand because all of us have at one time or another, been a participant in a professional development program. During this phase, a schedule of the professional development program is implemented, materials are distributed/used, and professional development is implemented by an instructor/facilitator. Tests, or better for an audience of teachers, checks on understanding are employed by the instructors. Such checks on understanding are called *formative assessment.*

Formative assessment is essential during the delivery of teacher professional development as it helps the instructor to understand the participants' grasp of the content in real-time and make necessary adjustments to the instruction. Here are some methods of formative assessment that the professional development instructor can use:

- **Quizzes:** Short quizzes at the end of each section or module can help the instructor to assess the participants' understanding of the key concepts (Zepeda, 2015).

- **Polls and Surveys:** Using online tools to conduct polls and surveys during the session can provide immediate feedback on the participants' understanding and opinions.

- **Interactive Activities:** Engaging participants in interactive activities such as group discussions, case studies, and hands-on exercises can provide insights into their ability to apply the concepts being taught (Guskey, 2002).

- **Question and Answer Sessions:** Allocating time for participants to ask questions and providing answers can help clarify any misunderstandings or misconceptions.

- **Observations:** Observing participants as they engage in activities, discussions, or exercises can provide valuable insights into their understanding and skills.

- **Self-Assessment:** Asking participants to assess their own understanding and skills can provide insights into their perceived strengths and areas for improvement.

- **Peer Assessment:** Having participants assess each other's understanding and skills can provide additional perspectives and insights.

- **Online Discussion Forums:** Creating online discussion forums where participants can post questions, share ideas, and engage in discussions can provide insights into their understanding and application of the concepts.

At the end of a professional development, it is recommended to assess overall participant learning based on the previously written measurable learning objectives. This is known as *summative assessment*. Traditional methods can be used, such as tests or rubrics to evaluate teacher-created deliverables. Some teachers may not appreciate being asked to take a test at the end of their professional development, but more will appreciate being asked to produce a deliverable that will be evaluated based on a previously shared grading rubric, especially if the deliverable can be redone multiple times, if necessary, to achieve the learning objectives and it is even better if the deliverable will be used by the teachers in their classrooms after the professional development is done.

Tech Leader Profile

Pattie Morales, Instructional Technology Specialist

Pattie Morales has been the instructional technology specialist for the Indian Community School (ICS) in Franklin, Wisconsin since 2017. ICS is a private, faith-based school serving around 360 intertribal American Indian students from kindergarten through 8th grade. Pattie started working at ICS after beginning her career as a classroom teacher in the Milwaukee Public Schools where she was a technology champion for two school buildings. Trained as an educator, she was first licensed for grades 1–8 with endorsements in science and language arts for middle school. Pattie eventually earned an M.S. in K–12 Special Education, and an M.Ed. in Learning and Technology. She has also earned a Google Level 2 certification, is an ISTE Certified Educator, and a Certified Education Technology Leader. Two others work in the technology department at ICS, but neither is supervised by Pattie. She reports directly to the director of instruction. Her main responsibilities include developing plans for using technology to improve teaching and learning, coaching teachers to use various instructional strategies to enhance, extend, and engage students, and facilitating the PowerSchool standards-based grading system while also troubleshooting that system. While ICS is in a suburban area, the school serves students from urban, suburban, and rural areas. Pattie's biggest challenge every day is balancing the back-end work required by her position while maintaining a consistent presence in classrooms and throughout the building. That classroom presence is essential for sustaining collaborative relationships with staff members. Her satisfaction comes from seeing teachers develop confidence in their ability to use technology purposefully. Pattie recommends that those who aspire to be a technology leader make sure they do not lose their connection to the end user. Teachers and students know what does and does not work for them. A cross section of school representation is needed at the table when making decisions. You can follow her work at: @MoralesPattie.

Retrospective pre-post self-assessments are a valuable tool for summative assessment to measure changes in participants' knowledge, skills, and attitudes after a professional development program. This type of an assessment is an alternative to administering a test or producing a deliverable product. It is easy to administer, and teachers are unlikely to be put off by such a self-assessment as they might be if asked to take a test. Unlike traditional pre-post assessments, where participants are asked to assess their knowledge or skills before and after the training, retrospective pre-post assessments ask participants to assess their knowledge or skills both before and after the training, but only after the training has been completed.

In a professional development program, retrospective pre-post self-assessments based on written learning objectives can be designed and used in the following way:

- **Clearly Defined Learning Objectives:** At the beginning of the professional development program, clearly define the learning objectives. These objectives should be specific, measurable, achievable, relevant, and time-bound (SMART) (Zepeda, 2015).

- **Introduction of the Assessment:** At the end of the program, introduce the retrospective pre-post self-assessment. Explain to the participants that they will be asked to assess their knowledge or skills both before and after the training, but only after the training has been completed.

- **Design of the Assessment:** The assessment should be designed to measure the participants' perception of their knowledge, skills, and attitudes related to the learning objectives. For each learning objective, ask participants to rate their knowledge or skills on a scale (e.g., from 1 to 5, where 1 is "no knowledge/skill" and 5 is "expert knowledge/skill") both before and after the training (Lamb, 2005).

- **Administration of the Assessment:** Administer the assessment at the end of the training. Ask participants to complete the assessment independently and honestly.

- **Analysis of the Assessment:** Analyze the assessment data to identify any changes in the participants' perception of their knowledge, skills, and attitudes. This can provide valuable insights into the effectiveness of the professional development program and identify areas for improvement (Guskey, 2002).

- **Feedback and Reflection:** Share the results of the assessment with the participants and encourage them to reflect on their learning journey. This can help them to identify their strengths, areas for improvement, and strategies for implementing what they have learned in their teaching practice.

Remember that the retrospective pre-post learning self-assessment should be designed to assess each measurable learning objective used in the design of the professional development. This assessment is administered at the end of professional development before teachers are released. An example retrospective pre-post self-assessment instrument can be accessed using the QR code or visiting bit.ly/3u4bE4u.

In addition to the retrospective pre-post assessment, it is also a common and best practice to get participant reactions to the training at the end of a professional development. Such feedback forms should be designed to improve the design and delivery of the professional development in the future. An example form is provided at the QR code or visit bit.ly/49kPnj9.

A useful and comprehensive evaluation model will be presented in the next section of this chapter.

Evaluation Phase

The evaluation phase is not only the final phase of the ADDIE model but also a continuous process that loops back to the other phases. The feedback and data collected during the evaluation phase are used to make revisions and improvements to the instructional program, which may involve revisiting the analysis, design, or development phases. This iterative process helps ensure the instructional program remains relevant and effective over time. This phase involves two different types of evaluation: formative and summative.

Formative Evaluation

This type of evaluation is conducted during each phase of the ADDIE process. During the analysis, design, and development phases, instructional designers gather feedback on the instructional materials, activities, and assessments to ensure they are aligned with the learning objectives and are effective in facilitating learning. This feedback can be obtained from subject matter experts, other instructional designers, or a small group of learners who are part of the target audience. The purpose of formative evaluation is to identify any issues or areas for improvement before the instructional program is fully implemented.

Summative Evaluation

This type of evaluation is conducted after the instructional program has been implemented. It assesses the overall effectiveness of the instructional program in terms of achieving its intended learning outcomes. This involves assessing learners' performance on assessments, gathering feedback from learners and other stakeholders, and analyzing data on learners' engagement and satisfaction with the program. The results of the summative evaluation are used to make decisions about whether the instructional program should be continued, revised, or discontinued.

Both formative and summative evaluations are essential for ensuring the effectiveness of the instructional program. Formative evaluation helps to identify and correct issues during the development of the program, while summative evaluation helps to assess the overall success of the program after it has been implemented.

Kirkpatrick's Model

The summative evaluation portion of this phase is commonly conducted using a framework known as Kirkpatrick's evaluation model. It was originally developed by Donald Kirkpatrick in the 1950s and has been refined and expanded over the years. The model includes four levels of evaluation, each of which assesses a different aspect of the training program (Kirkpatrick & Kirkpatrick, 2006).

1. **Reaction:** This is the first level of the evaluation process. It assesses the participants' immediate reactions to the training program. This includes their feelings about the content, the trainer, the method of delivery, and the overall environment. Evaluators usually collect this information through questionnaires or surveys given to participants at the end of the training session. This level of evaluation is crucial because if the participants do not find the training engaging or relevant, they are less likely to pay attention or apply what they have learned (Kirkpatrick & Kirkpatrick, 2006). *An example of this level of evaluation has been provided previously in the Professional Development Form.*

2. **Learning:** The second level of the evaluation model focuses on the extent to which participants have learned the material presented in the training. This can be measured through tests, quizzes, or other assessments that are given before and after the training. The difference in scores can help evaluators determine how much knowledge or skill has been acquired. This level of evaluation is important because it helps to determine if the training content was effective and if the participants were able to understand and retain the

information presented (Kirkpatrick & Kirkpatrick, 2006). *An example of this level of evaluation has been provided in the Professional Development Session Retrospective Pre-Post Self-Assessment form.*

3. **Behavior:** This level of evaluation assesses the extent to which teachers change their behavior because of the professional development program. This can be observed by school administrators or colleagues in the classroom or can be self-reported by the teachers themselves. It involves assessing whether the teachers are implementing the technology tools and strategies they learned during the training in their teaching practices. It is important to note that a change in behavior may not be immediate and may take time to manifest. Therefore, this level of evaluation is often conducted a few weeks or months after the professional development program has been completed. This level is critical because the ultimate goal of any professional development program is to change behavior and improve teaching practices (Kirkpatrick & Kirkpatrick, 2006).

4. **Results:** The fourth and final level of the model evaluates the overall results of the professional development program. This includes assessing whether the program has had a positive impact on the school or district, such as improved student achievement, increased engagement, or more effective use of technology in the classroom. This level of evaluation is often the most difficult to measure because it involves many variables that are outside the control of the professional development program. However, it is also the most important level because it helps to determine the return on investment (ROI) of the program, in terms of improved educational outcomes and more effective teaching and learning practices (Kirkpatrick & Kirkpatrick, 2006).

Each level of Kirkpatrick's model builds on the previous one, and it is important to conduct evaluations at all four levels to get a comprehensive understanding of the effectiveness of the training program. However, it is also important to note that not all training programs may require evaluations at all four levels, and the specific needs and goals of the organization should be considered when designing the evaluation process (Kirkpatrick & Kirkpatrick, 2006).

Measuring evaluation level three, behavior, is commonly done using a self-report form or an observation instrument. Level three evaluation is usually done one to three months after the professional development is over. For an example of a professional development self-evaluation, visit bit.ly/3FHB22P or scan the QR code.

For an example of a teacher observation instrument, visit bit.ly/3Qw7OJk or scan the QR code.

Effective Teaching with Technology Professional Development Report.

Effective Teaching with Technology Teacher Observation Instrument.

Measuring Results with Kirkpatrick's Model

Level four of Kirkpatrick's model, Results, is the highest level of evaluation and measures the overall impact of the professional development on the organization or broader context. It involves assessing the extent to which the professional development has achieved its intended outcomes, such as improved student learning, increased teacher efficiency, or improved classroom management.

Here are some ways to measure Level 4 results:

- **Student Performance:** Compare student performance data before and after the teachers participated in the professional development training. Improvement in students' grades, test scores, graduation rates, attendance rates, or other performance indicators can be attributed to the improved teaching practices.

- **Teacher Performance:** Analyze teacher performance data, such as classroom observations, teacher evaluations, or self-assessments. Improvements in teaching practices, technology integration, or classroom management can be indicators of the professional development's effectiveness.

- **Organizational Outcomes:** Assess organizational outcomes such as reduced costs, increased efficiency, or improved student satisfaction. For example, if the professional development aimed to improve the efficiency of technology use in classrooms, an indicator could be a reduction in the time teachers spend on administrative tasks.

- **Surveys and Feedback:** Conduct surveys or interviews with key stakeholders, such as school administrators, parents, and students, to gather feedback on the perceived impact of the professional development.

- **Long-Term Goals:** Analyze the alignment of the outcomes with the long-term goals of the organization or educational institution. For example, if one of the goals is to improve digital literacy among students, the outcomes could be measured by assessing students' digital skills before and after the training.

It is important to note that Level 4 evaluation should not be conducted immediately after the training but after a reasonable period, based on the impacts listed in the logic model, allowing for the changes to take effect. Also, it is crucial to establish a baseline before the training to have a reference point for comparison.

On Time, On Target, Ongoing PD

The integration of technology in teaching and learning is a vital aspect of the contemporary K–12 educational environment. For teachers, professional development related to teaching and learning with technology transcends merely enhancing technical skills; it also involves adapting their pedagogical practices, mindset, and attitudes to the ever-evolving digital world. Studies have consistently indicated that effective professional development programs must be ongoing, context-specific, and actively involve the participation of teachers (Darling-Hammond, Hyler, & Gardner, 2017). Additionally, collaboration and sharing of best practices among teachers can lead to a more cohesive and effective implementation of technology in the classroom (Trust, Krutka, & Carpenter, 2016).

The ADDIE model provides a useful structure for planning and implementing professional development programs related to technology integration. The logic model, a graphical representation of the resources, activities, outputs, and outcomes of a program, can also be employed to articulate the underlying theory, assumptions, and expectations about the relationships among these elements (W.K. Kellogg Foundation, 2004). By incorporating both the ADDIE and logic models into the design and implementation of professional development programs, educators and administrators can ensure that these programs are well-planned, relevant, and effective in achieving the desired outcomes.

Moreover, it is crucial to assess the effectiveness of professional development programs. Kirkpatrick's Evaluation Model offers a comprehensive approach to assess the impact of professional development programs (Kirkpatrick & Kirkpatrick, 2006).

Ensuring equitable access to high-quality professional development opportunities for all teachers remains a challenge. Schools and districts must allocate adequate resources and provide the necessary support to ensure all teachers, regardless of their starting skill levels or the contexts in which they work, can effectively integrate technology into their teaching and learning processes. Policymakers and educational leaders should also advocate for a systemic approach to professional development that recognizes the complex interplay between technology, pedagogy, and content knowledge (TPACK) (Mishra & Koehler, 2006).

In the digital age, the teacher's role is more critical than ever, not only as a facilitator of knowledge but also as a guide who can help students navigate the digital landscape safely and responsibly. Continuous professional development in technology integration is essential for empowering teachers to fulfill this role effectively. As teachers become more proficient and comfortable with technology, they can create more engaging and meaningful learning experiences for their students, thereby contributing to better educational outcomes.

Answers to Essential Questions

1. **What does the literature say are the elements of effective teacher professional development?**

    Effective teacher professional development is (a) content focused, (b) employs active learning, (c) promotes collaboration among teachers, (d) provides teachers with models of effective practice, (e) provides support through coaching and expert mentoring, (f) provides time for teachers to reflect upon the new information and how it relates to their practice, and to solicit feedback on implementation, and (g) is sustained over a time period of weeks or months rather than being a one-off event.

2. **How does the technology coordinator design and evaluate a professional development program?**

    Based on the logic model of your choice, the characteristics of an effective professional development programs, an agreed-upon and resourced logic model, you would use the ADDIE Instructional Design Model as your guide to designing and implementing the professional development program, and use Kirkpatrick's Evaluation Model to guide all four levels of evaluation.

Chapter 5

SUPPORTING EDUCATIONAL TECHNOLOGY

Essential Questions

1. What essential functions does the technology coordinator support?

2. What processes must a technology coordinator implement to ensure that comprehensive technical support is provided?

3. How can the technology coordinator prioritize numerous and simultaneous support issues or requests?

4. For what security and protection issues must the technology coordinator monitor and establish systems?

5. What key elements should be included in an Acceptable Use Policy?

6. What technology systems must the technology coordinator ensure are installed and are continuously functional because of their importance to a school or district?

7. How can the technology coordinator stay up to date on the latest digital learning innovations?

8. How can the technology coordinator support pedagogy involving digital learning tools?

9. What role should the technology coordinator play in helping the district to meet the legal requirements of the Children's Internet Protection Act (CIPA)?

10. What does the technology coordinator need to know about grant writing to locate and secure additional funding for technology projects?

Technology coordinators are key players in planning, implementing, and sustaining the use of technology for teaching and learning. Based on current trends, a technology coordinator must be prepared to provide or arrange for multiple types of support for the teachers, students, support staff, administrators, parents, and sometimes community members they serve. Figure 5.1 depicts the nine essential issues for supporting educational technology as considered in this chapter.

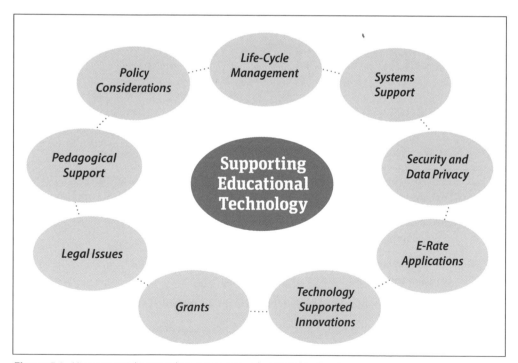

Figure 5.1. Nine essential issues when supporting educational technology.

Systems Support

Systems support ensures that the organization will be able to provide technical support and help desk assistance for issues such as software or application problems, hardware failures, or network issues. The technology coordinator must ensure that the right people, processes, and products are in place to provide the systems support called for based on the local conditions. These three elements may be something the school or district can provide using its own resources, or they may be elements that will need to be put in place through outsourcing.

Every school district requires many technology systems to operate and provide instruction. The technology coordinator is responsible for ensuring such systems are in place and properly managed, which requires a team of qualified people. No technology coordinator, even in a small operation, can perform all these functions and possess all these skill sets alone. A list of the most often implemented systems, and a description of each, is provided next. Most of these systems are functions provided by a school's network operating system, which manages the server, network, and the connection of the school or district to the internet as part of its client/server architecture. In some cases, on a limited budget, many or all these services can be provided using inexpensive or even free open-source software. Network operating systems (NOSs) that are commonly employed in schools include Novell Open Enterprise Server, Apache, various distributions based on or including Linux, and Windows Server. These systems enable a network administrator to configure and manage an email system, a directory management system that enables users to store and access files and software from the server, allows users to authenticate to the network and to the device in one login, enables the sharing of printers across the school's intranet, provides for the backup and retrieval of files, storage management, and usually provides other functionality such as a firewall. The systems mentioned below may be managed at a school or a district level. A school that is private, charter, or otherwise administratively independent of a school district would need to have most, if not all, of these systems in place.

People

Of the variety of people needed to support educational technology, the most obvious is the technology coordinator her- or himself. The technology coordinator has a big job to perform and, when all the duties and responsibilities are defined, the need for a full-time technology coordinator is usually clear. In some cases, the duties of a coordinator are distributed among a variety of people, but we conceive of the technology coordinator as the person with overarching responsibility for all these categories of support. In addition to a technology coordinator, there may be technicians, teachers, students, vendors, or even volunteers assisting with the enormous task of sustaining the technology support for teaching and learning.

Technicians are often needed who have specialized skill at managing a server at the center of a network that is usually used to serve a website to the public on the internet, provide networked storage, host the email accounts of everyone in the school or district, and provide other services that will be mentioned later in this chapter. Network support is another area in which a technician is needed, because installing, maintaining, and troubleshooting the devices and wiring that enable networks to function and communicate with other networks requires specialized skills. At least one other type of technician is critical—this is the desktop and device support technician. This type of technician supports teachers, students, and staff by installing and maintaining the hardware and software used throughout the organization on desktop computers and mobile devices.

Often teachers are used to perform various services, such as providing a variety of professional development to their peers, planning and reviewing progress toward technology plan goals, supervising students helping to perform support functions, providing pedagogical support to their peers, and even providing direct technical support. Given that teachers are the largest group of employees in a school or district, it makes sense to make use of any who are skilled and interested in helping out. It also makes sense to use teachers to supervise student helpers.

Students may also be used to staff a help desk. If the organization chooses to do this, the technology coordinator or another teacher typically supervises students who are asked to provide support functions. Students can be a significant resource for a school, and it makes sense to use those who are skilled and interested, especially if the students can be given class credit for their work and for what they learn in performing their duties.

Even if you involve teachers, staff, and students, the hiring of vendors to provide specialized services is common. When a large job is to be done, such as installing all-new computers or a brand-new network in a school, a vendor is typically hired to perform these time-sensitive and critical tasks. Hiring a vendor enables the technology coordinator to specify in a contract the services to be provided, the quality of those services, and the due dates for services to be completed. If services aren't completed according to the contract agreement, the technology coordinator is often able to withhold payment until the contract is met. A well-conceived contract gives the technology coordinator power and provides substantial value to the school or schools to be served.

Finally, some schools have had success using community volunteers who wish to use their technical skills or physical labor to help the school meet its technology goals. Volunteers may be used to provide technical services such as troubleshooting problems, depending on the skill level of the volunteer. Also, in other cases, volunteers lacking technical skills may be very useful in performing tasks such as moving computers around a school or plugging in cables in a computer lab.

Tech Leader Profile

April Burton, Instructional Technology Content Leader

April Burton has been working for the Francis Howell School District in Missouri since 2001. She was originally hired as a French and English teacher and then became an instructional technology content leader in 2015. The district is located on the far Northwest side of the St. Louis metro area, where it serves about 17,000 K–12 students in twenty-three schools. April received her initial training in French education and English, later earned a master's degree in information science and learning technologies, and is currently a doctoral candidate. She also earned designations as an ISTE Certified Educator and a Google Certified Trainer. Her main responsibilities are supporting the use of the district LMS, facilitating professional development, and training teachers to purposefully integrate technology. April and another content leader work on instructional technology initiatives for the district, while a separate group manages and supports the district IT operations. She reports directly to the director of adult learning. The Francis Howell School District is suburban, populated by mostly white students with fewer than 20% qualifying for free or reduced lunches. April describes her biggest challenge as successfully reaching all teachers to support them in using technology to transform learning. She points out that "it can be difficult to get the message across to all buildings, especially when teachers have different comfort levels in using technology. I rely on constructing relationships with building leaders to support teachers' needs." Her satisfaction comes from students who report that a tool or strategy was fun. A good day for April is when she's visiting the classroom of a teacher whom she's been mentoring, and the students are so excited and engaged that they don't want to leave. For those who wish to be educational technology leaders like April, her advice is to lead by example; try new things and share your successes; don't be afraid to innovate; and bring others along on your journey. You can follow her work here: @MmeBurton.

Processes

The technology coordinator must ensure that a variety of processes are in place to provide competent technical support. In some cases, these processes may need to be clearly formalized in a written policy or standard. In other cases, they can be less formal and more easily changed, such as in procedures or guidelines. Regardless of formality or approval method, such processes enable the technology coordinator to effectively manage technical issues ranging from the smallest technology glitches encountered on a day-to-day basis, to managing notifications and updates to stakeholders, to managing all higher-level aspects of support for teaching, learning, and computing.

An exemplary, easy-to-understand, and comprehensive set of best practices, called the Information Technology Infrastructure Library (ITIL), has been established in the United Kingdom. The ITIL is a joint venture between the government of the U.K. and a company called Axelos. It covers the life cycle of service management in five phases containing twenty-six processes that are just as useful in schools as they are in business or industry. These processes, based on the ITIL (ClydeBank Technology, 2015), are described next.

Event Management

When a technician monitors a system to make sure it is functioning normally, abnormalities are sometimes detected. If the conditions monitored do not result in a disruption of service, but are important for the management of the infrastructure, they are often called *events* and are treated similarly to incidents, below. Systems management software can be used to monitor for potential events, provide notification of potential problems, help to diagnose problems, and even help to remedy the situation before an incident occurs.

Incident Management

When a device or service does not work properly, causing a disruption or reduction in functionality, the end user of that device contacts a help desk for assistance in resolving the issue. This type of disruption is called an incident, and help desks typically use a ticketing system for their tracking and management. A ticket is created in the help desk management software describing the incident and assigning a priority to it, and someone is assigned to troubleshoot the issue. Previously created troubleshooting guidelines are followed—and updated based on experience—for network, desktop, or mobile device issues.

Problem Management

A collection of related incidents is called a problem. For example, if multiple teachers are reporting that their computers freeze when they perform certain tasks, this is an example of a problem. Similar to incidents, the technology coordinator must document the problem in the help desk management software, determine the extent and scale of the problem within the school, devise a plan to fix the problem with the least disruption to the end users, and implement the plan. Because a problem often affects multiple devices or systems, it is often appropriate to communicate with end users the nature of the problem, how the problem or its solution may affect them, the steps being taken to fix the problem, and an estimated date by which it will be fixed.

Change Management

Changes in technology are constant in schools. Therefore, the technology coordinator must have processes in place to manage routine change. Examples of change include adding new software to multiple computers, updating operating system software on all devices schoolwide, or installing a new email management system. Changes involve an upgrade in service of some sort for the end users of one or more systems. These upgrades represent changes in the configuration of items such as software, hardware, or systems of software and hardware, including network components. Configuration items also include a specific set of devices or all the devices in a specified area. When a configuration item needs to be changed to provide a needed upgrade in service to end users, this change must be managed in steps. First, it should be planned to minimally affect end users, and the plan should be well communicated. It should have administrative support and also have the support of a representative technology committee to help ensure the buy-in of teachers. Ideally, upgrades to devices and systems should take place over a weekend or holiday, when there is limited use of the affected systems. Finally, if the change means that teachers or staff must learn to use something new or different, job aids or handouts should be created and distributed, video tutorials created as needed, and even professional development planned in advance of the change to ensure continuity of productivity, teaching, and learning after the changes take effect.

User/Incident Notification

A process and system must be implemented to notify users of issues or incidents that may affect them. Such a notification system may be as simple as email, or it may be more complicated and involve automated telephone calling, text messaging, or a combination of these methods. User notification may also make use of social media such as the school's website, X (formerly Twitter), or Facebook. Notification systems are useful for technical issues, certainly, but they are also very useful for emergency situations such as school closures or crisis situations. Processes for notification should be mapped out in advance for every conceivable scenario and should include who is notified, in what sequence, and the process involved in deciding when and what to include in the notification. A series of template messages should be created so they are ready to be implemented when needed.

Stakeholder Updates

The technology coordinator must also be prepared to implement processes to update employees, parents, students, or community members about important changes or upgrades in technology services or capabilities at least once or twice a year. An emailed newsletter, also posted on the school's website, is an effective process for updating stakeholders. If the school sends out a printed newsletter, asking for a section in the newsletter at least once a year should help to keep stakeholders updated as well. Giving verbal reports at leadership meetings, parent-teacher organization meetings, student council meetings, or to teachers at staff meetings is also an effective way to keep everyone informed of major events in the technology life of the school. Having an article published in the student newspaper can also keep students updated.

Technology Support Priorities

A very important process the technology coordinator must establish concerns the prioritization of support requests. Everyone naturally wishes to have her or his request for assistance taken care of immediately. However, even in a school with robust staffing levels, this is impossible. Therefore, a process must be created, approved by administration and the technology committee, and communicated to all end users concerning the prioritization of support requests. Having a series of levels of urgency based on severity of impact is a common system. A system such as the ones depicted in Figure 5.2 and Table 5.1 may meet your needs.

		LEVEL OF IMPACT			
		URGENT	HIGH	MEDIUM	LOW
LEVEL OF URGENCY	**Extensive**	PL1	PL1	PL2	PL4
	Significant	PL1	PL2	PL3	PL4
	Moderate	PL2	PL2	PL3	PL4
	Minor	PL2	PL3	PL3	PL4

Figure 5.2. Help Desk Priority Matrix.

Table 5.1. Priority Matrix Definitions

PRIORITY LEVEL	RESPONSE TIME	URGENCY DEFINITION		IMPACT DEFINITION	
PL1	1 Business Day	Extensive	Affects all users and/or multiple systems	Urgent	• Service is out • Users are unable to work and no work-around is available • Immediate restoration is needed
PL2	3 Business Days	Significant	Affects significant percentage of users and/or systems	High	• Partial loss of functionality, access, or resources • Work-around may/may not be possible • Quick restoration is needed
PL3	5 Business Days	Moderate	Affects limited percentage of users or secondary systems or modules within a primary system	Medium	• Service not functioning properly • Work-around may/may not be possible • Users inconvenienced but can still perform tasks
PL4	Scheduled into Operations	Minor	Affects a specific group of users, system module(s), or function(s)	Low	• "Nice to have" functionality disrupted • Functionality or accuracy not affected • User experience can be improved

Equipment Standards

Schools often contain a mixture of old and new technology. The life span for most hardware and software is generally three to five years. Sometimes events make it a necessity to keep older computers, even as new computers are being deployed. For example, a school with several laptop carts and a smaller special-purpose computer lab may be able to acquire enough new equipment to replace some but not all devices in the building. At some point in time, older technology becomes costly in both time and resources, and may even become cost-prohibitive, to repair or upgrade. The technology coordinator must have in place standards for deciding which technologies are fully supported, upgraded, and repaired, and those that receive limited or no support at all. The technology coordinator should develop, approve, and communicate these standards in a way that is transparent to everyone in the organization. Such standards should include the operating system(s); specific makes and models of desktop and laptop computers; makes and models of mobile devices; and the minimum processor, RAM, and hard drive space. Similarly, standards are needed for the network, its speed, and its components. Having these standards in place allows the technology coordinator to make sure all educational and business functions are supported, and puts the school or district in a position to be able to adopt new technologies when needed. Finally, procedures or guidelines should be developed and put in place concerning staff-owned technologies. Bring Your Own Device (BYOD) programs are growing in popularity for schools who struggle to fund technology budgets and provide adequate technology resources. Still, such programs create a significant challenge for any school. You should make clear what support, if any, is available to a staff member or student regarding connecting a personally owned device to the network, troubleshooting issues, and ensuring the personal device is protected or screened for malware before connecting to the network.

Data Backup and Recovery

The technology coordinator should consider developing, communicating, and implementing a process for regular backups of all data stored on the school's servers, especially critical data. The frequency of backups—daily, weekly, or monthly—and the type of backups performed—incremental or complete—should be clearly defined. Critical systems, such as student information systems, should usually be backed up fully on a daily basis. It's common to run a full backup of all data once a week, while a daily incremental backup is also conducted. An incremental backup includes all newly created files not previously backed up. A full backup makes sure that all files are backed up, whether they were previously backed up or not. Backed-up data should be stored in at least two different locations off site to help ensure that all data and functionality can be restored following a catastrophic event, such as a fire or lightning strike. Make sure that backup files are stored for a minimum of several months, ensuring that data can be recovered from an older backup file, even if newer files have somehow become corrupted. All staff and students should also understand what happens with deleted files stored on a server. A procedure should be established and communicated so everyone knows when deleted files on servers are purged and under what conditions files might be recovered from a backup.

Image Creation and Management

The load of software on and the configuration of each computing device is called an image. Software such as Symantec's Ghost Solution Suite can be used to create an image for a particular kind of machine with a particular configuration (graphics cards, drives, etc.). Once a master computer is set up, an image can be made of that computer. Once made and stored, the image can be speedily deployed to all other computers having the same configuration through a network. An image can be deployed to many computers at the same time, depending on the capabilities of your network and server. Of course, the software contained in the image must be carefully monitored, because it is easy to install too many instances of a piece of software across multiple machines, exceeding the purchased number of licenses. The images created, the software contained in each image, and the deployment of each image must be accurately reflected in your configuration database.

Setting up a master computer as the basis for an image should be done with great care. Any imperfections in the image will be replicated on every computer using that image. Because the process of creating an image requires the technology coordinator to take a computer out of operation, it is best if at least one extra computer of each type can be purchased so it can serve as an image master computer. Once an image is created, it should be tested on at least one other computer before it is deployed. Consider using a checklist to make sure the image contains all the necessary software and is properly configured and tested. A library of images can be created and stored on a server for rapid deployment as needed. It may be advantageous to create one image for deployment to all teachers and a different image for deployment to all students.

Finally, the imaging process can be an important tool in addressing incidents and problems. Re-imaging can automatically replace all the software and configurations on a computer, and assuming the image has no defects, this method can be an important way to quickly solve problems. If you plan to use this method, it should be communicated to all end users that if you have to re-image their computer, they will lose any personal files or documents they have saved on the local hard drive. It is a good practice to encourage everyone to save any documents they wish to keep on the server (as opposed to the local hard drive) so they won't be deleted upon re-imaging.

User Management

Certain actions must be taken when a new staff member is hired, at various points during their employment, and when they leave the school. Upon hiring, processes must be established for collecting necessary information from new users, having them

them read and acknowledge acceptance of policies, and having them create usernames, passwords, and authentication procedures for systems such as the network and email accounts. You should create a process for distributing devices to staff members, too. At a minimum, staff members should sign a form acknowledging receipt of a device—identified on the form by make, model, serial number, and inventory tag number—and acceptance of any policies associated with using the device. Standards for secure passwords should be established, as well as standards for frequency of changing passwords and the reuse of old passwords while the user is employed. When a staff member leaves the school, processes must be established for closing their accounts, removing their personal files from all devices and locations, deactivating their accounts, and collecting any devices signed out to them.

Products

In addition to the processes that must be established, the technology coordinator must have in place a variety of products or systems to help manage the functions of technology support. These products range from database systems, to management software, to user-support systems.

Help-Desk Management Software

Perhaps the single most critical product needed by every technology coordinator is a system to track events, incidents, problems, and changes over time. In a small school with limited resources, these functions can probably be managed using sharable online documents. But free and open-source help-desk software is available, as well as low-cost alternatives. Help-desk software should assign a tracking number to each event, incident, and problem, often referred to as a "ticket." The software should enable a priority level to be established and allow the ticket to be assigned to a specific person. The best help-desk software will work with the school's website to allow users to view the status of their request for help, allow technicians and others providing assistance to see all tickets, provide a record of all tickets, have the capability to produce reports, and be able to perform an analysis of the data contained in the system.

Configuration Management Database

A configuration management database (CMDB) will help the technology coordinator keep track of the software installed on various images, the images installed on all of the various devices, and the configuration of devices located in specific facilities, such as libraries or offices. Functionally, the CMDB is an inventory system for all hardware, software, software licenses, installations, and locations of all configurable items the coordinator is responsible for. The CMDB enables the coordinator to make sure software licensing agreements aren't being violated. It also makes it possible to effectively manage the various versions of software in the inventory and track where different versions of a software product are located in the school or district. In addition, the CMDB allows tracking and management of devices signed out to individuals such as teachers, administrators, staff, or students. A database-savvy technology coordinator can create a home-grown CMDB, but free and low-cost options are available for educational institutions and require much less development and implementation time.

Knowledgebase

A knowledgebase, especially one linked to a school's website, can be an important tool for end users. This collection of information and answers to common questions can be a resource to allow end users to find answers to minor problems themselves. By providing a resource like this, the technology coordinator can reduce the number of questions and calls to the help desk and can provide a way to record and share common solutions and fixes as well as information and guidance about issues that appear less frequently.

Student Information Systems

Student information systems (SISs) are critical for school administration. They provide schools with the ability to enroll and register students in courses, maintain test scores, and track achievement on a variety of standardized assessments indicating student progress toward meeting educational standards. Schools also make use of SISs for providing transcripts, to build class schedules, and to track attendance. State laws often require the use of an SIS in schools, especially SISs that are interoperable with the state's system so that student data can be analyzed at the state level and students can more easily transfer from school to school. SISs enable teachers and administrators to analyze student achievement data to help improve teaching and revise curriculum. Some SISs have built-in analytic functions to automate some analyses. Free or low-cost SISs are available.

Learning Management Systems

Over the years many learning management systems (LMSs) have been developed, and there are some that can be used for free. Regardless of the LMS chosen, they provide similar services. They enable classes to be created within the LMS into which structured course content is uploaded as learning modules. Students log in to the LMS and access the content of their courses, such as text, audio, video, assignments, or interactive simulations. LMSs allow students to interact with each other, with the material, and with the teacher through assignments, discussions, text or even video

Toolbox Tip

Eight Digital Skills Every Teacher Needs

The Learning Technology Center of Illinois, a program of the Illinois State Board of Education, supports the use of technology for school districts and educators in the state. The Center developed an infographic titled Eight Digital Skills Every Teacher Needs. The infographic identifies and describes the eight skills and goes on to identify four popular programs that support learning in each of the digital skill areas. The digital skills are identified below. The infographic and more information

 about the Learning Technology Center of Illinois can be found at bit.ly/46Orj68 or by scanning the QR code.

1. Blend learning
2. Content creation
3. Video creation
4. Screencasting & recording
5. Presentations
6. Data collection
7. Assessment
8. Resource collection

chat, and email. Once an assignment is submitted, or a discussion takes place, the instructor can grade and/or provide feedback to the student(s) and record the grade within the LMS. It is best to find an LMS that can easily integrate with student and class enrollment data provided by the chosen SIS to make the configuration and enrollment of classes as easy as possible. Using an LMS is increasingly important, especially in secondary schools, as the use of online learning, flipped learning, and hybrid courses continues to increase and LMSs support and enable such models of instructional delivery.

Employee and Parent Notification Systems

Schools and districts are increasingly installing notification systems that can be used to notify any specific group of people, such as just parents or only teachers, or to notify all stakeholders, in the case of emergencies or urgent messages. Such systems enable a school or district to broadcast a one-way message to stakeholders. Other names used for such systems include emergency alert systems or emergency communication systems. In the wake of tragic events such as school shootings or bomb threats, it is more important than ever to have a way to communicate with a school's staff, students, parents, and community in an emergency. Notification systems can also provide routine notification to parents to ensure they are aware of key events, such as the start of final exams, a snow day, a make-up day, scheduling for parent-teacher conferences, when report cards are sent home, or a reminder of a long weekend due to a holiday. Such systems require schools to enter the email addresses, home phone numbers, and mobile phone numbers of all parents, staff, and other community members as necessary. Notifications may be sent via email, text message, or using an automated voice/recorded telephone message. Two methods of signup are common, opt-in or opt-out. If an opt-in system is used, stakeholders will have to sign a form indicating their desire to receive notifications. In an opt-out system, stakeholders begin receiving messages and may choose to click on a link or button to be removed from the notification system.

Employee Information Systems

Providing personnel tracking, payroll management, benefits administration, time and attendance tracking/management, management and tracking of sick and personal leave, performance review, job applicant tracking, and even on-boarding management, employee information systems (EISs) are critical to the functioning of schools. Additionally, managing and operating an EIS is a specialized skill area and may require hiring one or more skilled technicians.

Social Media Systems

Relative newcomers to the list of systems that may need to be supported and supervised by the technology coordinator are social media systems. Such technologies may include wikis, blogs, and other systems that are running from a school/district server. Other social media platforms may be employed that are not directly managed by the school/district, such as X/Twitter, Facebook, or YouTube accounts. Regardless of where the social media is hosted, the technology coordinator should make sure there are policies and procedures in place for the use of such platforms to avoid legal issues or potentially embarrassing public relations gaffes.

Technology Life-Cycle Management

The life cycle of any hardware or software in a school can be thought of in five stages: 1. Pre-procurement, 2. Procurement, 3. Deployment, 4. Support and maintenance (see the section on technical support, earlier), and 5. Disposal. Excepting support and maintenance, we discuss these stages next.

Pre-Procurement Stage

During this stage, in which a great deal of planning takes place, a needs assessment is conducted to establish what hardware, software, systems, or service functionality is needed. A set of specifications to meet the needs is then written, identifying features or capabilities that are required, desired, and optional. The specifications document should also include the maximum and desired budget to meet the identified needs. The budget specification should indicate whether this is expected to be a one-time purchase, an ongoing budget item, or a short-term series of purchases over a few years. The specifications document should also define the desired timeline for the procurement, deployment, disposal, and subsequent purchase of a replacement, if necessary. Of course, the specifications document should also include the quantity of items, or frequency of services, needed. A technology committee can be extremely helpful in this process. The resulting specifications and timeline can then be used to procure the technology or service directly, or as the basis for a request for bids to prospective vendors.

If managing the procurement in-house, the technology coordinator and committee can now use the specifications document to identify potential hardware, software, or services to meet the school's needs. At this stage, vendors should be contacted and asked to provide a price quote and to confirm that their technology or service meets the specifications. If the purchase will be large, vendors may be asked to provide an evaluation copy of the technology for comparison. An evaluation matrix can be created based on the specifications and then be used to evaluate and compare the technologies or services best matching the specifications and based on price. The technology coordinator and/or committee can then choose the technologies or services to purchase.

There are at least three other factors to consider at this stage. First, consider the value of an extended warranty. Buying on-site service for hardware may be the most cost-effective way to keep hardware running over the course of its early life. Second, consider the option of leasing hardware. Leasing equipment may allow you to permanently acquire the equipment in a few years when the terms of the lease end. Finally, the power to purchase hardware or software is greater when purchasing in bulk. If you are representing a single school, or a small school district, consider forming a technology consortium with other schools or systems in your area. Making purchases, or negotiating leases or software licenses, can be much less expensive when done as part of a consortium. The larger the consortium, the better the negotiated pricing deal is likely to be.

Procurement Stage

Once the technologies or services have been selected, the next steps depend on whether you are making a direct purchase or making a decision based on submitted bids. If a bidding process was used, the bids should be evaluated by the technology coordinator and committee. The best bid can be selected based on lowest price or best value, depending on the laws and policies of your state and school district. However, if the option is open, consider that the lowest bid is not always the best value. This is why using a "best value" criterion may be a more reasonable method of bid selection.

Ensure that licensing and contract details are clear and will be managed effectively over the life of the technology or service. It may be useful to have these contract documents reviewed by legal counsel to avoid problems. Shipping and delivery arrangements should be part of any agreement. Upon delivery, it is important to inspect products for defects and make sure replacements for any defective items are shipped as soon as possible. Upon receipt, each item must be inventoried and added to your configuration database. Additionally, items accepted for delivery should be bar coded and receive an asset tag for easy management and inventory going forward. It is important to stage newly received and inventoried items in a secure location, preferably one that affords easy deployment.

Deployment Stage

During the deployment stage, and before actual movement of products into place, the technology coordinator will ensure that the technology is configured and imaged. If any personalization, assembly, or customization is needed, it is often easiest to take care of these tasks while the technology is in a centralized staging location. Checklists are helpful during this stage. Placing a checklist on each piece of hardware may be a useful quality-control process. Was the computer imaged? Check. Was an appropriate and custom name set in the computer? Check. Was the correct IP address assigned? Check. Was the correct printer assigned? Check.

Once the technology has been processed for deployment, the next step is often distribution. Upon distribution, the technology should be tested for functionality in its final location and with its final configuration. If the items being deployed are computers or mobile devices, it is a good idea to make sure the end user can log in to the device and perform a few common tasks, such as check their email and print a document. Check. To complete the process, ensure that the inventory/configuration database is updated based on configuration and location. Check.

Disposal Stage

As the technology reaches its end of usable life, disposal is the final stage in the cycle. All assets identified for disposal (based on age or inability to perform their designated function) should be removed from deployment and staged for disposal. The inventory database can be an important tool to identify products that are ready for disposal. To avoid disruption to daily events, it is best if this process is done on a previously sched-uled and communicated day and time, such as after school or on a weekend. Notifying affected users ahead of time allows students, teachers, and staff members to make sure any valuable files they may need in the future are removed. Another checklist would be helpful here, because there are some critical steps involved in this process. Items most often disposed of are computers, laptops, and mobile devices. Ensure that hard drives are wiped clean. No one using the device after it is placed in surplus or the recycle heap should be able to access any software or information that had been previously stored on the hard drive. Remove asset tags and school markings, if possible. If the devices have any usable components that may be used to upgrade or keep another machine running, such as newer RAM or a high-speed drive of some sort, remove such items and store them for reuse. Remove the disposed item from your inventory. Based on the laws and policies in place where you are, consider transferring the device to a liquidation/surplus service or to a disposal service that will properly recycle all components. It may be possible for liquidation or disposal to generate a small amount of revenue to help pay for replacement technology.

Security and Data Privacy

The security of systems and protection of sensitive data, such as student and human resources databases, is among the highest of priorities for a technology coordinator. This is a complex and rapidly changing area. It may be advisable to hire a person with expertise in this area to help with these systems if one isn't already employed in your school or district. The following areas of policy or types of services, at a minimum, should be considered when taking steps to secure systems and data.

Physical Security

Of course, securing electronic access to your systems and data is important, but so is physical security. Physical security includes physical access to computing and network infrastructure, the ability to protect devices from theft or relocation, and the proce-dures for the access to keys or combinations for locks keeping devices physically secure. A plan for the physical security of all devices and infrastructure should be made, which may include locks, keys, and combination locks as well as key card systems. Rooms that should have restricted access include server rooms and main or intermediate network distribution rooms. It is important to keep a list of who should be able to access such rooms without being accompanied by authorized personnel. The keys for these rooms should be locked up and signed out to authorized personnel only when needed. After access is no longer needed, the keys should be signed in. Such a policy enables the coordinator to keep a log of who accessed which rooms, when they accessed the rooms, and the purpose for which the access was granted. Stationary devices, such as printers and desktop computers, need security, too. Consider locking all such devices to a post or heavy desk using a lock and cable to prevent theft or unauthorized relocation. Mobile devices, such as laptop computers or tablet computers, should have a designated storage cabinet that can be locked using a key or combination lock. If the storage cabinet is mobile, consider chaining the cabinet to a pole or wall to prevent its unauthorized removal. The devices to be stored in the cabinet should be locked up at the end of each day. A teacher or other responsible person should be assigned to secure the devices and the cabinet.

The regular and timely inspection of assets is an important step to maintain physical security of all devices. Such an inspection not only should account for the items themselves, but should also check associated security features. At these inspections, consider accounting for all keys and changing the combinations of the locks. If individuals are responsible for mobile devices, take the opportunity provided by the inventory inspection to update any forms and agreements signed by teachers and staff members to keep the inventory current and accurate. Consider keeping an inventory checklist to make sure you do a thorough inventory inspection each time. Update the checklist and its format so it gets better with each use.

Device Tracking and Recovery

All computers can be stolen, especially those that are considered mobile. To help protect your inventory and increase the chances you will recover devices if they are stolen, consider buying and activating anti-theft software that tracks the location of devices and allows them to be wiped and locked if they are stolen. Apple hardware comes with these capabilities, but they must be activated. Similar software and services are available for other hardware. If used, make sure the software images you install on your devices contain your preformatted anti-theft software and that it is installed upon receipt during your life-cycle management process. Another item for your checklist.

User Authentication

Only authorized people should be able to use your hardware and software. The primary way this is done is through an authentication process. Usernames and passwords must be created for each end user to enable access to devices and systems, such as email. For ease and consistency, a naming convention is often used to make up the username for accounts. Such a naming convention often includes at least the first five letters of a last name, the first initial, and the middle initial. Convention-driven usernames are commonly used, and often considered to be the best way to proceed. However, consider that usernames for some systems have to be known and used by many other people. An email address, for example, is not very personal if it is based on this sort of naming convention. For email addresses, consider following the recent trend and allow users to have an email address containing their actual name. This is not only more user friendly, it allows others to more easily discover someone's email address.

It is good to require passwords that contain at least one uppercase and lowercase letter, at least one symbol, at least one number, and at least eight total characters. These guidelines create a "strong" password, because such passwords are less likely to be guessed by another person or by a program written to hack into user accounts. Consider using a two-factor (also known as a two-step) authentication process to further ensure account safety. A two-factor system requires at least two pieces of information from each user to verify identity, such as a password and a small set of predetermined questions the user must answer to establish their authenticity as an authorized user upon login. A second factor may also be biometric, such as a fingerprint. Passwords should be changed on a regular basis, perhaps once a quarter or once every six months, and old passwords should not be reused for a period of least two years.

Malware

Malware, or malicious software, comes in many different forms. A technology coordinator must understand malware and take measures to prevent it from entering systems and devices, actively find and delete it, and educate all end users about it. One type of malware is a virus, a program that is usually hidden among other files and is designed to perform a malicious action, such as deleting data. Some viruses are programmed to replicate themselves on as many drives and devices as possible. Sometimes this replication is accomplished by inserting copies of the virus into other programs or files. This type of virus is usually referred to as a worm. Another type of malware is referred to as a Trojan horse. This is any program that invites a user to run it and, when executed, performs some malicious activity, such as encrypting the user's files or downloading other malicious software. To keep malware from being seen and deleted on a system, malware programmers sometimes use rootkits to modify the host's operating system to hide the presence of the malware. Rootkits often defend against malware removal by replicating the malware and changing the name of the replica. To combat a rootkit, both the malware and the rootkit must be deleted. Some malware creates a backdoor into a system, a way of bypassing the normal authentication procedures for access. Once a backdoor has been established, Trojan horses or viruses can be installed.

Protecting against malware is an important responsibility for all system users, but the chief responsibility belongs to the technology coordinator. Anti-malware software must be installed on each device—from network servers to desktop computers to mobile devices. Anti-malware software that is updated each day with the latest information about the newest known malware found "in the wild" should be uploaded to every device on the system daily when the user logs in. It should also be continuously running on the server. The internet firewall (see below) should also help screen out malware, locate infected websites, and block malware on those sites from reaching your system. Additionally, all users should be trained not to open or run attachments that are suspicious or that were sent from an unknown source. If they must be opened, users should be able to scan them for malware first, or a work ticket should be submitted to the help desk to scan the attachment. The email or internet access management software on your server can usually block websites or email addresses that are known for sending malware.

User Training and Responsibility

Institute a program of education and training of all end users. Such a program can be delivered through a series of in-person sessions or online videos. Everyone who uses the systems and technologies needs to know about the policies in place that affect (and protect) them, such as policies covering technical support, security, passwords, FERPA, email, netiquette, privacy, acceptable use, and social media. Requiring all users to pass a test on the content of the training—with an unlimited number of retakes until a passing score is met—will serve to establish the material as important and will allow the technology coordinator to document that everyone was trained and understood the policies and procedures. Consider having these training sessions available in an online video format so that busy staff members and students can take the course and pass the test at a time best suited for them. At the conclusion of the training, before the session officially ends, is a good time to collect signed acknowledgment forms for acceptable use and related policies that will be kept on file. This is another area where a checklist is useful to make sure everything is properly covered.

Data Privacy

Making use of technology to access network and internet resources is common in elementary and secondary classrooms today. To enhance their classroom instruction and to supplement classroom activities, teachers regularly turn to online applications, websites, and technology platforms to engage students. While laws such as the Family Educational Rights and Privacy Act (FERPA) and the Children's Online Privacy

Protection Act (COPPA) exist to protect student information, schools are experiencing data breaches and violations of data privacy. Classroom teachers using current digital technology resources often employ this technology to deliver content, access information, and interact with other students in order to enhance learning. Applications and social media platforms allow students to collaborate, and online applications allow teachers to customize the learning process for individual students. The rapid shift to online learning pushed schools to rapidly adopt the use of applications and tools that may not have gone through an extensive vetting process. Recently schools have been victims of hackers using ransomware and data breeches by software vendors such as the recent data breech by Illuminate Education.

While there are laws currently in place to protect student data privacy, these laws are somewhat out of data (FERPA dates to 1974 and COPPA to 2000) and often require parent interaction to gain permission for underage students. In practice, many applications have ignored COPPA requirements, and few have been penalized for violations. Kumar et al. (2019) points out there is often a lack of effective teacher training in this area and an ongoing need for more professional development directly addressing the protection of student data and privacy. Educational users described for the researchers that while they may have received professional development and training on the use of technology, this training did not include information addressing privacy and data security. Chanenson et al. (2023) "found that school officials, IT personnel, and teachers lack resources to deal with privacy and security incidents more generally and around EdTech, given that limited privacy and security training is offered on these issues."

Changes may be necessary in the way applications are considered and vetted for use in educational settings. Decision makers will need to more carefully consider the security and privacy implications of the products used by students in order to ensure that student data privacy is maintained. One issue is that decision makers often lack the necessary awareness of the privacy issue or the training necessary to deal effectively with the issue. Schools need to continue working to develop necessary policy and protocols to address these issues in future purchases and adoptions. Professional development offerings need to be enhanced in order to more comprehensively address the issue of privacy and provide teachers and decision makers with the background and information necessary to understand the issue and make effective decisions. Other educational leaders may also need to be involved to help enhance existing state or federal privacy legislation to enhance the protection offered in these two areas. For now, a good start will be to ensure that additional resources are devoted to development of additional resources and training on privacy and security related to educational technology for school district leaders, IT staff, teachers, and students.

Digital Safety

Another role of the technology coordinator should be to make sure that teachers and students understand the importance of guiding policies such as the district Acceptable Use Policy (AUP) and to ensure that teachers are reinforcing these policies when they teach. Teachers should be trained to respect privacy laws when digitally interacting with parents and students and especially third parties. The Family Educational Rights and Privacy Act (FERPA) protects student data and controls access to that data, especially data that individually identifies a student. FERPA is probably the better known of the two laws. The Children's Internet Protection Act (CIPA) requires that schools and teachers must: (a) adopt and enforce an Internet Safety Policy, (b) enforce the operation of a technology protection measure (filter), and (c) hold a public hearing of meeting to propose a technology protection measure and an Internet Safety Policy. The technology coordinator should reinforce the provisions of CIPA through professional development. It is also important to establish procedures to ensure that all parents and students acknowledge AUP requirements and to make sure the AUP contains provisions addressing cyberbullying, social media, chat rooms, texting, and other digital interactions. It is suggested that parents be asked to discuss these key provisions of internet safety with their children and to signify that they did so on the AUP agreement form. The technology coordinator should also emphasize to teachers the need to be vigilant and always supervise students when using the internet, to model safe behavior on the internet, and to notify the technology coordinator of inappropriate websites that need to be filtered or blocked.

Policy Considerations

The acceptable use policy (AUP) is one of the most important documents a technology coordinator can have in place. To create one, review the AUPs of other schools or districts in your state, get your technology committee to help (and make sure the committee has at least one member who is a parent), and have the final draft reviewed by legal counsel before it is finalized. *Education World* (2009) suggests that an AUP should contain six key elements:

1. A **preamble** explaining why the policy is needed, what it will accomplish, and how the policy was developed. It should also be clear in the preamble whom the AUP applies to, and that the overall code of conduct also applies to online activity.

2. A **definition section** that explains key words used in the policy.

3. A **policy statement** explaining which computing services are covered by the AUP, and the rules for using school or district computing devices and services. The policy statement should require successful completion of the training and responsibility program described earlier before use of school computing resources is allowed.

4. An **acceptable uses section** should define appropriate use of computing resources, including the network. Often, this section restricts student use of computing resources to "educational purposes," which should be defined in Element 2.

5. Next, an **unacceptable uses section** should clearly specify examples of unacceptable use, particularly for students.

6. Finally, a **violations and sanctions section** should tell students how to report violations of the policy, and specify whom to ask to clarify questions about the application of the policy. This section should reference and reinforce the school's disciplinary code and employee policies.

The technology coordinator may find it prudent to develop and implement an acceptable use policy related to the use of social media. Numerous resources for the development of these policies exist, but Williamson (2010) has written a helpful research brief and guide for just this purpose that contains a variety of online resources and links to templates that can be very helpful.

Training new network users is a critical aspect of the technology coordinator's job. Technology coordinators who provide a mandatory introductory class ensure that all new users receive a standard introduction to network use. This session can be offered at a variety of times and locations at the beginning of the school year. The session can be quite basic in nature and can be taught by the technology coordinator or technology contacts at school sites.

This mandatory class can be a useful way to help people learn how to connect to the network with a user ID and password. A formal introduction to the network helps new users understand how the network is organized. This training can show new users items such as public versus private storage of files and can help them learn what programs are available through the network, how to access such resources as the online library catalog, how to find out whom they can turn to when questions or problems arise, and so forth. This introductory class is also an ideal forum for introducing new users to the district's AUP.

AUP documents outline the district's intended uses of the network and internet. They set forth proper online behavior for users. A district's AUP should be one of the first technology-related policies developed. The technology coordinator is often the staff member who is charged with formulating, implementing, and communicating this policy to other district staff.

Including the AUP in student handbooks ensures that all students and families have a copy of the document and, therefore, the opportunity to review it before school activities begin. By having a document that is distributed to every user, the technology coordinator can educate users on potential pitfalls and provide guidance for students and parents. Some schools choose to have the AUP signed by both students and parents and kept on file in the office or classroom. This may be a difficult task for a large organization, but such efforts provide long-term benefits because this document defines boundaries of behavior and, more critically, specifies the consequences of violating those boundaries.

The Children's Internet Protection Act (CIPA) was passed by congress in December 2000. This act requires schools that receive federal funding for technology (such as E-Rate dollars) to meet certain requirements. CIPA requires schools to enact internet filtering to block obscene and pornographic materials to protect students from inappropriate materials. Schools are also required to enact an internet safety policy. This policy must address several student access issues:

- Access by minors to inappropriate matter on the internet
- The safety and security of minors when using electronic mail, chat rooms, social media, and other forms of direct electronic communications
- Unauthorized access including "hacking" and other unlawful online activities by minors
- Unauthorized disclosure, use, and dissemination of personal information regarding minors
- Restricting minors' access to materials harmful to minors

The act requires that the online activity of minors be monitored and that a public notice and hearing regarding the passage of the internet safety policy be documented by the school or district. Schools applying for and receiving E-Rate funds must be prepared to document their compliance with the CIPA requirements.

With the passage of the Protecting Children in the 21st Century Act in 2008, schools receiving E-Rate funds were required to teach students about appropriate behavior on social networking and chat room websites, as well as instruction on the dangers of cyberbullying. To be sure that their policies are in compliance with all of these requirements, schools and districts should carefully review the acceptable use policies, internet safety policies, and instructional plans to ensure that all necessary requirements are met.

Legal Issues

The Family Educational Rights and Privacy Act (FERPA) is a federal law that protects the privacy of educational records (U.S. Department of Education, 2015a), requiring, among other things, that student records be safeguarded. Because almost all student data is now stored and handled electronically, the technology coordinator must have an understanding of FERPA and related laws, because they specify what student information may be released, to whom, and for what purposes.

The Protection of Pupil Rights Amendment (PPRA) specifies that surveys of students may not ask certain kinds of questions. Students may not be asked, for example, about their political beliefs, the political beliefs of their parents, or family religious practices (U.S. Department of Education, 2015b). There are at least eight areas of questioning that students may not be asked about under PPRA:

- Political affiliations or beliefs of the student or parents
- Mental or psychological problems of the student or family members
- Sex behavior or attitudes
- Illegal, antisocial, self-incriminating, or demeaning behavior
- Critical appraisals of other individuals with whom the student may have close family relationships
- Legally recognized privileged or analogous relationships, such as those of lawyers, physicians, and ministers
- Religious practices, affiliations, or beliefs of the student or student's parents
- Income (other than as required by law to determine eligibility for participation in a program or for receiving financial assistance under such a program)

It behooves the technology coordinator to be aware of this law, because many surveys of students are administered, compiled, or analyzed using the computing resources of the school.

The technology coordinator is often responsible for systems that employees may use to transmit or store personally sensitive information. For example, a teacher may send information about her or his health through email to a friend. A staff member may download his most recent federal tax return and save it on his computer. An employee may accuse another employee of sexually offensive email activity. These sorts of situations should be covered in the annual user training and should be acknowledged in the signed AUP. But the technology coordinator should be aware of state laws and local policies that apply to accessing personal information related to incidents such as these. Typically, schools and districts have policies specifying that individuals have no expectation of privacy when using school or district computing resources. If so, this should be made clear to all students and employees.

Firewalls and CIPA

Your web-server software should have a firewall, a security system that protects your server from inappropriate access, hacking, or discovery by outsiders or robot programs crawling through the web to find open servers that can be exploited. A firewall should both monitor and control the incoming and outgoing traffic based on the rules you set. It creates a software barrier between your network and the rest of the internet. It's worth employing a network security professional who knows how to use, maintain, and upgrade your firewall, because they can be complicated to manage and require frequent updates.

One function performed by firewalls or related systems on a web server, is to screen out objectionable websites. If your school or district receives discounts for internet access or internal connections through the Federal E-Rate program, you are likely subject to CIPA. You will know you are subject to CIPA because you will have to certify that you meet its provisions before receiving E-Rate money. CIPA requires schools and libraries to certify they have an internet safety policy in place for protecting children from predators and for filtering access to obscene, pornographic, or harmful material. This applies to email systems as well as internet sites, chat rooms, and other communications systems. CIPA has implications for the training of all school personnel, and for the training of students (Federal Communications Commission, 2016). The fact that you are actively complying with CIPA should be clear on your AUP. Consider complying with CIPA even if your school or district does not receive E-Rate funds. Protecting students from the dangers of the internet is always is good idea.

Tech Leader Profile

Donna Noll, District Technology Director

Donna Noll has been the district technology director for the Atchison, KS school district since 1997, which is most of her 30-year career in education. Atchison is a city of around 11,000 on the Missouri River in Northeast Kansas and was originally the eastern terminus for the Atchison, Topeka, and Santa Fe Railway. Donna was initially trained as a math teacher and spent the first few years in the classroom as a math and computer teacher at high schools located in rural Kansas communities. Along the way, she earned a Master's in Instructional Design Technology. The district technology director is a district level leadership position and Donna is responsible for developing the technology budget and managing purchasing decisions, maintaining the operation of the district network, and making a wide range of decisions regarding the use of instructional technology in the district. The three other people who work in the technology department are all supervised by Donna. The Atchison district is a majority white, rural district made up of four schools that serve a student population of just over 1,500 with 68% qualifying for free or reduced lunches. She describes the biggest challenge in her position as prioritizing the many jobs she has. With technology key to so many different aspects of the operation, it is very important to know where to start. Donna gets satisfaction in her position from seeing how far the district has come over the years and how technology is seamless in the everyday flow of the learning process. Her advice for those who may aspire to a position as a technology leader is to remember the job is never fully defined. New branches are always forming, and you may find yourself responsible for phones, video cameras, security issues, copiers/printers, social media, and grants. You can follow her work here: @NollDonna.

Systems Support

Information and communications technology (ICT) has had a widespread presence in schools for decades now, but the changes in teaching and learning needed to take full advantage of ICT have not taken place beyond small pockets of good practice. However, a few innovative practices are gaining momentum that bear watching and consideration. Some of the most prominent digital learning innovations are mentioned here.

In 1:1 computing models, every student and teacher receives a computing device—usually a laptop computer or a tablet computer—in the hopes that transformative teaching and learning will be enabled based on the ubiquity of available technology. It is up to the teacher to make effective use of the technology.

In flipped learning models, teachers create recorded lectures and other instructional materials that students study and learn from at home, and then in school teachers build on what the students have learned by implementing classroom activities in which students apply the concepts or otherwise extend their knowledge in some way (Adams Becker, et al., 2016). In this way the learning is flipped: instead of the teacher delivering instruction in the classroom for students to apply at home as homework, students learn at home from teacher-created materials or texts and then come to school to apply their learning, deepen their understanding, and get clarification on things they may not have understood during the at-home instruction.

In online learning models, teachers upload and create instructional content in a learning management system and students then learn, interact, and complete all or a portion of a lesson or unit while online at home. Hybrid learning models have some elements in common with online learning and some with flipped learning. In a hybrid model, designated portions of a class are conducted online using the LMS, and the rest of the class is conducted in the classroom.

To help implement these digital learning innovations and others, schools are creating makerspaces (Adams Becker et al., 2016). A makerspace is a room that is equipped with all sorts of technologies and materials to enable teachers and students to build or create anything needed to support teaching and learning activities. Teachers and support staff use makerspaces to create instructional content. Students use makerspaces as a way of creating authentic projects as part of their classwork. The equipment in a maker-space might include three-dimensional printers; laser cutters; computers and printers; woodworking equipment; still and video cameras and photography studio equipment; electrical and metal shop equipment; materials for silk-screening; and a wide range of supplies such as paper, wood, three-dimensional printing material, glue, nails, circuit boards, electrical components, markers, and paint.

All of these digital learning innovations have unique features, but they likely need very similar support from the school and technology coordinator. While serving as both a teaching and learning leader as well as a technology leader, the coordinator must play a role in fostering teaching and learning with technology, if such efforts are to be positioned for maximum success and impact. Some of the key foundational principles shared by the above digital learning innovations are identified next. These principles are applicable to the successful implementation of most other digital learning innovations as well.

Vision

It is very important to establish a shared vision for your digital learning innovation with all stakeholders. Engage parents, community members, the technology committee, and your school board to gain support and guidance. Stakeholder engagement will help everyone understand how the innovation will affect teaching and learning and what it will take to make the endeavor successful. An often-overlooked partner might be a local college or university. Many faculty and staff members in the college, school, or department of education have expertise that can be useful at various stages of your project. Find places where your innovation has been successfully implemented and learn from their successes and mistakes. Finally, an important part of the vision is defining and measuring the criteria for success.

Infrastructure

Ensure that your infrastructure can fully support the innovation. Your network should be robust enough to handle the added stress of the new devices, technologies, and methods being implemented. Security policies and procedures must be adequate to meet the demands of the innovations taking place. Adequate storage will be necessary for the materials likely to be created and saved by teachers and students. It will be important to have the right firewall and security in place to support the needs of this innovation, and to provide the physical space needed to accommodate the components of the innovation.

Planning

One of the key elements of planning is to define the learning model. The technology configuration exists to support the teaching and learning. What will it actually look like when teachers and students implement this innovation? You must plan for the implementation of the technologies used in the innovation. New devices or systems will be required to work with your existing network and authentication system, and if this is not possible, you will need to select new network client software or an upgrade to your network. Changes may need to be made to your Acceptable Use Policies.

Hardware, Software, and Space

Ensure that the hardware is durable and powerful enough to perform its functions and run the desired software, and that it has sufficient memory, speed, and processing power to perform well with the intended use. Software should be chosen based on its ability to support the educational objectives of the program that were originally established in the vision. You will need to have enough software licenses in place that everyone implementing the innovation can legally use the software. It will also be important to make sure that the software will meet both your current and future needs. It will be helpful to select software that will help prepare students to use the tools they will likely use in business, college, or the workplace. You will also need to secure physical learning space that is both flexible and engaging and make sure that there is durable, comfortable, attractive, and functional furniture in place that can be arranged into different grouping layouts.

Professional Development Spotlight

Online training Opportunities from the Texas Computer Education Association

The Texas Computer Education Association (TCEA) offers a variety of professional development opportunities to members seeking to learn more about enhancing learning through technology. They offer a variety of self-paced courses on many different subjects, webinars to share ideas and techniques, certification-based courses, and on-site training. For those interested in working at the district level, the organization offers a certification course designed to develop leadership skills and prepare professionals to work in technology leadership positions. Their IT Director leadership certification course includes twelve modules covering important topics such as professional development, personnel, and budgeting. Part of the program is devoted to establishing a professional learning network with others in similar leadership positions. Over a twelve-month period, participants complete online coursework, develop a final project or portfolio, and receive feedback from a program coordinator. Completion of the certification process is recognized by a certificate awarded by TCEA. In addition to leadership training, the organization offers courses specific to becoming a certified educator, with tools and services from Google or other vendor-specific products. They also offer courses related to the management of various LMSs, a variety of device- and application-focused courses, along with a wide variety of teaching and learning topics, numerous STEM-related courses, and even courses on robotics. Some other state organizations, such as the Association of Computer Technology Educators of Maine and Louisiana Computer Using Educators, have partnered with TCEA to offer courses to their members. The offerings from this organization may be of interest to both technology leaders and to the teachers and staff members they work with in classrooms and programs. More information can be found here: tcea.org/learn/courses.

Pedagogical Support

When thinking about the role of the technology coordinator, with all its technical issues and leadership challenges, it is easy to overlook pedagogy. The promise of technology to positively affect teaching and learning is largely related to the support teachers get for their teaching. The technology coordinator is expected to effectively support teachers and their individual needs when teaching with technology.

In addition to technical issues and leadership, there are three key areas for which coordinators must ensure support: pedagogical support—how to implement instruction with technology, instructional design support—how to design and plan for instruction with technology, and instructional delivery model support.

The successful technology coordinator must at least consider when, where, and how pedagogical support occurs. Will the tech coordinator be able to provide or arrange for pedagogical support on demand (available on a drop-in basis)? Providing this level of support means that someone knowledgeable about teaching with technology must be available during business hours. Perhaps a teacher, or rotating group of teachers, could be provided with release time to staff a help desk to provide pedagogical support. A more traditional help-desk system is another possible way to schedule this type of support. A teacher could submit a help request and make arrangements for scheduled pedagogical help. Using the help-desk system has the added benefit of creating an analyzable record of pedagogical help requests. A third way to provide this support would be to arrange teachers into informal "teaching with technology" groups— perhaps a learning community in which one teacher in each group is designated as the pedagogical support person. Using this method, all members of the group benefit from discussion and sharing of pedagogical issues, questions, and methods. Finally, expert teachers who are recognized and respected by their peers may be good exemplars of pedagogy with technology. Consider asking such teachers to teach demonstration lessons for their colleagues. Teachers wishing to watch such demonstration lessons may be asked to sit in the back of the classroom to view the lesson, or demonstration lessons may be recorded and shared with larger groups of teachers for discussion and professional development.

Very closely related to pedagogy, instructional design support is needed to help teachers design lessons, interactions, projects, and assessments that are mediated by technology. Based on the instructional delivery model, the type of instructional design support will vary. Support for instructional design should probably follow the ADDIE instructional design model (see previous chapter). The technology coordinator, a peer teacher, or a dedicated instructional designer would first meet with the teacher to define what help is needed. Some teachers will just need help with ideas for teaching with certain technologies to achieve instructional objectives; others may just need help with identifying specific technologies to accomplish an instructional objective or with finding resources on the internet. Still others will need help writing lesson or unit plans from scratch. Regardless of the type or level of instructional design support that is needed, it can be managed using the same strategies mentioned earlier for pedagogical support: drop-in support, a help-desk request for scheduled support, and learning communities. If some sort of drop-in support model is used, consider using the same people and methods for both pedagogical and instructional design support.

The last consideration for supporting teaching and learning is the instructional delivery method. With changes in digital learning over the past few years, it is not uncommon to find that new and innovative delivery methods are being used in more and more schools. Some of the most common methods that will require support include traditional face-to-face instruction, the flipped classroom, and various hybrid models of instruction in which some instruction is face-to-face and some is online. Increasingly, fully online instruction is being used in K–12 education, especially at the high school level. Each of these delivery methods will require unique pedagogical and instructional design support.

Toolbox Tip

Buying Consortiums

Software and application costs are a challenge for any school or district. An effective way to reduce licensing costs is to look for organizations or buying consortiums that allow the district to become part of larger purchasing blocs. For example, state contracts may offer opportunities for reducing software costs, particularly for common programs. Educational service centers may also offer programs to assist schools with equipment purchases or the licensing of software. Service centers can use volume purchasing to secure a wide range of software packages or applications at prices often unavailable elsewhere. Before making a purchase from a commercial vendor, check pricing options available through a state contract purchase or a local educational service center.

Grants

Grants have become a regular part of the funding equation for educational technology leaders. Although grants should not be viewed as a routine component of the regular technology budget, they can provide useful dollars for exploring new technologies, funding innovative projects, and enhancing professional development opportunities. Grant applications often require considerable time and intense effort and commitment from the technology coordinator, but they can also provide welcome additional resources.

Two basic types of grants are available to schools: entitlement grants and competitive grants. Entitlement grants are those funds allocated to schools and districts primarily based on a formula. The formula is intended to distribute the available funds to districts based on an equitable funding method. Funding of entitlement grants is not competitive but is based on eligible student count and other data.

Examples of entitlement grants include Title I, Title VI, and Eisenhower funds. The purpose of entitlement grants is to provide funding to state and local educational agencies to help them implement educational programs. Entitlement grants provide funds mandated by law. Local educational agencies set up entitlement grant programs based on the criteria of the entitlement program. Appropriations are usually determined by formulas based on enrollment, high concentrations of low-income families, and other need factors. To receive entitlement funding from a state or federal agency, local school districts must report a variety of data about their student population—for example, enrollment and participation in the free and reduced-fee lunch program.

Competitive grants are programs in which the applicant designs a project that competes with others seeking funding. The agency that sponsors the grant program selects projects and determines grant amounts based on pre-established selection criteria. Some competitive grant programs are funded by state or federal education agencies. Other sources for competitive grant funds are private foundations or businesses. Whereas entitlement grants are usually based on financial need, competitive grants are most often awarded based on specific criteria specified by the funding source. Most competitive grant applications are evaluated on criteria such as the potential benefit to the students, how well the project addresses a particular educational need, and the integrity of the project's objectives, planning, and budget.

Although each grant is different, most grants tend to be made up of the same basic components: an executive summary, a statement of needs, the project's goals and objectives, a project narrative, and a budget for the project. The executive summary provides a clear overview of the project in a concise format. The statement of needs details the compelling reason for the project. The goals lay out the project's intended results. The objectives suggest ways to evaluate the success of the project. The project narrative provides a specific plan for what will happen and when. The project budget clearly explains, in concise terms, how the funding for the project will be spent and tracked.

Successful grant writing requires that the technology coordinator come up with a workable idea that fits the grant criteria, provide a project outline that will persuade the grant reader of the value of the idea, and list enough details to make it clear the project is feasible.

As mentioned, developing successful grant applications is a time-consuming process. The first step in the process involves developing a grant concept that meets both the criteria of the grant and the needs of the organization. Data must be gathered to support the organization's need. This data must provide information about how the grant project will support the purpose. When developing the grant concept, it is important that the technology coordinator communicate with, and gather support from, district staff and administration to ensure that it will be possible to carry out the project. A funded project may be based on an outstanding concept, but if the staff and administration do not support the project, it will have little chance for success.

Once a grant concept has been selected, and support for the project assured, the actual writing of the proposal can begin. A proposal usually starts with an executive summary, which is a brief synopsis of the entire grant proposal that gives the reader a general understanding of the project. As a first look, the executive summary provides information on the problem to be addressed, a description of the project and how it will deal with the problem, and a summary of the funding requirements of the project. The executive summary is the part of the proposal that gets a grant reader's attention and creates interest in the project.

The executive summary is followed by a detailed statement of need. This statement provides the facts and figures that support the need, and it helps the reader fully understand the issues involved. This statement also ties the identified need to the mission and goals of the organization. For example, if the grant is intended to strengthen the use of technology in the learning process, the statement of need shows how the grant would support the district goals for integrating technology in instruction. Although the statement of need must provide background and tie the project to the solution, it does not have to be long. Concise and persuasive writing will be more effective than a long and involved narrative.

The next section of the proposal is the project description. This section usually includes four subsections: objectives, methods, staffing/administration, and evaluation. Objectives are the measurable outcomes of the program. The project objectives must be specific, measurable, and achievable in a specified time period. The methods section describes the specific activities that will take place to achieve the objectives. You will need to devote a few sentences to discussing the number of staff who will work on the project, their qualifications, and specific assignments. An evaluation plan should not be executed only after the project is over; it should be built into all stages of the project. Including an evaluation plan in your proposal indicates that you take your objectives seriously and want to know how well you have achieved them.

Finally, a budget for the project must be prepared. The budget for your proposal may be as simple as a one-page statement of projected expenses or may require a more complex presentation of information. The budget is intended to help both you and the funding source understand how the money will be spent. For most projects, costs should be grouped into subcategories that are selected to reflect the critical areas of expense. You might divide your expense budget into personnel and non-personnel costs. Your personnel subcategories might include salaries, benefits, and consultants. Subcategories under non-personnel costs might include travel, equipment, and printing, with a dollar figure attached to each line.

Grants are all about meeting the needs of the organization. By taking the time to explore grant funding opportunities, working with others to develop the support needed to carry out a grant project, and crafting a winning grant application, the technology coordinator can secure the funding necessary to carry out a meaningful technology project.

E-Rate Applications

Securing adequate funding to support a technology program is always a challenge for schools and districts. Technology coordinators can help bridge funding gaps by participating in the E-Rate program, which was established by the Federal Communications Commission and made available through the Schools and Libraries Division (SLD) of the Universal Service Administrative Company.

The E-Rate program was established as part of the Telecommunications Act of 1996 to improve telecommunications services in schools, libraries, and hospitals. By participating in this program, the technology coordinator can help the school or district improve its telephone and internet connectivity, purchase computers and software, and provide additional training for teachers and staff.

The E-Rate program bridges funding gaps by offering schools discounts of 20% to 90% for telecommunications services they purchase or improvements they make to their network infrastructure. All schools can participate in the program by determining what services they currently use or wish to acquire, soliciting any necessary bids for those services, and awarding contracts based on the bids.

The technology coordinator begins the E-Rate funding application process by filing Form 470, which sets out the needed services and improvements. The number of free and reduced-fee lunches served by the school or district determines the amount of the discount. Districts serving students with greater levels of need receive the highest discounts. Bids must be solicited to determine the actual cost of these services and improvements.

After bids have been solicited, final negotiations completed, and agreements made, the technology coordinator takes the second formal step in the process: filing Form 471, the Services Ordered Confirmation form. This form describes the actual costs of the services selected, determines the level of discount available to the district, and formally completes the first phase of the E-Rate application. Form 471 must be filed according to the deadline determined annually by the SLD.

When the E-Rate filing deadline has passed, the SLD processes all Form 471 applications, determines the amount of funds requested across the nation, verifies applications, and decides the E-Rate awards for each applicant. All schools that apply within the eligibility window qualify for discounts on a variety of technology and telecommunication services. Once these services have been provided to all applicants, any remaining funds are distributed to schools for network infrastructure improvements, which are referred to as internal connections, beginning with those schools in greatest need.

When final decisions have been made on the discounts available to a district, an official Funding Commitment Decision letter is issued. This letter identifies the level of discount and the amount of funding available from each service provider identified on Form 471. Following the receipt of the funding letter, the district must file a Form 486, which acknowledges the receipt of services from the vendor and allows the district to officially begin receiving discounts or rebates on services.

To begin receiving the actual discounts on services, the district needs to work with service providers to determine the most appropriate method of receipt. Discounts may automatically be applied to monthly bills for services or received as a cash rebate. To receive cash payments, the district must, in conjunction with the service provider, complete Form 472, the Billed Entity Applicant Reimbursement (BEAR) form. This form identifies services that are received from a vendor and paid in full. Filing a BEAR form notifies the SLD to issue a rebate to the district.

Toolbox Tip

10 Tips for E-Rate Success

Following are ten tips for success with the E-Rate program application process:

1. Begin thinking about E-Rate early. Deadlines always arrive at busy times, and the application process can take longer than expected.

2. Spend time researching the current cost of services used by the district. This may help identify new areas in which to apply for E-Rate funding.

3. Be familiar with the products and services eligible for discount.

4. When in doubt about something related to the E-Rate process, call the USAC SLD for help, 1-888-203-8100, or visit their website for assistance: www.usac.org.

5. Be sure to read directions carefully, fill in all required blanks on forms, and file forms by the deadlines.

6. Include E-Rate in the technology planning process to ensure compliance with all program requirements and certifications.

7. Keep copies of all forms submitted in case they are needed for reference or program audit.

8. If you disagree with a funding decision, file an appeal. It will take time for a decision, but there will be no penalty, and the results may be to your advantage.

9. If necessary, hire an E-Rate consultant. These consultants offer management services and provide help with paperwork. They charge 5% to 8% of the discounts received and will assist with the application process.

10. Always budget fully for any services requested through the E-Rate program. Requests can be denied or funding reduced. If sufficient funds have not been budgeted, important services or projects can fail because of lack of funding.

There have been a variety of recent changes to the E-Rate program that should directly benefit schools and libraries. According to Herold and Cavanaugh (2015), annual spending on the E-Rate program was increased to $3.9 billion in late 2014. In addition to the increased spending, various rules governing the program were changed to make it easier for schools to concentrate on Wi-Fi and broadband network services in order to support increased student access through 1:1 initiatives, widespread use of online testing, and enhanced support for digital learning. These changes allow schools and libraries to use E-Rate funds to create their own fiber-optic networks. Creation of these networks is something that has been a particular problem for rural schools, according to a recent survey by the CoSN.

Answers to Essential Questions

1. **What essential functions does the technology coordinator support?**

   The technology coordinator must directly or indirectly provide in six essential areas: technical support, technology life-cycle management, security and protection of people and technologies, key systems that are used to manage necessary functions, teaching and learning initiatives, and pedagogy using digital learning tools.

2. **What processes must a technology coordinator implement to ensure that comprehensive technical support is provided?**

   The technology coordinator must ensure that there are people available and able to support the tracking and management of events, incidents, and problems. Also, the planning and implementation of multiple and continuous changes is an important set of processes to manage. Notifying stakeholders of incidents and updating them on important policies, procedures, and events should also happen in various ways at regular intervals. Having a system to prioritize support, policies, and procedures for managing the technology purchased through its entire life cycle, including data backup and recovery and image management, is also an important process. Finally, it is important to have regular processes in place for employees at various stages of their employment.

3. **How can the technology coordinator prioritize numerous and simultaneous support issues or requests?**

   A matrix-like tool showing a range of levels of impact across the top and a range of urgency levels down the side is useful for assigning priority. When well understood and communicated, such a prioritization matrix lets all stakeholders understand how needs are prioritized, instills confidence that requests are being handled, and gives stakeholders a systems perspective to issues and support requests.

4. **For what security and protection issues must the technology coordinator monitor and establish systems?**

    Information and communications technology is a rapidly changing field. At a minimum, the technology coordinator should be concerned about physical security, user authentication, and training users on their responsibilities for security of property and information.

5. **What key elements should be included in an Acceptable Use Policy?**

    Following the guidelines from Education World (2016), we suggest that an AUP should contain six key elements: a preamble, definitions, a policy statement, an acceptable uses section, an unacceptable uses section, and a violations and sanctions section.

6. **What technology systems must the technology coordinator ensure are installed and continuously functional because of their importance to a school or district?**

    Examples of such systems are internet services, the network, the student information system, the learning management system, VoIP telephony, employee and parent notification systems, the employee information system (human resources system), and external communication tools including social media such as X/Twitter, Facebook, and YouTube.

7. **How can the technology coordinator stay up to date on the latest digital learning innovations?**

    The technology coordinator can stay up to date by joining professional organizations and attending their conferences. Examples of such organizations would include the International Society for Technology in Education and the New Media Consortium.

8. **How can the technology coordinator support pedagogy involving digital learning tools?**

    The promise of technology to positively affect teaching and learning is largely related to the support teachers get in their teaching. The technology coordinator must ensure pedagogical support (how to implement instruction with technology), instructional design support (how to design and plan for instruction with technology), and support for a variety of instructional models.

9. **What role should the technology coordinator play in helping the district to meet the legal requirements of the Children's Internet Protection Act (CIPA)?**

    The technology coordinator should work with the district administration and board of education to develop and put in place any policies and procedures required by CIPA to ensure that all legal requirements are met for student use of district technology resources.

10. **What does the technology coordinator need to know about grant writing to locate and secure additional funding for technology projects?**

    By involving a variety of people in the planning process and constructing an effective grant application, the technology coordinator can help locate needed funds for innovative projects.

11. **What should the technology coordinator know about the E-Rate program and application process?**

    By understanding the various steps and forms involved in the E-Rate application process, the technology coordinator can help the district acquire discounts on products and services that will assist in the support of the district technology program.

Resources

Sample Acceptable Use Agreements and Policies from the National Center for Education Statistics (bit.ly/3ZUXiiJ)

AUP information and resources from the Virginia Department of Education (bit.ly/45zBWsp)

Guidelines for creating Acceptable Use Policies from the Kentucky Department of Education (bit.ly/3FbKCuy)

Chapter 6

NETWORK OPERATIONS

Essential Questions

1. How can the technology coordinator ensure that the network infrastructure meets users' needs?

2. What issues will confront the technology coordinator when providing wireless (Wi-Fi) and Voice over IP (VoIP) services to district users?

3. How can the technology coordinator assist with the management of network user accounts?

4. How can the technology coordinator ensure that appropriate backup and disaster recovery procedures are regularly carried out?

5. How can the technology coordinator use remote management tools to provide better network service and support?

The school building network is, for all practical purposes, the central nervous system of a school building or district. This network ties together the many different offices, classrooms, and other locations so that a school can make effective use of technology and provide quality educational services to students and their families. A school network should support efficient digital communication and convenient access to data and files, should provide security for confidential documents and information, and should facilitate access to shared resources such as printers and network-based programs. The school network also makes it possible to connect the building to the wide variety of information and resources that can be found on the internet.

Network Operations and the Technology Coordinator

A computer network has a variety of important benefits for the technology coordinator (see Figure 6.1). The network makes it possible to supervise and manage resources, as well as monitor use by staff and students. The technology coordinator can use the network to create a shared storage area for staff members that remains invisible to student users. A network can also provide regular backups of both critical data and personal files. In addition, the network can be used to oversee the various devices and resources that are linked to the network.

A network also has a variety of advantages for staff and student users. A common storage area can be created so that staff or students can share documents and other information. Teachers can create a class folder on a shared network drive in which all students can save their work in individual folders. The files stored there can be made available to students in any location with network access: a science or computer lab, a classroom, the library, or even the gym. These files can be automatically backed up on a regular basis. The network makes it possible for users to work from many locations and to access, share, and manage information efficiently.

Access to the internet has quickly become an indispensable resource for schools. Such access provides a wealth of information and allows students and teachers to learn and communicate in new and different ways. Innovative methods of accessing information, such as cloud computing, make it possible for the teacher to share information and assignments with students in a convenient way across the network and over the internet. The teacher can easily access all files requiring their review. This sharing model makes it possible to "share and access data and information across platforms and devices, and more information is available to more users" (Katzan, 2010).

Access to a computer network and the wide-ranging resources available through the internet allows users to connect to information sources in their local area, in other states, or on the other side of the globe. Students have the opportunity to communicate with people from different cultures and political systems, and in a variety of physical locations. By establishing quality network access for both wired and mobile devices, making sure the network is properly managed and administered, and providing the support and training necessary for all users, the technology coordinator can ensure that students, teachers, and other staff members have the resources they need to work and learn in our technology-fueled world.

Schools have been very successful in completing both wired and wireless school networking projects and in providing quality internet accessibility to teachers, students, and staff. The E-Rate program has been a critical factor in this progress. The funds provided by this program have allowed almost all schools to be connected to the internet. The program has also allowed many schools to develop the robust network infrastructure necessary to deliver this access to classrooms in multiple ways. Schools now have wired networks to connect computers as well as wireless connectivity that allows access to tablets and other handheld devices. This connectivity makes possible mobile access and on-demand learning from multiple locations. The development of a comprehensive learning structure is one of the goals of the 2016 National Education Technology Plan (U.S. Department of Education, 2016): "A comprehensive learning infrastructure (aside from wires and devices) includes digital learning content and other resources as well as professional development for educators and education leaders. Key elements of this infrastructure include high-speed connectivity and devices that are available to teachers and students when and where they need them."

The National Education Technology Plan was instrumental in the development of school infrastructure, the widespread availability of internet access, and the establishment of new ways in which digital content and networked applications could be used to transform teaching and learning. The U.S. Secretary of Education was the main individual charged with the development of a National Education Technology Plan specifically to address the needs of the educational community. The 2016 version of this plan establishes a national vision and plan for learning enabled by technology intended to improve student academic achievement and prepare students for life and work in the digital age. More information about the plan can be found here: tech.ed.gov/netp.

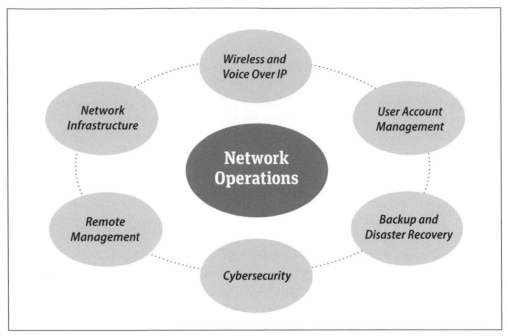

Figure 6.1. Network operations issues.

Network Infrastructure

The success of a school computer network is dependent on the design and durability of its infrastructure. The wiring, patch panels, file servers, hubs, routers, print servers, high-speed communications lines (such as T1, T3, frame-relay, and fiber-optic lines), wireless access points, and other parts of the network system must work together seamlessly. A poorly designed or inadequately maintained network will always fail at the worst possible moments.

Dealing with network infrastructure issues often requires highly specialized and advanced technical skills and knowledge. The technology coordinator may not be trained in all areas or have specific responsibility for these operations but should be willing and able to learn about them in order provide leadership in these areas. This knowledge allows the technology coordinator to plan and implement an effective network infrastructure and manage project installations and upgrades. A school or district's technology plan should include a detailed analysis of network resource needs and plans for developing, expanding, and improving the infrastructure. The tech coordinator should work with school or district staff and the board of education, as well as with outside vendors and consultants, to develop a network plan that will meet current and future curricular and administrative needs.

It is also important to plan for and secure adequate technical assistance for network equipment. A single person may not be able to handle server administration, user account setup, personnel training, equipment failures, and all the other requirements of network management. As a school or district's network becomes more complex, the technology coordinator may need to work with administration to recruit and hire a certified network administrator. If the technology coordinator is the only person in the district responsible for technology, a plan must be in place for handling routine network maintenance and for repairing critical components when they develop problems or experience failure. A variety of service and support contracts are available from various vendors.

Significant investment in technology infrastructure, often thanks to the E-Rate program, has allowed virtually all schools to install local area network (LAN) capabilities. Some technology coordinators may be called on to design, install, and configure networks for their districts or buildings, or to expand the capabilities of an existing network. A coordinator who is planning to install or expand a network will face a variety of

Toolbox Tip

Implementing Essential Cybersecurity Protections

Cybersecurity is an important issue for all technology leaders, including those in Kansas. Dean Mantz, the Technology Coordinator for Sterling USD 376 in Sterling, Kansas, has been working with a group from the Kansas Council of K12 Technology Professionals to develop a planning document and related checklist of items to prevent cybersecurity threats for Kansas schools and districts. The checklist and related documentation will make use of the K12 Security Information eXchange (K12 SIX) Essential Cybersecurity Protections framework as a baseline for K12 schools. This documentation will align with current versions of the Center for Internet Security Critical Security Controls and the National Institute for Standards and Technology Cybersecurity Framework. A list of the K12 SIX Essential Cybersecurity Protections appears below. More information about K12 SIX is available here: k12six.org.

- Sanitize network traffic to/from the internet.

- Safeguard student, teacher, and staff devices.

- Protect student, teacher, and staff identities.

- Practice continuous improvement.

issues and decisions. Because the networking needs of each organization are different, a network installed in one location may be quite different from that in another location, even in the same district.

One of the first tasks that a technology coordinator must perform is determining the type of network to be installed. At one time, the only choice for installing network capabilities was to run wire to all endpoint locations—essentially creating a hardwired network much like that of the old landline telephone system. This method requires installing copper wire from point to point and connecting all the different endpoints with a central location where the central network equipment (servers, routers, and switches) is installed. Today, other, more cost-effective options exist. Installation of fiber optic cable may be an attractive option if large amounts of bandwidth are needed. Another option is the installation of Wi-Fi that connects devices to the network using only wireless access points that communicate with the devices through radio frequencies.

Regardless of the network type, it is critical that a technology coordinator work with experienced technical experts to design and install the most appropriate network for a particular location. Some expertise may be available from staff with networking knowledge and experience. Most schools, however, will need to engage contractors with expertise in this area. These contractors will work with the technology coordinator and other technical staff to design and install the network.

For most schools, the LAN located in a school building will be connected to a larger network such as the district wide area network (WAN) and to the internet. When choosing how the school network will be connected to the outside world, the technology coordinator faces a variety of high-speed connectivity choices and issues. Schools can be connected through ISDN, T1, T3, broadband cable, or fiber optics. Each of these connection types has different speeds and costs.

ISDN connection. This digital transmission technology supports voice, video, and data communications applications over regular telephone lines capable of speeds from 57.6k to 128k. Integrated Services Digital Network is a telecommunications standard.

T1 connection. This type of digital data connection can pass data at a rate of 1.544 megabits per second.

T3 connection. This type of digital data connection can pass data at a rate of 44 megabits per second. T3 lines are often used to link large computer networks, such as those that make up the internet.

Broadband cable connection. This type of digital data connection, provided by a cable company, can reach speeds of up to 10 megabits per second.

Fiber-optic connection. This connection via a thin strand of glass that carries light transmissions is used for high-speed voice or data transmission. Fiber-optic connections can support 30,000 times the traffic that can be carried on copper wire.

Several factors should be considered when determining the appropriate connectivity scheme for an organization or site. The first consideration is the number of potential connections. The second consideration is what types of services will be delivered over the network. For example, a site that will be accessing video-on-demand services will need higher capacity and connection speeds than a site that will be sending email and browsing web pages. The available budget is a third factor to consider. Finally, the types of connections available must be determined because connectivity service may vary by location.

To determine the best service option for providing network connectivity, the technology coordinator should consult with the district's administration and business operations staff, network services vendors, network design consultants, and other stakeholders. It is of critical importance to make sure the school has adequate and reliable network connectivity for conducting research, connecting with experts outside the school, and collaborating with other students in remote locations. For most schools, high-speed network and internet access is considered a standard utility in the same way that water and electricity are expected services that are part of the standard building infrastructure.

With the proliferation of internet-dependent devices in classrooms and offices, reliable high-speed network connections are becoming critical to schools. A recent publication entitled "The Broadband Imperative" from the State Educational Technology Directors Association included several recommendations for addressing K–12 needs for broadband network infrastructure. Of critical importance was the recommendation to provide an external internet connection to the internet service provider of at least 1 gigabit per second per 1000 students/staff by the 2017–18 school year (Fox et al., 2012, p. 2). This publication clearly explains the importance of broadband access in schools and how such access can enhance learning in a variety of different ways. The authors conclude that this access "allows our teachers and students to exploit the full spectrum of online educational content and evolving best practices available to every nation via the internet" (Fox et al., 2012, p. 26).

Tech Leader Profile

Drew Lane, Executive Director of ICT

Drew Lane is the executive director of information and communication technologies (ICT) for the Shawnee Mission school district, a suburban Kansas school district on the west side of the Kansas City metro area. The district serves almost 28,000 students in 45 schools and is the third largest school district in the state of Kansas. Drew joined the district in 2014 where he reports to a deputy superintendent. He supervises seven people who in turn manage a team of more than 50 people in the ICT department. Originally trained as a secondary social studies teacher licensed in several states, following five years in the classroom, he completed an MS degree in Information Technology and has been working in educational technology for most of his career. The main responsibilities in his job are building and maintaining teams, strategic planning for all areas of technology, and building and maintaining bridges between stakeholder groups within the organization. He points out that there must be an open line of communication between educators and the technicians who support them; the IT people need to have a strong customer service focus. Drew shared that while the pandemic created a variety of obstacles for his organization, familiarity with technology helped to lessen some of them. He identified that some of his biggest challenges are maintaining a balance in communication with stakeholders and knowing what information to provide to be helpful without being overwhelming. Drew gets satisfaction from knowing he is helping young people become the best people they can be. His advice for people who wish to work in his field is to "take every opportunity to learn, practice, and perfect skills in leadership, negotiation, communication, and effectively speaking to diverse groups of people." You can follow his work here: linkedin.com/in/drewlane/

Wireless Network and Voice over IP Technologies

Wi-Fi technology has become faster, less expensive, and more reliable in the past several years, and its capabilities and speed continue to improve. It is now possible to create a wireless network by installing a minimum of wired connections throughout a building and then installing wireless access points that allow desktop and laptop computers, tablets, and other mobile devices to connect to the network using radio frequencies. In certain cases, this solution may be a more convenient and cost-effective choice than installation of a hard-wired network. In a newer building with false ceilings and easy access to conduits in walls, it may be possible to install a copper wire network with minimal intrusion and nominal expense. But for older buildings with solid ceilings, it is often much more difficult and expensive to install a hard-wired network throughout the facility. The installation of a wireless network may be a much more sensible choice in such a location.

Many schools are using wireless networks to offer connectivity to teachers and students throughout the school building and in key locations around the school campus. According to Market Data Retrieval, some 10% of schools reported using wireless networks in 2001, but by 2005 that number had increased to 45% (Borja, 2006). That number has continued to increase, in many cases driven by the widespread implementation of 1:1 laptop or 1:1 tablet projects to put devices in the hands of students. The National Center for Education Statistics, in their fall 2008 report on educational technology in the public schools, noted that 78% of schools reported the availability of wireless networks in some part of the school building (Gray, Thomas, & Lewis, 2010). In addition to allowing connections from virtually any campus location, wireless networks make possible the connection of a variety of different devices. Students and faculty can connect to the network with laptops, tablets, or other mobile devices such as smartphones. The adoption of wireless network capabilities makes it possible to simplify the lives of teachers and students by providing ubiquitous network access.

A technology coordinator must consider a variety of issues when implementing a wireless network. Steps must be taken to ensure that wireless connections are secure and that unauthorized users cannot make use of the connections. It is also important to make certain the network access points are carefully placed throughout the building to avoid interference and ensure there are no gaps in the coverage area. Although older buildings pose a challenge for the installation of both wired and wireless networking, careful planning and strategic access point placement can help avoid weak signals and dead spots in network coverage. For complete coverage of a school building, numerous access points will be necessary, and the ability to actively and easily manage these devices should be a consideration. Careful planning should be used when designing, installing, and implementing these networking systems.

Schools are also beginning to use their data networks to handle other types of communication, such as telephone calls. In an effort to save money, schools have begun to install telephone systems that use VoIP to handle telephone call traffic. VoIP uses the existing infrastructure of computer data lines to route phone calls within a building or across the school district. Districts can sometimes realize considerable savings from implementation of VoIP systems. Keith Seher, an information manager for the 10,000-student David Douglas district, in Portland, Oregon, estimates his district saved about $70,000 the first year the district used the local area network that the district already had in place, instead of local telephone lines (Davis, 2009).

There are a variety of issues that must be considered when implementing VoIP systems. A primary consideration is emergency backup. If, for some reason, the data system goes down, the phone system goes down, too. To accommodate emergencies, many schools continue to have at least one traditional analog phone line running into the building to handle calls. Cost is another factor that technology leaders should consider when investigating a VoIP solution. Some school districts do not have the wiring capability or the desire to switch all district calls to VoIP at once. It is also important to consider that analog phones tend to cost only about $12 each on average, compared with the smarter phones for a VoIP system, which can cost many times that amount.

If a district is considering the installation of a VoIP system, it is important for the technology coordinator to consider several questions and issues:

- Does the district have the appropriate network capacity to handle the data demands of district users, as well as the added capacity necessary to provide voice services?

- Does the district have the technical expertise needed to manage the new system?

- Will the potential savings in service costs be offset by the cost of the new system and the increased technical demands and support necessary from district staff?

Ultimately, any change to the phone system should not result in diminished or frustrating service for district phone users. It is important for the technology coordinator to work with district administration, technical staff, and vendors to carefully answer these questions when an investment in this type of system is being considered.

User-Account Management

The success of any network is best measured by the end users' level of satisfaction and productivity. A network's infrastructure may be of the highest quality, but if users have difficulty making use of the resources available, the network will not be viewed as a good investment of limited technology dollars. A user who is unable to log onto the network cannot access stored files, use network programs, visit a website, send an email message, or make use of a network printer or other resource. Problems with user accounts could cause a teacher who is already uncomfortable with technology to abandon the network altogether—and forego all the many benefits it can offer. Effective and efficient management of user accounts is, therefore, crucial to network operations.

Although technology coordinators may not be directly responsible for user account management, it is important that they establish standard procedures and understand issues related to typical user-account challenges, such as how to request accounts for new users, whom to contact when account access problems arise, what to do when a password is forgotten, and how to help users access network resources that are most useful to them. These procedures should be specified and communicated to all users of the network so that they know what to do when issues like these arise.

New account requests and problems with passwords are part of the day-to-day management of any network. At the beginning of each school year it may be useful to work with administration and school offices to compile a list of new staff members who will need user accounts. These lists should serve as the basis for new account requests. Lists of employees who have left the organization should also be shared so that those accounts can be removed. Password problems can arise at any time and need to be dealt with in a timely manner. Often these problems can be solved quickly by simply resetting a password that has been forgotten. The technology coordinator or network administrator should designate a contact who can assist with these routine questions and problems. This person might be given some extra training and the authority to create new accounts and reset passwords as necessary.

Tech Leader Profile

Christopher Fletcher, Director of Technology

Since 2020, Christopher Fletcher has been the director of technology for the Lansing Unified School District 469 in Kansas. Lansing is a city of just over 11,000 located on the Missouri River border in the east; the city is on the northwest edge of the Kansas City metro area. Christopher comes from a business background; he earned an undergraduate degree in management information systems. His entire twenty-year career has been spent working in technology operations for school districts. He recently earned a master's degree in instructional technology. Christopher is part of the 21-member district leadership team made up of the superintendent, building administrators, and other department directors. He is responsible for managing a four-person technology department, supervises all department personnel, and reports directly to the superintendent. His main responsibilities include balancing immediate district needs like trouble tickets with long-term planning issues, managing staff so priorities match district needs, and ensuring users have the resources needed to effectively do their jobs. Lansing is a suburban district with an enrollment of around 2,600 students in five school buildings serving grades early childhood–12. The district schools serve a population that is over 70% white and experiences limited poverty. The biggest daily challenge Christopher faces is developing systems and processes that work for users of all ages and knowledge levels. He must be able to "right size" systems to make them work for most people and provide effective training and useful documentation that help users work through unfamiliar systems. His satisfaction comes from getting to know district users and having the opportunity to visit classrooms. Christopher points out that technology leaders must balance requests with what they can successfully provide. Everything is a compromise of resources and results, so choosing a compromise that you are confident will be best for students should also be the best outcome for the system. You can follow his work here: @cfletcher.

Backup Procedures and Disaster Recovery

One of the most important procedures for ensuring network stability and integrity is the regular backup of files and information that network users access and modify. When a network file server is installed, the network administrator and technology coordinator must develop and implement a comprehensive plan for the daily backup of critical information. They must ensure that the necessary backup equipment and software are installed and working properly. The backup plan should also include disaster recovery procedures to be used in the event of a natural disaster, an attack on the system, or a critical failure, so that vital data are not irretrievably lost.

Typically, files on the server are copied to a backup system in the early morning hours when use of the system is minimal. After the backup is complete, the daily backup tape will need to be removed and stored, then replaced with the next day's tape. It is usually best to have a separate tape for each day of the business week. A designated person at each server location should be trained to switch the tapes daily.

As part of the disaster recovery plan, it is important to send a copy of the tapes to an off-site location each week. When a copy of the tapes is located off-site, a disaster such as flood or fire will not destroy all copies of important files. As copies of backups are sent for off-site storage, the original tapes can go back into the pool for daily backup.

An essential part of the backup plan is training users to save copies of important data and other files to the file server so that they can be backed up. Most computers today have large quantities of local storage space, and users may not feel the need to store important files on the file server. Helping users understand the importance of data backups and training them to make regular network backups of critical information, such as grades, will help the backup plan succeed. Asking users to take a few minutes at the end of each work session to back up important work to the server will save later frustration. Although computer equipment is often quite reliable, a single hard-drive failure with no backup can lead to the loss of important documents and information.

Although technology coordinators may not be personally responsible for setting up and managing the backup system, they can play an important role in ensuring that the system is implemented and working properly. The backup system and software should be monitored daily to make sure that important files have been backed up successfully, that the backup is complete before users arrive in the morning, and that an adequate supply of backup tapes is available as needed.

Cyber Security

A recent report from the Privacy Rights Clearinghouse identified 788 data breaches having occurred in K–12 schools and higher education institutions since 2005. These data breaches resulted in more than 14 million compromised records. With the increase in technology use and reliance by schools resulting from the COVID-19 pandemic, the number of these breaches is likely to increase. Schools need to be vigilant in their efforts to guard against network intrusions intended to acquire data, software installations that block access, or interruptions in video conferencing and disruption of online classrooms.

Toolbox Tip

Tech Support

Nearly all schools and districts struggle to provide an adequate level of technology support to district users. Funding these positions is often a challenge, and with the expansion of 1:1 device programs, there is often a growing need for technical support staff. If additional technical support for the district's hardware devices is needed, here are some actions that may help secure and provide that support:

- Create partnerships with local businesses that have technical staff positions.

- Tap the expertise of the staff of local colleges.

- Contract with local vendors for regular and emergency technical support visits.

- Work with existing custodial and maintenance staff to provide assistance as needed.

- Provide technical training for existing staff or hire additional staff with specialized technical training.

- Make use of parent volunteers who work in technical fields.

- Solicit help from a local technical school's computer-repair program.

- Recruit student helpers. They may have unexpected technical expertise and be able to provide useful assistance.

Schools can do a variety of things to provide the necessary security to protect themselves and prevent future problems. The Readiness and Emergency Management for
Schools Technical Assistance Center (rems.ed.gov) Cybersecurity Considerations for
K–12 Schools and School Districts publication identifies several actions schools can
take to prepare for such incidents. This list includes:

- Develop and promote policies.

- Store data securely.

- Create firewalls and list individuals with access to data.

- Implement effective and constant network monitoring.

Due to the nature of their work, schools have large data sets that are of interest to
criminals and may not have invested the resources necessary to protect themselves in
the same way as business and government operations.

It is important for schools to be vigilant in keeping up to date and learning from the
experiences of others. Organizations willing to take steps to protect themselves will be
successful in their efforts, but those who do not and assume it won't happen may be
unpleasantly surprised. District leaders can set an important example by emphasizing
the importance of appropriate cybersecurity and working with staff to improve culture
and practice. Any organization will benefit from monitoring and blocking inappropriate sites, safeguarding equipment, focusing on identity protection for staff and
students, and working toward continuous safety improvement.

Professional Development Spotlight

Cybersecurity Awareness Program from the Cybersecurity and Infrastructure Security Agency

The Cybersecurity and Infrastructure Security Agency (CISA) is charged with leading the
federal government's efforts to protect against threats and collaborate with partners
to create a more secure infrastructure for the future. The CISA Cybersecurity Awareness
Program is a national public awareness effort aimed at increasing the understanding of
cyber threats and empowering the American public to be safer and more secure online.
The agency develops and distributes a variety of programs and publications for the
government, businesses, educational institutions, and the public. Their website offers a
collection of free resources and tools to provide assistance, exercises, and free training.
The Cybersecurity Awareness Program Toolkit contains resources that include information
and training for K–12 students, educators, and parents. For students, the Savvy Cyber Kids

program has activity sheets, books, and in-school program sessions for educators and supplemental resources for families. The toolkit has links to the FBI-sponsored Safe Online Surfing activity websites for grades 3–8. It also includes various resources for parents and educators through the ConnectSafely website. This site offers resources for educating teachers, parents, and students about online safety, privacy, security, and digital wellness. They provide safety tips and guidebooks related to various tech topics, including social media, gaming, and cyberbullying. There are links to a variety of web and video resources related to Safe Internet Day. The toolkit links can be found here: tinyurl.com/2ubehp6w

Remote Management

The management of a school district's network technology resources is a critical function that is usually handled by a small staff. Most districts have multiple servers, often located in different buildings (and even different communities), that must be serviced and supported by a small staff or a single individual. A server that goes down at a particular site may be miles away from an available technician, and the time necessary to drive to the site to provide support may result in lost learning time or lost office staff productivity.

A district with multiple servers in various locations should seriously consider acquiring the tools and resources necessary to allow remote management of servers and network equipment via the internet. These tools provide a variety of resources to network administrators and technology coordinators who are responsible for maintaining the integrity of the network and keeping the servers up and running.

Remote management software tools for most types of network equipment are available from a variety of vendors. These tools allow a technician at a central location to monitor the operation of the network in multiple locations and report on the operating condition of devices such as servers, routers, and switches. When a problem is found with a piece of equipment, the technician can connect to the equipment from a remote site and take a variety of actions to resolve the problem. The technician may:

- Connect to the server console to complete diagnostics and access control software

- Reboot the server by recycling server power

- Recover or reinstall operating system software, applications, or user data

- Troubleshoot hardware problems
- Update drivers
- Install patches
- Manage rights, groups, and user accounts

The use of remote management software tools offers a variety of advantages to those organizations willing to implement them. First, they can reduce the need for technical staff to personally visit a site to resolve network problems. Also, before an actual system failure occurs, it is possible for support staff to identify hardware components that are experiencing performance problems. Such tools can also warn of an impending server problem before it happens, leading to fewer service interruptions.

Answers to Essential Questions

1. **How can the technology coordinator ensure that the network infrastructure meets users' needs?**

    The technology coordinator should work with administration and the board of education to create and carry out a network infrastructure plan that will meet the current and future needs of the school or district and achieve the goals of the technology plan.

2. **What issues will confront the technology coordinator when providing wireless (Wi-Fi) and Voice over IP (VoIP) services to district users?**

    The technology coordinator must be prepared to work with the network administrator to provide the necessary capacity and technical expertise needed by users of the district Wi-Fi and VoIP services and equipment.

3. **How can the technology coordinator assist with the management of network user accounts?**

    The technology coordinator and the network administrator must work together to ensure that effective procedures are in place for managing network accounts and solving user problems. The technology coordinator must also plan and conduct training to help users understand the network and how to use it.

4. **How can the technology coordinator ensure that appropriate backup and disaster recovery procedures are regularly carried out?**

    The technology coordinator must work with the network administrator to ensure that a disaster recovery plan is in place, equipment and software are appropriate for regular backups, and the system is monitored regularly. Users must also be trained to follow appropriate backup procedures for important files and data.

5. **How can the technology coordinator use remote management tools to provide better network service and support?**

    The technology coordinator can use remote management tools to solve network-related problems in a timely fashion, often without a site visit. These tools are also used to constantly monitor the network, diagnosing potential problems that may diminish network performance or create service interruptions.

Resources

Cisco Product Support and Downloads (bit.ly/3M2H5lY)

Consortium for School Networking (cosn.org)

Google Workspace for Education (edu.google.com)

Microsoft Office 365 education plans (bit.ly/45yOfVZ)

Microsoft Product Support Services (support.microsoft.com)

Chapter 7

ADMINISTRATIVE COMPUTING

Essential Questions

1. What must the technology coordinator know about the selection, implementation, and support of the student information system (SIS) for the processing of grades and attendance data, as well as other student records and information?

2. What is data-driven decision making, and how can the technology coordinator support district personnel in this process?

3. How can the technology coordinator assist with the management of human resources information?

4. How can the technology coordinator ensure that administrators have the technology resources they need to manage the school or district's business operations?

5. What issues must the technology coordinator consider when implementing and supporting a system for document imaging and management?

Although a school district is primarily concerned with teaching and learning, it is nonetheless a business organization and must be concerned with business functions. In terms of technology, a school district must use technology to manage and streamline its business operations. This type of technology, called administrative computing, includes information management, data processing systems, and software programs. The technology coordinator has an important role to play in the administrative computing operations of the district.

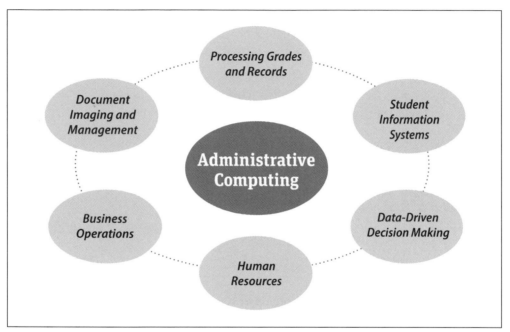

Figure 7.1. Administrative computing issues.

Administrative Computing and the Technology Coordinator

Schools and districts use administrative computing tools and software in a number of ways (see Figure 7.1). It is regularly necessary to create and manage student records, set up master course schedules, enroll students in courses, gather and analyze data about student progress to guide instructional decision making, and develop systems for keeping personnel and business records. Administrative computing software can help schools in the district handle a variety of information processing and distribution needs, from making decisions about the purchasing of classroom textbooks and supplies to the management of menus, meals, and other food service provisions.

Technology coordinators should be prepared to analyze, understand, and assist with the administrative computing needs of the organization. The coordinator will work with administrators and staff members to consider needs, develop technology solutions, consult with vendors about available products, and conduct professional development training sessions for business software users. Through involvement in these activities, the tech coordinator can have a positive impact on the efficiency of a school or district's business operations: "The use of technology, especially an easily-accessed, web-based system, can make process efficiency and increased parental involvement a more comfortable, favorable development for all involved" (Bird, 2006).

Tech Leader Profile

Jill Baker, Director of Field Support Services

Jill Baker has spent almost twenty-five years with the Metro Nashville Public Schools (MNPS), the second largest district in Tennessee. MNPS is an urban district, diverse in student ethnicity and socioeconomic status, serving 80,000 students speaking 132 different languages in more than 150 schools with a billion-dollar operating budget. Jill began her career as a first-grade classroom teacher and transitioned into working with federal programs and technology support. She earned a master's degree in educational leadership and was promoted to director of information technology support in 2014. Her office serves school locations across her district by providing staffing, training, and technology services for the various sites. There are almost 200 employees in the Technology Services and the Digital Strategy and Implementation (DSI) divisions. DSI is the instructional technology operation, with a staff of about 80. Jill's department is called Field Support Services, where she supervises 54 staff members, including field support technicians who work directly with classroom teachers and principals. She also collaborates with learning technology specialists who provide instructional support. The goal of all these people is to provide excellent customer service and technical support to MNPS users. Jill reports directly to the executive director of technology services and digital strategy and implementation. Her daily challenges include providing quality and timely technology services with trained technicians while having limited resources, and assisting schools with their need to share technician assignments. Jill's job satisfaction comes from having satisfied customers with students who can use technology to enhance their learning. For those who aspire to a position like hers, she offers this recommendation: "Build your foundation with education, training and experience; network with others in and out of your organization; attend conferences; and read widely. Be present for your job, communicate well, and engage in lifelong learning." You can follow her work here: linkedin.com/in/jill-baker-80413320.

Processing Grades and Student Records

Managing and processing everyday school data such as grades, student and employee records, and payroll figures are common administrative computing tasks. This data processing occurs routinely in all schools and districts, and managing both the necessary technology and the related processes is a recursive task for technology coordinators.

An administrative information system revolves around the management of many different types of records. A variety of records are created for every employee who works for the district and for every student who is served by the district. These records need to be created, updated, and archived on a regular basis. The technology coordinator should work with staff and administration to implement a system that adequately meets the needs of teachers and administrators for data creation, collection, storage, and reporting.

A centralized system usually offers advantages to a school or district with multiple buildings. Implementing a centralized system allows student and employee records to be kept and maintained in one location, but also to be easily accessed by users throughout the organization. When a centralized record is updated, the update is immediately available to all users of the system. If a school is using an information system that maintains unique records in separate locations, it is important to ensure that all records are updated simultaneously so that current information is available to everyone.

Student Information Systems

The processing of data concerning grades and other student records is an ongoing administrative computing function. Student information systems (SISs) often include a component for managing grade information for transcripts and other student records. At one time, the most common method for entering grade data was scanning bubble sheets that had been filled out by teachers. Computerized grading and attendance programs have become integral parts of SISs, used to manage the daily information necessary to accurately and effectively track student attendance and progress. Accurate and up-to-date information is available to teachers, administrators, and parents, thanks to these systems.

According to the Department of Education report "Use of Education Data at the Local Level" (Means, Padilla, & Gallagher, 2010), nearly all school districts have some sort of SIS and maintain at least some school data electronically. This data often includes the following student information: family information, courses taken, special program participation, immunization records, attendance, assessments, and grades. A comprehensive SIS allows stakeholders to easily communicate and make timely and effective decisions. Reporting requirements from the federal government and accreditation requirements at the state level require districts to gather and manage large amounts of student information, with the assumption that this data will lead to positive changes in instructional practices.

Numerous SISs have been developed by vendors for the K–12 educational market. Although some differences exist from product to product, certain basic features are included in all of them. A SIS should have the following basic features so that a school district can effectively manage student data:

> **Student records**. The ability to securely store information about each student enrolled in the district, such as address, phone number, name of guardian, emergency contact, and so forth.

Toolbox Tip

Creating a District Knowledge Base

School district administrators, teachers, and staff members need easy access to a variety of technology information and resources, particularly for those new to an organization. To provide easy access for his district employees, Lansing, Kansas, USD 469 Technology Director Christopher Fletcher created an online knowledgebase of technology information and resources. The knowledgebase contains a collection of resources on a variety of useful topics. These resources can be accessed from any district computer or any device with an internet connection. Following are examples of the kinds of topics covered in the knowledgebase:

- Details regarding the onboarding process for new employees

- Links to online professional development opportunities

- Tips for using the macOS, iPads, and Apple TV

- Tips for using Zoom

- Curriculum resources

- Technology integration information

Master schedule. The ability to create a master plan of classes and sections offered by a school.

Individual scheduling. The ability to enroll students in particular classes based on a master schedule developed by the school.

Grade reporting and records. The ability to create progress reports, grading-period reports, and transcripts.

Attendance. The ability to provide student and class attendance records needed for state reporting requirements.

Flexible reporting. The ability to generate a variety of reports based on the data in the system. With the increased data reporting requirements, this feature should be robust and provide a great deal of flexibility.

Student information systems can have a variety of other features and add-on components. These features include the ability to post, on a protected website, assignment information and grades. Parents and students can log on to these protected sites and view the data. Some vendors include this feature as a standard part of their SIS. Other vendors make such features and capabilities available as an add-on component.

Other SIS features, or add-on packages and components, include special-education record keeping, IEP tracking, fee management, and textbook rental and inventory tracking. Additional products can be purchased to work in conjunction with the SIS to provide teachers with aggregated assessment information. These products can assist teachers in tracking standards and indicators.

All of these features, and often many others, can be found in programs such as PowerSchool, a SIS used in a variety of schools in North America and around the world (www.powerschool.com/powerschool-sis). Other systems include Aeries from Eagle Software (www.aeries.com), School Information Systems products from Tyler Technologies (www.tylertech.com/solutions-products/tyler-sis-product-suite), and Infinite Campus (www.infinitecampus.com).

When selecting a SIS and a grade management program for district use, the technology coordinator, IT staff, administration, and project planning committee should make sure the system under consideration fully meets the needs of the organization. This selection process should include an analysis of all the features the organization needs at present as well as those anticipated for the future. The organization also should ensure that students and parents can access information remotely by logging on to a protected website. Pay careful attention to data security, equipment requirements, and concerns about privacy. Many of these systems also allow access by mobile devices. Choosing the right system will ensure that staff, students, and parents have convenient access in a format that is easy to use, while ensuring data security and records privacy.

The technology coordinator plays an important role in training users on use of the SIS. Users need to understand how the system works and how they can use it to perform their jobs more effectively. They must know how to get assistance when they have questions or encounter problems. Although the system may be maintained by IT staff or supported by outside vendors, the tech coordinator must serve as the local organizational contact.

Data-Driven Decision Making

Making instructional decisions based on the appropriate data to support those decisions is a common part of the school improvement process. The data-driven decision making process occurs when teachers and administrators base educational decisions on the analysis of student and program data. This data informs and guides the decisions necessary to improve student performance and school success. The Department of Education's National Educational Technology Trends Survey (NETTS) of 2008 revealed that access to electronic systems for gathering and managing student data increased from 48% in 2005 to 74% by 2007. As a result of increased federal and state reporting requirements, schools are collecting and analyzing more data than ever before.

Data from the school, district, and state levels is becoming more readily accessible and available (often on district or state department of education websites), and there is increased interest in using this data to make informed, effective decisions. Teachers currently use existing student information systems to monitor student progress and to inform parents about student progress. The NETTS survey indicates that although teachers may have some of the data analysis skills necessary for refining instructional practice, they would benefit from ongoing support and assistance. NETTS data also reveals that teachers felt they would benefit from a process that allows them to regularly use data more systematically and effectively to guide instruction.

The technology coordinator can play an essential role in the data-driven decision-making process. Educational users of data (both teachers and administrators) need initial preparation and ongoing professional development in the use of student information systems. The successful use of data for decision-making purposes is not possible if staff members lack the skills necessary to organize and understand the data. The technology coordinator can partner with other district leaders, such as school improvement leaders, district administration, and board of education members, to provide the necessary preparation, training, support, capacity, and even the time to analyze, interpret, and make decisions. These decisions can be instrumental in creating effective changes in instructional practice.

Tech Leader Profile

Laurie Guyon, Coordinator for Instructional Technology

Laurie Guyon is the lead coordinator for instructional technology programs for a five-county region in East-central New York. Originally trained as an elementary classroom teacher, she also served as a technology integration specialist before earning her administration degree and beginning her work for a Board of Cooperative Education Services (BOCES) office serving 31 suburban school districts and approximately 38,000 students. Her office is responsible for professional learning related to technology, implementation of the state computer science and digital fluency standards, and providing support to area educators and administrators for the implementation of educational technology products. Laurie is assisted by one technology integration specialist. Because she serves a large school population and a geographic area of over 2,500 square miles, finding the time necessary to meet the needs of all the educators she serves can be a challenge. One of the things Laurie enjoys most about her work are the smiles on the faces of teachers and students who are doing something new and exciting with technology. The pandemic had a profound impact on her work. Change has been continual during transitions to and from virtual learning. Post-COVID, teachers may not be as fearful of technology, but they are often left wondering when it is best to use technology. In 2023, Laurie was the recipient of the Leader in Digital Education Award presented by the School Administrators Association of New York State. She was also acknowledged by ISTE as one of 20 to watch for 2023, an award that recognizes 20 up-and-coming individuals who are making a difference through their work and exemplify excellence that others can replicate. For those aspiring to a position like hers, Laurie offers this advice: "Be resilient and willing to try new things. Just because something is hard, that doesn't mean it is not worth it. Supporting children is always worth it." She goes on to point out that "one must be flexible as no two days are ever the same and technology is always changing. It is critical to stay connected, stay current, and be willing to pivot when necessary." You can follow her at: @smilelearning.

Human Resources

The management of human resources records is another area of administrative computing in which technology coordinators are likely to be involved. Information management systems used for student records can often be used for employee records as well. This system can track such details as salaries, wages and hours, benefits, and supplemental contract agreements.

Technology coordinators can work with HR staff in the analysis and planning of technology purchases and implementation. The technology coordinator may also play a significant role in supporting the technology functions of a school's or district's human resources department. Coordinators can work with vendors to select the appropriate hardware and software, and they can provide training and ongoing support for users as needed.

Implementing an HR information management system can be a complex and time-consuming undertaking. However, the benefits of a properly implemented system can be significant. Let's take a look at the procedures one school district followed to effectively implement a new electronic time clock system.

The district began by organizing a team made up of the technology coordinator, staff from district administration, and staff from the personnel and business offices. The team then reviewed current procedures and established project goals.

Team members found that current hourly record keeping was done on paper time cards. Every month, two payroll staffers spent twenty hours overtime apiece resolving problems and correcting time card errors. When processing yearly contract renewals, three people entered teacher contract information by hand in three different systems.

In meeting and reviewing this information, the team established goals for implementing an entirely new system. The most desirable system would use electronic time clocks to enter data directly into the payroll system. Contract information would be easily shared between different offices and systems that needed access to the data.

Once the goals for the project had been established, the technology coordinator contacted various vendors, providing them with a project description and requesting an informational product presentation. The team spent nearly six weeks viewing product demonstrations, comparing system features, and gathering additional information. The purpose of these informational sessions was to compare products and select several vendors from which to secure bids.

After the initial list of potential products had been narrowed, the technology coordinator worked with the purchasing department to develop a request for proposals from vendors. The resulting document described the district project, outlined the project goals, and requested a proposal from each vendor that specified how the vendor might design a complete solution, along with the cost. Requests for proposals were sent to four of the vendors who had presented informational sessions. The team also spent time developing an evaluation process to help rate each proposal, including project scope, timeline for completion, how well the product met the project criteria, and the cost of the solution.

Each of the proposals was evaluated by the team according to the pre-established criteria. Ultimately, a single vendor was selected to provide the system and was contacted to meet with the team to begin detailed project planning. Timelines were developed and communicated to district schools and staff. The implementation of the electronic time clocks would be rolled out in phases, beginning with two sites and expanding, in phases, to all sites.

As the system was being installed at the district office site, initial user training took place for those who would directly use the new system to manage information on a daily basis. As the two pilot sites came online, various problems were discovered. Repairs and changes were made, and procedures were refined. As the district prepared to bring additional sites online with the time clocks, more users were trained to use the new system. Within a period of four months, all district sites were online.

After the completion of the project, the team continued to meet for several months to review progress and identify the benefits of the new system. Feedback

Toolbox Tip

Network or Cloud Backups

Users should be trained to store all their important documents on a network storage resource or in cloud-based storage. By doing so, they can be assured that their information will be backed up, even if there is a device failure or loss. When stored in this way, information can be accessed from any network computer or device connected to the internet. Storing files on a local hard drive means that access to the files is limited to the computer where the files are stored; storing files in this way does not guarantee the regular backup of the information. By training all users to have effective storage habits that ensure backup, the technology coordinator helps users avoid losing critical data due to equipment failure or other unforeseen problems.

from office employees indicated that processing hourly employee data for payroll no longer required overtime. Hourly employees indicated they liked having sick leave and vacation data available to them whenever they accessed the time clock system. Contract information now flowed much more efficiently between offices and systems.

In this case, the technology coordinator provided important leadership and assistance in facilitating a project to benefit district staff and improve the management of information. By using a simple seven-step process, problems with the current human resources system were addressed, and procedures improved, to the satisfaction of both the district staff and the employees. These seven steps were: review current procedures, set goals, gather information, get proposals, plan project, implement carefully, and evaluate progress.

The technology coordinator can also assist with employee recruitment. A system can be implemented for posting job opportunities on the district's website and other employment websites. Postings can be placed with university placement offices. States also offer online job listing sites, such as those of the Kansas Education Employment Board (www.kansasteachingjobs.com) and the Florida Department of Education (www.teachinflorida.com). National listing sites such as the Regional Educational Applicant Placement website (www.reap.net) are also good places to post openings. By listing job opportunities on these sites, a school or district will have a better chance of hiring qualified candidates for open positions.

Business Operations

Purchasing is an important part of a school or district's daily operations. The business office must generate purchase orders, track the filling of these orders, acknowledge the receipt of merchandise, manage the inventory of district assets, and arrange for the payment of accounts. In addition, a district is often required to generate requests for proposals and bids involving large purchases and then manage the bidding process to award contracts.

Although business officers usually manage these purchasing operations, the technology coordinator often plays a role in supporting the technology they use. This technology usually takes the form of a centralized information management system. Such a system may be an add-on component of the student information management system, or it may be separate. An example of a business operations system is the LINQ Integrated

K–12 Business Platform (www.linq.com). This product includes components to manage purchasing and receiving, fixed assets, HR, accounting, and warehouse inventory.

It is the responsibility of the technology coordinator to ensure that appropriate technology resources—such as connectivity, workstations, or mobile devices for accessing the system and training for users of key programs—are available to business office staff. For example, to access the information management system effectively, all offices must have the necessary network connections. In addition, office staff who work eight hours a day with purchasing or accounting data may need workstations with multiple or larger monitors to maintain a highly productive work environment.

The effective use of technology to support the purchasing operations of a school or district will result in better financial management. An information management system enables the school or district to have better access to financial data and other critical information necessary for decision making. This system also allows for better use of available school resources.

Document Imaging and Management

School districts, like many other organizations, generate vast collections of paper records as part of their day-to-day operations. Management and storage of business records, student records, transcripts, student portfolios, required reports, and other paper documents is a major challenge for many schools and districts. Records must be maintained in accordance with state and federal law, as well as to meet the record keeping and business needs of the school or district itself. The technology coordinator can help streamline this task by assisting in the planning and implementation of a system for document imaging and management.

Document imaging is the conversion of a paper document into an electronic image that can be accessed by a computer. After a document has been converted into an image and stored in the system, it can be retrieved quickly and efficiently. An imaging system is made up of several separate yet important elements. These elements include scanning, storage, retrieval, indexing (creating a system for document filing), and user access.

When evaluating a document management system, a technology coordinator must consider two critical elements: storage and retrieval processes. Many different types of scanners are available, and they are capable of scanning anywhere from a few pages per minute to several hundred. As part of initial planning, conducting a careful needs analysis will help determine the number and types of scanners needed and where these scanners should be located. A variety of storage options are available. Most organizations will benefit from recording information on some kind of optical drive and using a jukebox device to distribute and arrange information on several different discs.

Document management software can be used to organize and index documents so that they can be retrieved easily. Documents can be indexed in several ways: field and keyword indexing, full-text indexing, or a file or folder system. Good document management software allows information to be indexed in a variety of different ways at the same time so that users can easily retrieve needed information regardless of how they search for it. Some users may wish to retrieve information by keyword, while others need to find documents through use of full-text searches.

The final component of the document-imaging system is control of access to the archived documents. This system must provide users with easy access to the information they need while restricting access to sensitive information that is not within their purview. Some users need access to student records, others to employee files, and still others must be able to access business records stored in the system. The system should be flexible enough to meet all these different needs without compromising security.

A variety of important questions must be asked when planning and establishing a document imaging system that will meet a district's document management needs. Among them are the following:

- What problems will this system solve, and how will the system improve the productivity of the organization?
- How many documents will the system store, and for what purpose?
- How many users will need to use the system at the same time?
- Which offices will need access to the system, and where are the users located?
- Is the necessary network connectivity available for users of the system? Is this connectivity adequate for the system's successful use?

For some districts, the planning, purchase, implementation, and support of a document imaging system will be a viable project. For others, the implementation of such a system may be out of the question because of budget constraints, lack of staff to install and support such a system, or limited return on investment due to the size of the district.

Outsourcing may be a possible solution for those districts that want to implement such a system but have limited resources. Outsourcing document imaging can provide electronic storage and access to information and documents while avoiding the upfront costs of acquiring and supporting such a system. This is a possibility that must be explored when considering the implementation of an imaging and management system for a district.

By working with administrators and office staff to determine the answers to the previous questions, the technology coordinator can design a document management system that meets user needs. The coordinator will then need to work with vendors to select the appropriate hardware and software, plan the installation of the system, create a training program for users, and address issues of system administration and ongoing support.

The successful planning and implementation of a document management system can have many benefits for a school district. Archived documents are more easily accessed by users, thus increasing productivity. Document access is more easily regulated, ensuring employee- and student-record confidentiality. Records are readily available precisely when they are needed. Principals, for example, can review employment applications on their personal computer rather than having to visit the personnel office to review them. A document management system also saves considerable space in the storage of archival files, and electronic documents can become part of a disaster recovery plan. Archived records can be copied and stored off site to allow the re-creation of the data archive system should a disaster destroy the paper records of the organization.

Although administrative computing may not be the chief focus of the technology coordinator's job, the leadership, support, and guidance that tech coordinators can bring to these activities will help ensure the success of the organization and maximize the return on investment in technology in support of a school or district's business operations.

Answers to Essential Questions

1. **What must the technology coordinator know about the selection, implementation, and support of the student information system for the processing of grades and attendance data, as well as other student records and information?**

    The technology coordinator should have a detailed understanding of the system used to manage grades and student information in order to provide training, offer assistance, and give ongoing support to users of this system. All those who work with students and grades, as well as those who manage this data at the district level, will need this training and assistance.

2. **What is data-driven decision making, and how can the technology coordinator support district personnel in this process?**

    Data-driven decision making is the process of getting student data (especially assessment and background data) into the hands of teachers—the primary instructional decision makers—for the purpose of planning and implementing strategies that will lead to increased student achievement. The technology coordinator plays an important role by providing the technology resources, professional development, and support necessary to help teachers make effective decisions based on the data available.

3. **How can the technology coordinator assist with the management of human resources information?**

    In addition to user support and training on the information management system, the technology coordinator should be prepared to assist with the posting of employment opportunities to various websites to attract quality teacher candidates and applicants for other positions.

4. **How can the technology coordinator ensure that administrators have the technology resources they need to manage the school or district's business operations?**

    In supporting the purchasing process for a district, the technology coordinator must ensure that users have the workstations, software resources, network connectivity, training, and support they need to perform their jobs efficiently.

5. **What issues must the technology coordinator consider when implementing and supporting a system for document imaging and management?**

    In implementing a system for document imaging and management, the technology coordinator must discuss the documentation needs and overall scope of the system with administrators and staff, work with vendors to select the appropriate hardware and software, and develop a comprehensive plan for successful training and support of system users.

Resources

Aeries Student Information System (aeries.com)

Infinite Campus products (infinitecampus.com)

ISTE Standards for Education Leaders (bit.ly/45yfxMc)

Educate Kansas (educatekansas.org)

Laserfiche Imaging and Management for K–12 Schools (bit.ly/45CNQBU)

PowerSchool Student Information System (powerschool.com/solutions)

Regional Educational Applicant Placement (usreap.net)

State Educational Technology Directors Association—National Trends Reports and other resources (bit.ly/46Omh9R)

Tyler Student Information System (bit.ly/48YRdGb)

Chapter 8

PLANNING AND BUDGETING

Essential Questions

1. What should the technology coordinator know about developing a comprehensive and successful technology plan?

2. How can the technology coordinator assist administrators in creating and carrying out a sound technology budget?

3. How can the technology coordinator assist in evaluating the effectiveness of technology use in the school or district?

4. What must the technology coordinator do to ensure proper licensing of software?

5. What must the technology coordinator do to make sure equipment is properly maintained, upgraded, and repaired as necessary?

6. What role should the technology coordinator play in the recycling and disposal of computer equipment?

7. What can the technology coordinator do to assist the district in hiring the appropriate IT staff?

The primary function of most technology coordinators is to serve as the technology leader for the school or district. The importance and challenge of this leadership role are most evident in the areas of planning and budgeting. The technology coordinator can best fulfill this role by articulating a vision for technology use in the school or district; establishing a clear, achievable plan for making that vision a reality; and working with administrators and the board of education to find the resources necessary to make it all happen. By developing a comprehensive and appropriate technology budget; securing grants and other outside funding to move demanding and resource-intensive programs forward; and applying for discounts and refunds from the E-Rate program, the technology coordinator can have a tremendous impact on the successful implementation of technology in the school or district (see Figure 8.1).

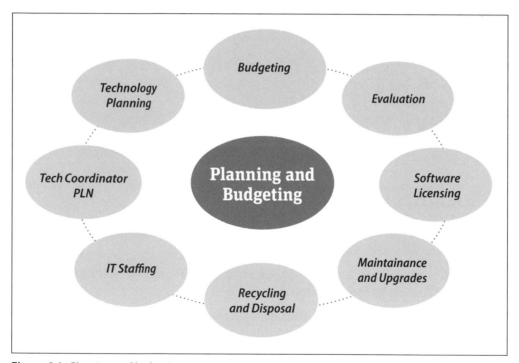

Figure 8.1. Planning and budgeting issues.

Technology Planning

Since computers first appeared in libraries and classrooms in the 1980s, schools have spent vast sums of money purchasing technology for classrooms and offices. While exact figures are difficult to come by, David Nagel, writing in *Campus Technology*, estimated in 2008 that Educational IT spending would exceed $56 billion by 2012, with K–12 accounting for over $20 billion of this spending (Nagel, 2008). Yet even with dramatically increased technology investment, there has often been a lack of essential planning regarding what purposes the technology would serve and how it would be used to accomplish those purposes. The expectation has commonly been that simply placing technology tools and other resources in the classroom leads to exciting results and improved student learning.

Any school or district that wants to make sure technology expenditures have the intended impact for students and staff must have a carefully-developed technology plan. This plan represents a three- to five-year road map of where the school or district wishes to go with technology. It also represents the results of many conversations among board members, administrators, teaching staff, and community members regarding how technology can support the learning process. Consideration is given to how pedagogy and the learning environment must change in order to make better use of the available technology tools and, in so doing, provide richer experiences for students. The technology coordinator plays an important role in fostering and sustaining these conversations.

Most schools and districts today develop technology plans. Until 2015, districts were required to periodically submit a technology plan for approval if they were seeking funding for certain services under the federal E-Rate program. Beginning in 2015, the FCC has chosen to eliminate the technology plan requirements in an effort to both simplify and streamline the application process for E-Rate funds.

While submission of a district technology plan may no longer be a requirement for E-Rate funding, development and monitoring of a technology plan is a good idea for any school organization and may still be required by other organizations such as state agencies. In many cases, these plans originally concentrated on the acquisition of hardware or the development of network infrastructure. Although these are certainly important components of an effective technology plan, an effective technology plan should encompass much more. Barnett (2001) has clearly and succinctly defined ten essential elements of a successful technology plan:

1. Create a vision.
2. Involve all stakeholders.
3. Gather data.

4. Review the research.

5. Integrate technology in the curriculum.

6. Commit to professional development.

7. Ensure a sound infrastructure.

8. Allocate appropriate funding and budget.

9. Plan for ongoing assessment and monitoring.

10. Prepare for tomorrow.

Barnett's list of elements ensures that a technology plan goes beyond devices and network connections to consider the overall vision of where the organization is trying to go, an idea of what resources will be needed to get there, and a plan for what will happen when these resources are in place. In many ways the planning process looks both forward and back continuously, and the planning process is ongoing.

Any educational organization should consult some of the wide variety of planning resources available before beginning the process of developing or updating a technology plan. One source of information about planning might be the National Educational Technology Plan developed by the Office of Educational Technology at the U.S. Department of Education (tech.ed.gov/netp). In addition to this plan, a number of other resources and publications are available from the site.

While some of the documents and information found on the site may be dated, the National Center for Technology Planning (NCTP) provides information about a variety of models and approaches for planning technology. Founded by Larry Anderson in 1992, the NCTP (www.nctp.com) serves as a clearinghouse for information. The website makes available a wide range of plans from schools and districts across the nation. It also contains articles, brochures, checklists, and other items to assist in the planning process.

The technology coordinator should enlist the aid of a variety of stakeholders when beginning the planning process. When teachers, administrators, board members, community representatives, parents, and students are all involved, a wide range of needs and ideas can be expressed and vetted, and a broad base of support can be established for the plan. The coordinator should work with these stakeholders to develop a vision that defines what the technology program will look like in three to five years. The vision statement should include how students and teachers will be using technology to support and enhance the learning process.

No planning process can be effective without data to support decision making. The technology coordinator must provide the planning group with up-to-date information about a school or district's technology inventory. This current summary of the hardware, software, and network resources currently used in district classrooms, offices, and other facilities is important to inform decision making. It is often useful for the technology coordinator to conduct a system-wide survey of technology use by teachers and students and to share the results of the survey with the planning group in advance of the planning activities. Arranging site visits so that stakeholders can see how teachers and students in other locations use technology in unique and compelling ways is an excellent way to raise awareness and interest.

The technology planning committee will also benefit from providing members with access to current research on the use of technology in learning. The technology coordinator can help to facilitate this process by creating a summary review of the literature, by identifying and collecting useful articles that address the issues and tasks at hand, and by making sure these resources are easily available to the planning committee. By emphasizing current research, the technology coordinator can help focus the committee's planning efforts. The focus should be on how to integrate technology successfully into the curriculum rather than on hardware specifications, software titles, or network infrastructure. Powerful computing devices, the latest applications and software, and high-speed and large-bandwidth internet connections are great, but these things alone are not enough to ensure successful technology integration or improved teaching and learning. Enhancing the processes for student learning should always be the focus when creating or revising a technology plan.

One component that is sometimes overlooked in the planning process is the allocation of resources for professional development and training. While considerable attention is often paid to the purchase, upkeep, and replacement of equipment, the need to train teachers and staff to effectively use that equipment is sometimes overlooked—a critical mistake. To ensure that the investment in technology resources and infrastructure is maximized, the training and support of teachers and support staff must be included in the planning. The technology coordinator must be sure that an ongoing professional development program is integrated into the technology plan. Failure to include this element, or an emphasis on isolated events for staff development, will make the success of the plan much more elusive. The development of a comprehensive and ongoing system of technology training and instructional support for effectively using technology in the classroom will maximize results.

The technology plan must also address technical support and infrastructure needs. The technology coordinator is usually responsible for identifying those needs and

Toolbox Tip

Budget Allocation Formula

Providing funding for the various technology needs of an organization can be a challenge. A successful technology budget will allocate dollars for a variety of different needs. A budget plan that follows an allocation formula can help to ensure that the various needs of a school or district are being sufficiently addressed. Following is one example of an allocation formula used by a school district for technology funding:

- Hardware and equipment 35%
- Software and apps 15%
- Contracts and services 10%
- Professional development 20%
- Support and maintenance 10%
- Upgrades and other needs 10%

drafting a budget that will support them in a stable and sustainable way. Some organizations have found it challenging to devote the resources necessary to provide a quality technology infrastructure, while others have been hesitant to hire the support personnel necessary to properly support the technology. It is critical to the success of the organization that these important needs both be met through effective technology planning and budgeting. Attempting to fund these needs in a haphazard way or relying on uncertain funding will only lead to problems and frustrations. By working with the board and administration, the technology coordinator can make sure necessary financial support is in place to carry out all components of the technology plan.

No technology plan is complete without an evaluation component: staff, teacher, and student use of technology must be regularly monitored, and assessments must be used to determine progress. The technology coordinator should assist in developing and administering surveys, defining learning outcomes, and implementing evaluation rubrics throughout the school or district. The information gathered from these assessments should be compiled and shared with stakeholders for further analysis and use in future planning. To stay on top of exciting new developments in technology that may improve learning outcomes, the technology coordinator should also regularly read about new products and developments, attend conference presentations and trade shows, and discuss products with vendors.

For the experienced technology coordinator, a technology plan is much more than a shopping list of hardware and software needs. It is a comprehensive plan that includes a variety of critical components that "craft a flexible framework that allows schools to implement systematic changes that support 21st century learning and greater academic achievement. The bottom line is that technology should be an essential means for supporting 21st century learning and achievement; it is not, however, an end unto itself" (Virginia Department of Education, 2010).

Budgeting

Securing and supporting technology to enhance learning requires considerable financial commitment from a school district. For a comprehensive, districtwide technology program to be successful, the technology coordinator and administration must ensure that an adequate budget is available to provide all necessary equipment, software, connectivity, technical support, and training. Although few businesses would ever try to implement technology solutions without the necessary funding and resources, school districts sometimes implement programs and equipment without identifying and obtaining adequate financial resources to complete and support these projects and initiatives. The technology coordinator must make sure this does not happen; funding must be allocated in both the current and future budget cycles for hardware, software, maintenance, connectivity, supplies, and professional development.

The technology coordinator can ensure that the school or district technology plan is suitably funded and sustained by budgeting carefully; assessing administrative, curricular, and infrastructure needs; and working with the board of education and administration to develop funding that adequately meets those needs.

Developing an effective budget for district technology can be a time-consuming process for the technology coordinator. Considerable time may elapse from the initial needs assessment to the actual approval of a budget; therefore, the earlier the start, the better the outcome. Although each district will have a budgeting process that is unique to that organization, some common themes can be recognized.

One of the first steps in the budgeting process is data collection and needs assessment. In this phase of the process, the technology coordinator, usually working with the planning committee, gathers data such as inventory and professional development statistics, as well as any other information that provides a current picture of technology in the district. It is also useful for the technology coordinator to review the current technology plan to determine what progress has been made and how the plan is proceeding. In addition, it is important for the technology coordinator to communicate with district and building administration, curriculum committees, and other constituencies to identify perceived technology needs and wants throughout the district.

When data has been collected and a list of needs determined, the actual work on a preliminary budget can begin. This budget must provide resources in two general areas: an operations budget, which provides the funding to pay the ongoing costs of providing technology services and support, and a capital improvements budget, which provides the funds to purchase new technology resources and provides upgrades and improvements to existing ones.

Operations funding includes the funds necessary to pay technology staff, provide network services, settle contract costs for support agreements and software licensing, purchase day-to-day repair parts, and furnish professional development services. Capital improvement costs are those associated with the purchase (or lease) of new computing devices (desktops, laptops, or tablets), servers, and network equipment; replacement and upgrades for existing devices and equipment; and various hardware purchases such as projectors, document cameras, or electronic whiteboard systems used in classrooms.

At this point in the process, the technology coordinator works with technology staff, administration, and other groups to identify specific areas of need. The coordinator will attempt to fit these needs into a workable budget plan. Part of the budget will be made up of fixed costs that will be ongoing, and so must be factored in first. Fixed costs include such items as salaries, network connectivity, and support contracts. Part of the budget will likely be devoted to equipment replacement and upgrades because machines eventually wear out and must be replaced. The final part of the budget will likely be made up of new initiatives that may be defined by the technology plan or advocated for by the administration. There may also be initiatives that are suggested by an individual building or group of faculty that promote the implementation of some new hardware or other technology resource. It is the responsibility of the tech coordinator to create a workable first draft of the budget by successfully balancing the various needs and wants along with their related costs.

After an initial draft of the budget has been developed, the budget will usually be submitted to central administration for consideration. During this time, all departments and units of the school district will be in the process of developing draft budget proposals, and a period of negotiation and revision will take place. The technology coordinator will need to work with central administration to help them understand the various elements that went into the draft budget proposal, including the needs outlined in the technology plans, targeted in the needs assessment, and expressed by the building staff or departments.

As budget negotiations continue, the technology budget, along with all other departmental and school budgets, will go through a process of revision. A considerable amount of give and take occurs during this period. Each department will have identified needs, wants, and goals for their budget. Their draft budgets will reflect these different goals, and there will be some level of competition for budget funding. Through negotiation and compromise, the district must find a way to successfully balance the needs of all the departments while dealing with the realities of a limited budget.

Following the negotiations with central administration and other departments, the final draft of the technology budget will be developed. The actual budget will be set by the local board of education, so it is important that the technology coordinator be both able to justify the budget as presented and able to make decisions about budget requests based on data that show the benefits of technology spending for the district. By beginning early, using data to determine need, developing a draft budget based on realistic expectations, considering the needs of others, and being willing to negotiate and compromise, the technology coordinator can ensure that a successful technology budget is developed for the district.

Evaluation

Significant educational resources have been invested to install and implement educational technology in classrooms. In the past, it may have been possible to evaluate this investment in terms of either numbers of students per device or level of internet connectivity, but today boards of education and school leaders often focus on finding ways to determine whether this investment is paying off in terms of student learning. Accountability has become an increased focus for all schools, and it has never been more important for schools to be able to demonstrate the beneficial impact of educational technology on the learning process. An increasing number of schools have chosen to implement 1:1 models to put a device in the hands of each student. When changes like this are made, schools must find ways to demonstrate that this investment is paying off in terms of student learning. The development of assessment tools and techniques that reliably evaluate the effective use of technology for learning is a considerable challenge for the technology coordinator. Nonetheless, this process is crucial for demonstrating that the integration of technology is making a positive impact on both teaching and learning.

As with any other part of the educational program, technology evaluation must be a systematic process. The technology coordinator must begin by identifying how the evaluation will be structured and what is to be learned from it. Assessment tools should be selected or developed based on the fundamental goals of a school or district's technology plan. They may include surveys, interviews, observations, focus groups, checklists, paper and pencil or online instruments, and analysis of additional data such as standardized test scores or results from state or local assessments. Many resources on technology evaluation and assessment can be found on the internet. The resources section at the end of this chapter identifies examples of several useful tools.

After data has been collected from either existing sources or new assessments, the information must be analyzed in order to draw conclusions and make judgments about the program, and to guide future decision making. The data collected during this process can be important in making long-range decisions about future technology purchases and initiatives. Assessment must be an ongoing process, because both the technology and the way users employ it are constantly changing. The evaluation process must be continuously revised, adapted, and improved to successfully gauge performance and growth.

The technology coordinator must also work to make sure that assessment results will be shared with a variety of different audiences—the administration, the board of education, the teaching faculty, and the community. These results should be tailored so that the information will fit the particular needs of each of these groups. Doing so helps each group understand the importance of the district investment in technology and the ways in which students benefit from this investment. Visual representations such as graphs and charts, for example, can be far more effective with a community group or the local board of education than a long, detailed report or narrative would be. On the other hand, state departments of education may require both a detailed narrative and plenty of supporting data. It is important that a technology coordinator carefully consider the intended audience when planning each assessment report.

Meaningful technology assessment can offer a variety of benefits. Results from the assessment help demonstrate whether the technology program is making progress, determine if the investment has been worthwhile, and assist in making adjustments in the way the program is operating. The conversations that result from planning and implementing the assessment also help everyone involved to better understand the program and its focus. By offering leadership in this process, initiating the conversations, working with administrators and teachers to design or select assessments, and helping analyze and share the results, the technology coordinator can play a critical role in the continuous improvement of a school or district's technology program.

Toolbox Tip

Using an Evaluation Rubric for Purchasing Decisions

Like many technology leaders, Jennifer Freedman, coordinator of instructional technology and library media specialist for Lindenhurst Union Free School District in New York needed assistance in establishing quality control for the educational technology tools used by district teachers. In a recent reply to Jennifer's question posted on the ISTE Connect discussion forum, Pattie Morales, instructional technology specialist for Indian Community School in Franklin, Wisconsin, suggested using the Triple E Evaluation Rubric for Educational Applications. The framework was developed by Professor Liz Kolb at the University of Michigan School of Education in 2011. It is designed to help K–12 educators connect research on education technologies to teaching practice in the classroom. The Triple E Evaluation Rubric supports schools and teachers in making informed choices about which educational applications to purchase and use to meet specific teaching and learning goals. The rubric helps to evaluate the connection between the technology in a lesson plan and the learning goals of the lesson plan. While all purchasing decisions in her organization begin with the rubric evaluation, Pattie also uses a decision-making flow chart (shown in Figure 8.2) to visualize how application and program requests are handled. The Triple E evaluation rubric can be accessed here: bit.ly/47wVv6A.

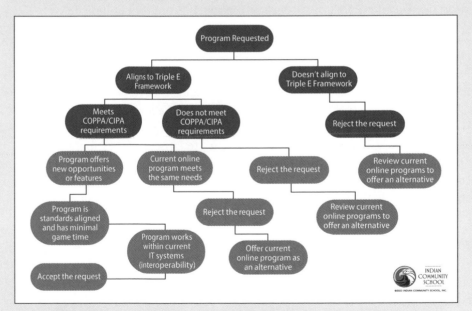

Figure 8.2. FHSD District technology application gameboard. Reproduced with permission.

Software Licensing and Installation

Although the installation and setup of equipment is important, the equipment is of little use without an operating system and software programs appropriate to the needs of end users. As discussed in Chapter 2, the technology coordinator is concerned with the selection, purchase, installation, and management of a standard set of programs for each computing device, including desktop, laptop, and tablet devices. The selection of a software suite ensures that all users will have access to the tools and software they need for their productivity and learning activities. It should not matter if the user sits down to use a desktop computer in an office, opens up a laptop from a cart in the library or a science lab, or makes use of a tablet in a classroom; the appropriate programs should be available for use in any of these situations.

Several options exist for licensing the programs and applications necessary to meet the needs of educational users. Some organizations may choose to purchase equipment that includes the required resources already installed. The advantage of doing so is that it allows capital outlay funds, which normally cannot be used for the purchase of software alone, to be applied to the purchase. The result is a computer with pre-installed software that is rolled into the price of the machine. Alternatively, organizations may choose to license and install the programs separately from the equipment.

The choice an organization makes depends primarily on what software packages they wish to have installed on their devices and whether these packages are available as a standard option. If, for example, a district wishes to have Microsoft Office installed as a standard package, and the software can be purchased already installed on a computer, then doing so will save the district installation time and allow it to use capital outlay dollars to make the purchase. If the district wishes to install a software package not available as a standard option, it may be necessary to either license the software separately and then install it, or set up a master machine and have the new equipment cloned. Today, many organizations are choosing a cloud-based suite of programs accessed through the internet. This makes installations and individual licensing of these programs either unnecessary or more convenient.

In addition to looking at price options available through consortiums, technology coordinators should check to see what manufacturers are offering. Most manufacturers have academic licensing programs that make their software relatively inexpensive for educational organizations to take advantage of. Such purchasing programs may offer licensing of specific numbers of machines at a particular cost per machine; alternatively, all devices throughout a building or district could be covered by a site license for a specific price.

No matter which path the organization chooses, it is important for the technology coordinator to ensure that an appropriate number of licensed copies have been purchased for all commercial programs and applications that will be installed on school or district equipment.

Once software is selected and installed on district devices, one of the challenges for the technology coordinator will be record keeping. Just as with equipment purchases, an accurate inventory of software and application installations should be established and carefully maintained.

The software versions that are installed in various locations must be tracked and accounted for to ensure that a standard version is in use. This can be a time-consuming task. Tracking the number of licenses installed for compliance with current licensing agreements can also be challenging. Many districts have chosen to provide a suite of cloud-based applications for student (and sometimes faculty) use. Both Google Workspace and Microsoft Office 365 provide access to software tools from an internet-connected device, along with cloud-based storage and access for documents. The main advantage for a district when choosing to implement either of these software suites is that they are available at no cost to schools. These suites provide applications and tools for productivity, file storage, file sharing, email, calendars, and collaboration. In addition to providing a variety of tools that can be accessed from either school or home, these products can save money in a time of tight budgets and liberate schools from the time-consuming task of tracking and maintaining productivity software installations.

Tech Leader Profile

Lakisha Brinson-Thomas, Director of Instructional Technology

Dr. Lakisha Brinson-Thomas has served as the director of instructional technology for the Metro Nashville Public Schools since 2017. Her responsibilities include supporting instructional technology and digital learning for nearly 80,000 students in the roughly 150 schools that make up this diverse, urban district. Initially trained as an elementary teacher, she went on to study school library science and earn a doctorate in instructional leadership. With her love of technology and experience as a teacher and librarian, Dr. Brinson-Thomas is uniquely qualified to support technology and provide professional learning for district teachers. In 2015, she was a selected as a finalist for the *School Library Journal* Librarian of the Year, and in 2022 she was recognized by ISTE as one of "20 to Watch"—up and coming professionals who are already making a difference through their work. EdTech Focus on K–12 recognized Dr. Brinson-Thomas as one of thirty K–12 Influencers to Follow in 2023.

Her main responsibilities include leading her team in various initiatives; participating as an active leader in building relationships with organizations and stakeholders; and collaborating and communicating with stakeholders on the selection of instructional technologies, digital content, and pedagogy. Dr. Brinson-Thomas is part of a senior leadership team made up of four people, and she supervises two management-level (coordinator) positions. She reports directly to the executive director of technology services and digital strategy and implementation. Dr. Brinson-Thomas describes a major challenge as successfully promoting instructional technology in all subjects. Sometimes, content experts have a hard time seeing how technology can help meet the academic needs of students. She wants to ensure instructional technology is not viewed as an "extra." Dr. Brinson-Thomas finds satisfaction in helping to ensure every district student is personally known. She advises those who aspire to leadership positions in technology to remember that power and wisdom come from building relationships with stakeholders. The goal should always be to provide ideas on how collaboration will provide greater success for everyone. You can follow her work here: @lakishabrinson.

Establishing a Professional Learning Network for the Technology Coordinator

The technology coordinator is often the district leader responsible for planning and implementing district professional development activities related to educational technology. As part of the planning and budgeting process, it is important for the technology coordinator to consider their own personal needs for professional learning and growth as part of the planning and budgeting process. To be prepared to take advantage of technology to successfully impact learning, strong and capable leadership is needed to create a vision shared by all. Leaders must be well prepared and supported in their work in the same way that administrators, teachers, and staff members are prepared for their work with students. As part of the budgeting and planning process, it is critical to provide and secure the resources necessary for the district technology leader to participate in personal learning to prepare them to effectively lead others in the district.

Building a professional learning network (PLN) is an important step for the district technology leader. An easy first step is to identify an area of interest and determine what online resources may be available. This may be as simple as doing research to find useful articles to read, identifying blogs or online videos that might share useful information, or following people on X/Twitter. If more formal learning is necessary, the technology coordinator may want to take part in webinars or online classes. Connecting with people through social media can be a first step in identifying sources of information and determining who might be helpful in the quest for professional learning.

Once professional connections are made and professionals of interest identified, it may be useful to determine ways to tap into these resources. Scheduling time for short online or phone meetings may be useful ways to have important conversations or ask questions. Scheduling visits to the workplace of local mentors for tours can be a useful way of understanding how other organizations operate and find success. The opportunity to see other organizations in practice and ask questions is a great way to gain ideas to carry back to the workplace.

Workshops and conferences are an ideal place to learn from other professionals in the field. Attending a conference like the annual ISTELive conference offers multiple opportunities to interact with, learn from, and socialize with others who are working in similar positions and have similar professional learning needs.

In order to ensure that the technology coordinator will be able to make good use of the PLN, make sure to devote both time and funding to the professional learning process. The budgeting and planning process needs to include both time and funding the technology leader can use to enhance their own personal learning and then share this learning with others in the organization.

Equipment Maintenance and Upgrades

While they are regularly concerned with the day-to-day technical problems encountered by users, the technology coordinator must also be concerned with the ongoing maintenance, upgrades, and eventual replacement of equipment used by the organization. A regular and rigorous maintenance plan allows equipment to remain trouble-free and operational as long as possible. This planned maintenance should include the regular update of virus protection files, cleaning and repair of peripherals, and periodic maintenance to ensure maximum performance.

Mission-critical hardware such as servers and other network equipment should receive special maintenance and support consideration. The purchase of extended warranties to cover such equipment, and service contracts to support it when problems do arise, can be a wise use of technology-support dollars. Such equipment should also be protected with uninterruptible power supplies that include battery-backup capabilities.

This will protect sensitive hardware from fluctuations in power and provide emergency power should a general service failure occur.

It is also important for the organization to have a long-term plan for upgrading equipment. As the memory and processing demands of new software and peripherals increase, it may be necessary to replace a computer's CPU or increase its memory to make use of the most recent software or operating system. It is a good idea, consequently, to establish guidelines for the planned upgrade of equipment.

Some districts may plan for equipment upgrades after a period of three years, with a maximum life expectancy of five years. Other districts may choose to phase out devices at the secondary level and then transfer them to the elementary level. Regardless, it is useful to have the procedures for the upgrade and maintenance of equipment clearly defined in the district technology plan. Well-defined procedures for equipment upgrades and replacement will help to ensure that this process occurs smoothly at regular intervals and is built into the annual technology budget.

Tech Leader Profile

Sonal Patel, Program Manager for Digital Learning and Computer Science Education

Since 2019, Sonal Patel has been the program manager for digital learning and computer science education for the San Bernardino County Superintendent of Schools. Originally trained as an elementary teacher in the United Kingdom, she was a classroom teacher and instructional coach prior to becoming a district administrator and joining the county office. She holds a master's degree in Educational Technology, and earned a California administrative credential. In the Spring semester of 2023, she completed her doctoral studies in Leadership for Educational Justice at the University of the Redlands in California and earned her Ed.D. Sonal has earned additional certifications as a Google Certified Trainer, a Microsoft Innovator, and an ISTE Community Leader. Her office includes a digital learning project specialist, a computer science project specialist, and an e-sports coordinator; all are supervised by Sonal. She reports directly to the chief technology officer. The San Bernardino County Superintendent of Schools serves a diverse mixture of urban, suburban, and rural districts serving a largely Latinx student population of approximately 400,000 in 33 different school districts. Sonal describes her biggest challenges as a lack of coherence between districts and school sites making it difficult to engage staff in high quality professional learning, a lack of technological resources creating challenges in sharing the power of technology online with staff, and the fact that digital learning and computer science are sometimes not a priority in school districts, making change a struggle. Her job satisfaction comes from regular opportunities to share promising practices for using technology with staff so they may personalize learning and provide opportunities for students. For those who aspire to a job like hers, Sonal offers this advice: "Build a personal learning network, collaborate with multiple educational partners and take a team-based approach in creating equitable outcomes for all students. Technology is beautiful. Think carefully about how technology can be used to remove barriers and create innovative solutions." You can follow her work here: @Sonal_EDU.

Equipment Recycling and Disposal

The technology coordinator must also be prepared to deal with computers and other equipment that has reached the end of its usable lifecycle. Obsolete and discarded electronic equipment is normally referred to as e-waste. E-waste often contains a variety of hazardous materials and must be disposed of in an appropriate manner. Components, especially now-obsolete tube-type monitors, contain environmental contaminants such as lead and mercury, in addition to a variety of other toxic elements. Examples of e-waste generated by a school district might be computers, monitors, DVD players, network hardware, and cell phones. Discarding such equipment through the normal waste system is not appropriate. Special planning and arrangements are often required for dealing appropriately with disposal of such equipment.

A total of twenty-eight states have passed legislation that mandates the recycling and special disposal of e-waste, and a number of other states have begun to pass laws regulating this process. Several more states have required electronics makers to help pay for local drop-off centers set up to collect and correctly dispose of e-waste. In many cases the cost of such programs is paid by the manufacturers, but laws differ depending on the state. It is important for the technology coordinator to research state law to see what procedures must be followed and what costs may be involved in the process.

In addition to implementing special procedures for dealing with e-waste, computer hard drives and other storage devices may require special handling to ensure data security. When disposing of computer hard drives, special care must be taken to completely wipe sensitive data from the storage devices. Special programs may be needed to accomplish this. Some organizations choose to remove hard drives for separate destruction before disposing of computer equipment.

The technology coordinator may also want to explore recycling programs offered by computer manufacturers. Apple Computer and Dell, for example, offer services that allow for the recycling and disposal of unwanted computer equipment. In some cases, manufacturers assist an organization in evaluating equipment for resale and may be able to help with data destruction to ensure that no confidential records or important information is stolen. Such services may be free, or charges may be incurred depending on the services required. The technology coordinator should work with computer vendors and recyclers to see what types of services are available and what the potential cost may be to the organization. Considering these costs upfront, at the beginning of a purchase cycle, may make it easier for the organization to plan for equipment obsolescence, and then have the resources in place to safely and effectively deal with disposal of equipment that is no longer needed.

Meeting IT Staffing Needs

Every technology coordinator faces the challenge of hiring and managing a staff that can provide effective technical support services. During lean budget conditions, technology support positions may be identified as places where personnel costs can be reduced. The technology coordinator must establish necessary levels of technical support services and provide an effective rationale to leadership for why these service positions are necessary and should be maintained, even when budgets are tight.

School districts spend considerable funds developing technology infrastructure, establishing networks, and installing educational technology resources. As Lesisko and Wright (2007) point out, "staff should be in place for hardware, network, and infrastructure support." To make effective and efficient use of technology resources, technology coordinators must ensure that equipment works properly and that problems are addressed in a timely manner. The development of technology resources is an investment that must be attended to and supported in an ongoing fashion. "For technology to impact student learning, appropriate resources must be in place to support and maintain networks and equipment. Technical support is also essential so that all systems work 24/7" (Barnett, 2001).

Technical support is a critical requirement for successful use of technology in schools and classrooms. It is an unfortunate fact that many districts do not allocate the necessary resources for districtwide technology support. Districts facing budget shortfalls also regularly look to technology departments as places to make cuts when money is tight. These decisions are justified with arguments that such personnel do not have a direct impact on students. However, when a district is unable to provide the necessary level of technology support personnel, service requests may take weeks to complete, and equipment problems may inhibit the use of technology in the classroom. The technology coordinator must work with district administration to guarantee that adequate support personnel are available to ensure rapid responses and timely problem resolutions. It is essential for the technology coordinator, along with other district planners, to determine ongoing funding sources for a technology plan, which in turn affords the necessary personnel to effectively support technology on a long-term basis.

Professional Development Spotlight

Certified Education Technology Leader from Consortium for School Networking

The Consortium for School Networking (CoSN) is a membership organization created to support and assist K–12 education technology leaders. The organization offers members the opportunity to assess their peers along with industry leaders, and to take part in leadership activities with others from around the U.S. working in similar situations. The goal of the organization is to provide K–12 educational technology leaders with the tools needed to support and lead change in their organization. One of the resources offered by the organization is the opportunity to become a Certified Education Technology Leader (CETL). CETL certification provides a program to technology leaders that combines technical knowledge; understanding of educational issues; leadership and vision training; and management of technology and support resources necessary to advance student learning through the integration of technology. A professional who earns the CETL credential has demonstrated mastery of the knowledge and skills necessary to create and support technology-rich learning environments. Those choosing to become CETL certified must have demonstrated experience in the educational technology field and must become familiar with the Framework of Essential Skills for the K–12 CTO. This framework includes the broad categories of leadership and vision, understanding the educational environment, and managing technology and resources. After becoming familiar with the framework, which also includes ten essential skills, participants are encouraged to join a study group to prepare for the CETL exam. Successfully passing the exam leads to certification that lasts for three years. More information about the program, exam, and requirements can be found here: cosn.org/careers-certification/cetl-certification.

Answers to Essential Questions

1. **What should the technology coordinator know about developing a comprehensive and successful technology plan?**

    The technology coordinator must work with administration, staff, and community members to develop a comprehensive plan that will address all aspects of the technology program implemented in the district.

2. **How can the technology coordinator assist administrators in creating and carrying out a sound technology budget?**

    The technology coordinator must work with administrators, curriculum committees, and school constituencies to identify technology needs. Funds must be carefully allocated to support fixed costs, equipment purchases, maintenance, upgrades, and new initiatives.

3. **How can the technology coordinator assist in evaluating the effectiveness of technology use in the school or district?**

    The technology coordinator should be familiar with resources and tools that can be used to assess technology use and integration. It is important to share evaluation results with stakeholders to guide ongoing planning efforts.

4. **What must the technology coordinator do to ensure proper licensing of software?**

    By keeping an up-to-date inventory of equipment and software and working with teachers and schools to purchase and license the necessary programs and applications, the technology coordinator can ensure that software programs are properly licensed, installed, and maintained.

5. **What must the technology coordinator do to make sure equipment is properly maintained, upgraded, and repaired as necessary?**

    The technology coordinator must work with the school or district administration to establish plans for the necessary maintenance and replacement of equipment. An established plan for regular equipment upgrades will maximize performance and minimize the chances of equipment failure. A system for reporting problems, answering questions, and providing needed assistance and repairs must be established. Creating a set of standard procedures for requesting services and repairs ensures that problems are documented in a systematic manner and resolved in a timely fashion. Implementing a standard reporting and tracking system for repair requests also makes it possible to gather data about departmental performance. This data can be used in a variety of ways for technology planning and staffing considerations.

6. **What role should the technology coordinator play in the recycling and disposal of computer equipment?**

The technology coordinator should be familiar with state laws regulating the proper disposal of e-waste. The technology coordinator should work with local, state, and national recycling and disposal programs to ensure that equipment is disposed of according to procedures that protect the environment and guarantee the appropriate destruction of confidential data.

7. **What can the technology coordinator do to assist the district in hiring the appropriate IT staff?**

The technology coordinator must work with district administration to guarantee that adequate support personnel are available to resolve problems rapidly and accurately. This work includes identifying key positions to be filled, developing clear job descriptions and expectations, and hiring candidates with the appropriate skills for positions in hardware, network, and infrastructure support.

Resources

ALTEC ProfilerPro—technology surveys available (profilerpro.com)

Apple Recycling Program: (apple.com/shop/trade-in)

Dell Recycling (bit.ly/3M5kKV0)

Institutionalization of Technology in Schools Checklist (bit.ly/3FiJmpl)

Technology Integration Observation Instrument (bit.ly/46yxCuP)

Chapter 9

THE FUTURE OF TECHNOLOGY LEADERSHIP

The work of the technology coordinator has evolved and expanded since the position was first described by David Moursund four decades ago. During this time, the variety of technology resources and the ways these resources are used for teaching and learning has grown and expanded as well. Teachers have come to rely more on digital resources, and in turn, technology coordinators have been asked to wear a variety of hats as they work to support the technology used for teaching and learning. Technology leaders who were once concerned with wiring school buildings and outfitting server closets are now asked to provide and maintain Wi-Fi networks, manage telephone systems, and plan for the cybersecurity protection necessary for district systems. The modern technology coordinator must be able to balance the different demands of being an educator, innovator, and technologist all at the same time.

In the future, the pace of change for the technology coordinator is likely to increase along with the variety and uses of technology in classrooms and schools. As districts rely more and more on technology as an important part of the learning process, the demand for technology leaders able to assist users and support the systems necessary for digital-age learning will only increase too. As one of the technology leaders interviewed in the preparation of this manuscript pointed out, technology coordinators are an important part of the organization and their importance is likely to grow in the future.

Impact of the COVID-19 Pandemic

The COVID-19 pandemic disrupted normal educational processes in nearly every way. When most school buildings were closed and students sent home in the spring of 2020, many schools had to make a very rapid shift to an educational model that many were poorly prepared to implement and support. While some districts had previously successfully implemented 1:1 device programs for students, many others did not have such a program in place or were only in the beginning phases of implementation. As teachers and students struggled with the transition to online learning, technology coordinators worked diligently to help familiarize teachers with instruction through video conferencing, attempted to solve problems with connectivity issues, and assisted with the selection of the best tools for delivering online instruction along with the training necessary to make successful use of them.

This rapid transition to online learning created a huge need for professional development. Even teachers who had at one time been reluctant to use technology were faced with learning to use new tools and resources to deliver instruction to their students. The shift to online learning had a huge impact on both the learning process and the people responsible for delivering it. This major change happened virtually overnight, without a normal transition period that would have allowed people the time and experience necessary to gain comfort with the new procedures; everyone had to work within the new system with no preparation. This shift caused a great deal of stress for students, teachers, parents, and technology leaders alike. Technology coordinators were asked to step up in order to provide the training and support necessary to make the change possible.

Many folks struggled during this shakeup, but shifting to online instruction did allow an important change to take place. The online learning model required most organizations to adopt and implement a device for every student. While some organizations had already taken this step, others were only thinking about it and determining how to move forward. The overnight transition to 1:1 student device programs highlighted the need to provide both the support and training necessary to ensure the new resources would successfully impact the learning process. In addition, these new resources needed to be reliable. Problems with the devices could lead to frustration in students and parents and a lack of engagement at home. The shift required having the necessary support staff in place along with significant cooperation from vendors. Everyone involved in the educational process was responsible for making the new paradigm work for the benefit of the students.

Technology leaders worked diligently throughout the pandemic to provide the training and support needed by classroom teachers responsible for delivering online, and later hybrid, instruction to students. In the background, tech coordinators worked to provide the devices and the network capacity required, and to resolve issues with providing internet access at home for both teachers and students. They also were responsible for carrying out ongoing training and instructional support for the teachers, who had to quickly implement an educational model that some were not yet comfortable with. In the past, some staff had opted not to make regular use of technology resources and had not developed a level of comfort in successfully using them. With the new reality of teaching in the age of COVID, there was no longer any way to avoid using technology. Many teachers made a great deal of progress during this time and learned to master new tools in their classroom instruction. Over time, teachers were able to focus more on how to structure a virtual classroom, rather than how to simply use the equipment and resources that were unfamiliar to them. In the beginning, much of the focus had been on the basics, but as time went on, teachers quickly began to think about how to make this new learning process better and get students more involved. The teachers began to seek out and develop instructional frameworks and identify new ways of thinking about how to do online or hybrid learning more effectively. The one constant for educators during this time was change.

Recent interviews with technology leaders indicate that a different challenge presented itself as schools began to transition back to in-person learning as the pandemic went on. Recently, many technology leaders have found it challenging to maintain the same level of effective use of technology as students returned onsite. While significant progress had been made in using technology resources, as pandemic policies relaxed a bit, some teachers were ready to let things return to "normal" and allow their teaching model to shift away from technology and back to how they had taught before the pandemic. On the other hand, for organizations that had made a significant investment in technology and resources, there was often an expectation that the use of this technology would continue.

Going forward, organizations should be clear about their expectations around technology use while also providing professional development, encouragement, and support. For some organizations, it may be a challenge to continue to support and manage the technology resources as they age and require replacement. Many schools and districts were able to purchase technology resources through an influx of federal pandemic relief funding. Finding the funding necessary to support and maintain this equipment in the long term may be a significant challenge. These challenges will likely fall to the technology coordinator. These important leaders are poised to have a significant impact on how the technology investments of schools will be used in the next few years.

The Impact of Artificial Intelligence

While it is often easy to think of artificial intelligence (AI) as something currently emerging from science fiction and making its way into the classroom, it is already part of a variety of technology currently used in classrooms including intelligent search engines, automatic lecture transcription tools, autocomplete text options in applications, and learning management systems (Blair Black, 2023). Nancy Blair Black, an ISTE-certified educator, describes how currently "students are growing up in a world where AI is embedded in the technologies they encounter at home, at school, and out in the world" (2023).

AI is an arm of computer science whose purpose is to create machines that mirror human intelligence, allowing machines to perform tasks that would seem to require human thought. This type of computing can generally be divided into three areas: generative tools that create new content (ChatGPT), predictive tools that analyze data and use it to forecast future events (credit scoring systems), and reactive tools able to respond to situations without learning from past events (robot vacuum cleaners). Generative AI is getting the most attention in 2023, but the other two tool segments probably have more everyday applications (Bringing AI to School: Tips for School Leaders, 2023). While AI is helpful and can provide a variety of constructive uses, it is important to remember that it is not human intelligence, capable of emotion or ethical judgement.

As a result of the COVID-19 pandemic, 1:1 device programs have been implemented in 90% of middle and high schools across the country and nearly 85% of elementary schools (Bushweller, 2022). Due to this rapid influx of technology across all grades, the use of generative AI tools by students is a growing concern for K–12 schools. In a recent interview with *Education Week*, ISTE CEO Richard Culatta referenced the promise and challenge of using devices and AI tools in his statement "there's no longer an excuse to be scanning and uploading worksheets. We have a set of tools that we got largely because of the pandemic. The clock is ticking. The world is looking at us to say, "alright, you got all the technology you've been asking for all these years. Show us the magic." (Klein, 2023). This moment in education offers potential but will require creativity along with time and sustained effort from the teachers and technology leaders in schools to turn these new tools into useful educational resources.

While schools are scrambling to effectively implement the technology in creative and engaging ways and seeking to develop effective policies and establish best practices, the federal government is working to assist schools by providing meaningful guidance. In its report "Artificial Intelligence and the Future of Teaching and Learning," the US Department of Education (DOE) digs deep into AI's potential for improving the classroom experience (Stone, 2023). In this report, the DOE "addresses the clear need for sharing knowledge and developing policies for Artificial Intelligence" and "… seeks to engage teachers, educational leaders, policy makers, researchers, and educational technology innovators and providers as they work together on pressing policy issues that arise as AI is used in education" (Artificial Intelligence and Future of Teaching and Learning: Insights and Recommendations, 2023).

A major AI focus for schools is currently directed at the issue of cheating. Many schools have become concerned about student use of generative tools to produce written assignments and have struggled with how to discourage students from using these tools to assist with homework assignments. As the 2023–24 academic year gets rolling, a growing number of school leaders are concentrating on "setting rules around acceptable use and preaching the benefits of the emergent technology" (Jones et al., 2023). Many educational professionals recognize that a variety of the jobs of the future may well incorporate AI and will demand skills that haven't even been dreamed up yet. It would be a mistake for teachers and administrators to waste their time trying to keep students from making effective use of the technology resources already available.

Perhaps it would be better for teachers and educational leaders to concern themselves with ethical issues. AI tools raise a variety of new questions and a whole host of related concerns. Lane (2023) describes these issues like this: "it's important to understand that this is a socio-technical challenge that impacts every single person on the planet. AI is absolutely pervasive. It's in our daily lives whether we realize it or not. It transforms our lives in ways that are often times outside our control, such as when a hiring decision is made for or against you due to an AI workforce progression platform being used by the employer." The students currently attending K–12 schools will be impacted in a variety of ways by these AI implementations and will need a set of ethical principles to guide decisions about use of AI. Teachers and technology leaders would do well to concern themselves with some of these ethical issues rather than attempting to simply keep students from completing assignments using tools like ChatGPT. Technology leaders of the future will need to keep AI on their radar and be thinking how best to manage and make positive and effective use of it in the learning process.

An Educator or a Technician

How should educational organizations go about seeking leadership for their technology resources and operations? District technology systems have grown more complex as technology use has expanded. This complexity creates an increased need for technical expertise. Smaller organizations have sometimes chosen to outsource management of some of their systems to vendors to provide the support needed for maintaining these systems. Other organizations have chosen to hire a leader with a technical rather than educational background to ensure there is an appropriate level of technical expertise on staff. Larger organizations tend to have leadership and expertise in both areas. One staff component may be made up of technicians who are responsible for handling repairs and managing network operations while a separate staff component offers expertise in professional development and instructional methods. Hiring technical expertise is likely the easier part of the equation; find a leader with the necessary understanding of effective teaching and learning with technology is much trickier. Most districts will want to hire an instructional technology leader who has a clear understanding of the challenges that teachers face daily when using technology for teaching and learning— put simply, a leader with a background in education. Some districts have found that technology leaders who were not educators struggled at times to understand some of the challenges inherent in the classroom. The successful technology leader must provide three distinct functions:

1. Serve as head of the department that provides technical functionality to the organization,

2. Operate with a collaborative mindset and a willingness to provide technical as well as instruction leadership, and

3. Deal with the policy and planning responsibilities for the organization.

To succeed and meet the needs of the organization, there should be a balance between the two different domains: technical and instructional. The successful technology leader may not be required to carry out the technical tasks but must be able to appreciate the challenges facing the technical side of the operation. The successful leader will also need to balance the requirements of education policy and needs along with consideration of the technical issues. If the technology operation is made up of both technical and educational staff, they will need to ensure that both sides of the operation can work together effectively and make good decisions collaboratively. To do this will require both good communication and trust. There must be familiarity and trust from both the technical and the instructional staff. Educators must be capable of developing working relationships with technical staff, and a technician needs to be sure they have solid working relationships with the educators.

The Invisibility of an Effective Technology Leader

One of the things that makes sports fun is watching people who make difficult feats look easy. That idea can be useful to the technology leader as well. An effective technology leader should aspire to create a system where things fit together well and just work without a great deal of intervention. In many ways, such a leader should aspire to be invisible, working towards making the use of technology for teaching and learning a natural part of the everyday experience in the same way that we in the U.S. do not have to think about standard utilities like water and electricity. Users should be able to expect, without thought or worry, that the tools they need will be available, the professional development will be provided, and the support supplied as needed. The ancient Chinese philosopher Lao Tzu was one of the first to identify the idea of the invisible leader. His wisdom: "A leader is best when people barely know he exists." Being invisible does not imply that a job is unimportant, rather it means that the leader has been successful in doing the job and has provided everything necessary for the activity or program to be successful. We know the technology leader is getting the job done when we don't have to think about it.

Decades of Technology Leadership and Counting

Technology coordinators have been an important part of school technology leadership since the early 1990s. Thanks to their efforts, computer labs were established, networks installed, professional development programs created, and 1:1 device programs rolled out to students. Over the past four years, during the COVID pandemic, these mission-critical leaders struggled in many ways to provide administrators, teachers, staff, parents, and students with the resources, training, and support necessary to operate in a rapidly shifting educational landscape. From helping teachers with the development of an online classroom, to posting helpful how-to videos for students, to helping teachers with new tools or techniques by co-teaching lessons, to holding online office hours, technology coordinators stepped up to provide leadership and support for schools. These technology leaders demonstrated their importance by providing the support, training, advocacy, planning, and guidance necessary to integrate technology in the teaching and learning process.

While the type of work they do has changed drastically since the first computers were installed in libraries and classrooms, and they are now asked to wear many different hats, these technology leaders continued to play an important part in the successful integration of technology. Without their ongoing guidance, the changes to the teaching and learning process would have been less successful and the significant invest-ment schools have made in technology resources might not have been so impactful. Technology coordinators (who now have many different titles) have evolved from quasi-teacher positions spending part of their time working on technology to cabinet-level leadership positions that are a mission-critical part of any successful educational organization.

Professional organizations like ISTE and CoSN have developed resources and services to connect and support professionals working in district technology leadership roles. The CoSN Certified Educational Technology Leader program was designed to provide training and establish certification for these important leadership skills. At the federal level, the Office of Educational Technology in the Department of Education is now responsible for developing and updating the National Educational Technology Plan and providing aid and assistance to technology leaders at both the state and local levels. At the state level, organizations like the Learning Technology Center (a program of the Illinois State Board of Education) provide district-level support to K–12 teachers. State-level professional organizations like the Texas Computer Education Association and California's Computer Using Educators are useful in providing activities to connect people who want to share resources and providing professional development opportu-nities to teachers and district leaders.

Technology coordinators and others in educational technology leadership positions have come a long way since they first appeared in schools. The organizations have recognized the important role technology plays in their operations and have responded by adding technology leadership positions to their organizational charts. Technology coordinators and directors are now part of district level leadership teams and have planning and decision-making responsibilities for significant parts of the school budget. Their importance in an organization has been recognized and proven, and this recognition had led to significant influence. The leadership they provide for an organization has grown over the past three decades, and with the expansion of technology within the organization, their influence is likely to grow even more.

The Technology Coordinator in 2030 and Beyond

As the importance of technology leadership positions has grown, state departments of education and universities have recognized the importance of these positions. Some states, Georgia and Louisiana, for example, have established licensure requirements for those wishing to serve in district-level educational technology leadership positions. Universities have worked with state-level departments to create licensure and endorsement programs to meet professional standards. As time goes on, these types of licensure requirements will only become more common.

Security will continue to be an ongoing concern for the technology coordinator. Many districts are exploring ways to ensure the safety and data security of students and employees as they work to protect them from phishing and ransomware attacks which could cause problems that would be catastrophic for a school district. Many organizations are implementing single sign-on solutions for their networks and requiring two-factor authentication to allow another layer of protection beyond username and password as is required for insurance coverage.

For many organizations, securing the funding necessary to maintain current technology and continue to innovate will be an ongoing challenge. Pandemic aid has allowed many organizations to make significant investments in technology and infrastructure. How to continue those investments and maintain the progress made over the past two years will be a significant challenge as equipment ages. For many districts, devices were purchased with federal funds and the question remains exactly how they will be replaced as they wear our or need to be upgraded? Organizations will have to juggle technology decisions that need to be aligned with curricular decisions and balanced with the ongoing demand for professional learning opportunities for both faculty and administration.

The importance of the technology coordinator position has grown and expanded considerably since first appearing in schools. Leaders serving in this position have been repeatedly asked to take on new areas of responsibility and provide support for additional services. Schools need effective leaders with the ability to manage a resource that impacts all parts of the operation. These leaders must have a clear understanding of this impact and have a sense of the importance of technology to the success of the whole operation. The technology leader must balance a variety of variables because there are so many different operations, processes and services that rely on technology to make the organization function. The technology coordinator must be the one who can see the big picture, balance all of the different demands, and help the leadership team to make the best decisions to support and enhance the technology program for the district. This leader must be on the cutting edge and have a vision for what is coming, be familiar with the innovations and help guide the superintendent and district leadership on where they need to be in the next three to five years. There is always going to be a need for someone to think about and advocate for the ideas and issues related to technology and be able to juggle all these issues along with having a high-altitude perspective about where the organization is headed and how they are going to get there. This leader will likely be the one to help maintain the momentum gained during the pandemic and encourage the leadership team and the instructional staff to continue their efforts to use technology to improve the instructional process and maximize student learning.

The issues facing technology coordinators continue to expand and evolve along with the demands of the position. These important leaders will be expected to juggle a variety of different challenges daily and will continue to be asked to wear a variety of different hats and manage different roles. The position of technology coordinator is a challenging one, facing many different demands for time and resources and having a great deal of promise for impacting and improving the teaching and learning process. It is a position offering an opportunity to lead and direct change, influence the classroom experiences for teachers and students, assist in supporting the educational mission of a school district, and to learn something new every day. The adventure awaits those willing to step into this challenging and promising leadership position.

REFERENCES

Adams Becker, S., Freeman, A., Giesinger Hall, C., Cummins, M., & Yuhnke, B. (2016). *NMC/CoSN Horizon report: 2016 K–12 Edition.* Austin, TX: New Media Consortium.

Adobe. (2020). *Create and verify PDF accessibility (Acrobat Pro).* [Adobe Accessibility Products]. bit.ly/3rSFf0i.

Americans with Disabilities Act of 1990, Pub. L. No. 101-336, §2, 104 Stat. 328 (1990).

Anderson, L. W., Krathwohl, D. R., & Bloom, B. S. (Eds.). (2001). A Taxonomy for Learning, Teaching, and Assessing: A Revision of Bloom's Taxonomy of Educational Objectives. New York: Addison Wesley Longman.

Anderson, N. (2020). School administrators' technology leadership. In G. D. Caruth (Ed.), Encyclopedia of Educational Innovation (pp. 674–679). New York: Springer.

Anderson, R., & Dexter, S. (2000). *School technology leadership: Incidence and impact.* (National Survey Report No. 6). Irvine, CA: Center for Research on Information Technology and Organizations. (ERIC No. ED449786)

Artificial Intelligence and Future of Teaching and Learning: Insights and Recommendations. (2023). In *tech.ed.gov.* U.S. Department of Education, Office of Educational Technology. Retrieved from tech.ed.gov/ ai-future-of-teaching-and-learning.

Aurora Institute. (2018). Quality online learning and teaching. Retrieved from aurora-institute.org/resource/quality-online-learning-and-teaching.

Barnett, H. (2001). *Successful K–12 technology planning: Ten essential elements.* (ERIC Digest). Syracuse, NY: ERIC Clearinghouse on Information and Technology. (ERIC No. ED457858)

Bergmann, J., & Sams, A. (2012). Flip your classroom: Reach every student in every class every day. International Society for Technology in Education.

Bird, K. (2006). How do you spell parental involvement? SIS: Student information systems are engaging parents, benefiting kids, and—finally—winning over teachers, too. *THE Journal (Technological Horizons in Education), 33*(7), 38.

Blair Black, N. (2023). *AI in the Classroom: Strategies and Activities to Enrich Student Learning* [Jump Start Guide]. ISTE. iste.org/aijsg.

Bloom, B., Englehart, M., Furst, E., Hill, W., & Krathwohl, D. (1956). *Taxonomy of educational objectives: The classification of educational goals. Handbook I: Cognitive domain*. New York, NY: Longmans, Green.

Borja, R. (2006). Technology upgrades prompt schools to go wireless. *Education Week, 26*(9), 10–11.

Borup, J., West, R. E., & Graham, C. R. (2012). Improving online social presence through asynchronous video. *Internet and Higher Education, 15*(3), 195–203. doi.org/10.1016/j.iheduc.2011.11.001.

Boudett, K. P., City, E. A., & Murnane, R. J. (Eds.). (2013). *Data wise: A step-by-step guide to using assessment results to improve teaching and learning*. Revised and expanded edition. Cambridge, MA: Harvard Education Press.

Bower, M. (2016). Deriving a typology of web 2.0 learning technologies. *British Journal of Educational Technology, 47*(4), 763-777. doi.org/10.1111/bjet.12344.

Brame, C. J. (2016). Effective educational videos: Principles and guidelines for maximizing student learning from video content. *CBE-Life Sciences Education, 15*(4), es6. doi.org/10.1187/cbe.16-03-0125.

Bringing AI to School: Tips for School Leaders. (2023, July). ISTE. Retrieved from bit.ly/3RYgwCb.

Burgstahler, S. (2015). Universal design in education. In The SAGE Encyclopedia of Educational Technology (pp. 815-817). Thousand Oaks, CA: Sage Publications, Inc.

Bushweller, K. (2022, May 17). What the Massive Shift to 1-to-1 Computing Means for Schools, in Charts. *Education Week*. Retrieved from https://bit.ly/3ZYi6WM.

Bushweller, K. (2020, June 2). How covid-19 is shaping tech use. What that means when schools reopen. *Education Week*. Retrieved from bit.ly/3Gokld3.

CAST. (2018). Universal design for learning guidelines version 2.2. Retrieved from udlguidelines.cast.org.

Cavanaugh, C., Barbour, M. K., & Clark, T. (2009). Research and practice in K–12 online learning: A review of open access literature. *International Review of Research in Open and Distance Learning, 10*(1), 1-22. doi.org/10.19173/irrodl.v10i1.607.

Cavanaugh, C., Barbour, M., & Clark, T. (2020). Research and Practice in K–12 Online Learning: A Review of Open Access Literature. *International Review of Research in Open and Distributed Learning, 21*(1), 1–32. doi.org/10.19173/irrodl.v21i1.4665.

Cavanaugh, C., Hodge, E., & Barbour, M. (2019). Navigating the new pedagogy: Six principles for transforming practice. *Journal of Online Learning Research, 5*(2), 127–145.

Chanenson, J., Chee, J., Rajan, N., Huang, D. Y., Chetty, M., Sloane, B., & Morrill, A. (2023). Uncovering Privacy and Security Challenges In K–12 Schools. Proceedings of the 2023 CHI Conference on Human Factors in Computing Systems, No. 592, 1–28. doi.org/10.1145/3544548.3580777.

ClydeBank Technology. (2015). *ITIL for beginners: The complete beginner's guide to ITIL.* Albany, NY: ClydeBank Media.

Collum, P. T. (2015). *An exploratory study of Alabama district technology coordinators: their duties and the various pathways to acquiring the position.* Doctoral dissertation, The University of Alabama. Retrieved from tinyurl.com/a8r72m8n.

Conley, K. (Ed.) (2007). Student information systems buyer's guide. *Learning & Leading with Technology, 34*(4), 40–41.

Consortium for School Networking (CoSN). (2004). Essential skills of the K–12 CTO. *Learning & Leading with Technology, 32*(4), 40–45.

Consortium for School Networking. (2021). The CoSN SEND initiative: Smart education networks by design. home.edweb.net/webinar/supers20200713/.

Culatta, R., (2019, June 24). *Make Digital Citizenship about the Do's, not the Dont's.* [Video]. YouTube. youtu.be/tZeNr1q5QTU.

Cutts, J. (2019). *The Role of The Technology Coordinator in Supporting the Successful Implementation of a 1:1 Chromebook Initiative.* Doctoral dissertation, University of New England. Retrieved from dune.une.edu/theses/240.

Darling-Hammond, L., Flook, L., Cook-Harvey, C., Barron, B., & Osher, D. (2020). Implications for educational practice of the science of learning and development. *Applied Developmental Science, 24*(2), 97–140.

Darling-Hammond, L., Hyler, M. E., & Gardner, M. (2017). Effective teacher professional development. Learning Policy Institute. Retrieved from bit.ly/3S216wJ.

Davis, M. (2007). Revised federal archiving rules raise legal, logistical challenges. *Education Week Digital Directions, 1*(1), 12–15.

Davis, M. (2009). Districts dial into the internet to modernize phone systems. *Education Week Digital Directions, 2*(3), 18–21.

Deci, E. L., & Ryan, R. M. (1985). *Intrinsic motivation and self-determination in human behavior.* New York: Plenum Press.

Desimone, L. M. (2009). Improving impact studies of teachers' professional development: Toward better conceptualizations and measures. *Educational researcher, 38*(3), 181–199.

Dexter, S. (2018). The Role of Leadership for Information Technology in Education: Systems of Practices. In J. Voogt & G. Knezek (Eds.), *The second international handbook on information technology in primary and secondary education*, 560–574. New York: Springer-Verlag.

DuFour, R., DuFour, R., Eaker, R., & Many, T. (2010). *Learning by doing: A handbook for professional learning communities at work—Action guide* (2nd ed.). Bloomington, IN: Solution Tree Press.

Dweck, C. S. (2006). *Mindset: The new psychology of success*. New York: Random House.

Education World. (2009). *Getting started on the Internet: Developing an Acceptable Use Policy (AUP)*. Retrieved from www.educationworld.com/a_curr/curr093.shtml.

Federal Communications Commission. (2016). *Children's Internet Protection Act*. Retrieved from www.fcc.gov/consumers/guides/childrens-internet-protection-act.

Ferdig, R. E., Baumgartner, E., Hartshorne, R., Kaplan-Rakowski, R., & Mouza, C. (2020). Teaching, Technology, and Teacher Education during the COVID-19 Pandemic: Stories from the Field. Association for the Advancement of Computing in Education (AACE). www.learntechlib.org/primary/p/216903.

Fingal, D. (2022, October 17). *Infographic: I'm a Digital Citizen*. International Society for Technology in Education. Retrieved from www.iste.org/explore/digital-citizenship/infographic-im-digital-citizen.

Fingal, J. (2021, October 12). *The 5 competencies of digital citizenship*. International Society for Technology in Education. Retrieved from www.iste.org/explore/5-competencies-digital-citizenship.

Fonseca, B. (2007). E-discovery rules add summer IT work for schools. *Computerworld*. Retrieved from bit.ly/3FgHyxg.

Fox, C., Waters, J., Fletcher, G., & Levin, D. (2012). *The broadband imperative: Recommendations to address K–12 education infrastructure needs*. State Educational Technology Directors Association. Retrieved from www.setda.org/priorities/equity-of-access/the-broadband-imperative.

Fullan, M. (2007). The new meaning of educational change. New York: Teachers College Press.

Garet, M. S., Porter, A. C., Desimone, L., Birman, B. F., & Yoon, K. S. (2001). What makes professional development effective? Results from a national sample of teachers. *American Educational Research Journal, 38*(4), 915–945. doi:10.3102/00028312038004915.

Guskey, T. R. (2002). Professional development and teacher change. *Teachers and Teaching, 8*(3), 381–391. doi:10.1080/135406002100000512.

Gagné, R. M., Briggs, L. J., & Wager, W. W. (1992). *Principles of instructional design* (4th ed.). Fort Worth, TX: Harcourt Brace Jovanovich.

Garrison, D. R., Anderson, T., & Archer, W. (2000). Critical inquiry in a text-based environment: Computer conferencing in higher education. *The Internet and Higher Education, 2*(2–3), 87-105. doi.org/10.1016/S1096-7516(00)00016-6.

Garrison, D. R., & Cleveland-Innes, M. (2005). Facilitating cognitive presence in online learning: Interaction is not enough. *American Journal of Distance Education, 19*(3), 133–148. doi.org/10.1207/s15389286ajde1903_2.

Garrison, D. R., & Vaughan, N. D. (2008). Blended learning in higher education: Framework, principles, and guidelines. Hoboken, NJ: John Wiley & Sons.

Graham, C. R., Woodfield, W., & Harrison, J. B. (2013). A framework for institutional adoption and implementation of blended learning in higher education. Internet and Higher Education, 18, 4–14. doi.org/10.1016/j.iheduc.2012.09.003.

Granić, A., & Marangunić, N. (2019). Technology acceptance model in educational context: A systematic literature review. British Journal of Educational Technology, 50(5), 2572–2593. doi.org/10.1111/bjet.12864.

Gray, L., Thomas, N., & Lewis, L. (2010). Educational technology in U.S. public schools: Fall 2008 (NCES 2010–034). U.S. Department of Education, National Center for Education Statistics. Retrieved from nces.ed.gov/pubsearch/pubsinfo. asp?pubid=2010034.

Greer, D., Rice, M., & Dykman, B. (2014). Responding to the needs of at-risk students in online education: A relational approach to academic support. *Journal of Educators Online, 11*(1), n1. www.thejeo.com/archive/2014_11_1/greer_rice_dykman.

Guskey, T. R. (2014). Planning professional learning. *Educational Leadership, 71*(8), 10–16.

Gustafson, K. L., & Branch, R. M. (2002). Survey of instructional development models. ERIC Clearinghouse on Information & Technology.

Hall, G. E., & Hord, S. M. (2015). *Implementing change: Patterns, principles, and potholes* (4th ed.). Boston, MA: Pearson.

Harris, J., Grandgenett, N., & Hofer, M. (2010). *Testing a TPACK-based technology integration assessment instrument.* In C. D. Maddux, D. Gibson, & B. Dodge (Eds.), Research highlights in technology and teacher education 2010 (pp. 323–331). Chesapeake, VA: Society for Information Technology and Teacher Education (SITE).

Herold, B., & Cavanaugh, S. (2015) E-Rate undergoing major policy, budget upgrades. *Education Week, 34*(15), 10–14.

Hew, K. F., & Cheung, W. S. (2013). Use of Web 2.0 technologies in K–12 and higher education: The search for evidence-based practice. Educational Research Review, 9, 47–64. doi.org/10.1016/j.edurev.2012.08.001.

Hixon, E., Barbour, M. K., & Decker, A. (2020). The impact of online teaching professional development on the pedagogical practices of K–12 teachers: A narrative synthesis. *Journal of Online Learning Research, 6*(4), 333–364.

Hirsh, S. (2009). A new definition. *Journal of Staff Development, 30*(4), 10–16.

Hodges, C., Moore, S., Lockee, B., Trust, T., & Bond, A. (2020). The difference between emergency remote teaching and online learning. *Educause Review, 27.*

Hoffman, R. (2002). Strategic planning: Lessons learned from a "big-business" district. *Technology and Learning, 22*(10), 26–38.

Hord, S. M. (2009). Professional learning communities. *Journal of Staff Development, 30*(1), 40–43.

Horn, M. B., & Staker, H. (2015). *Blended: Using disruptive innovation to improve schools.* Hoboken, NJ: John Wiley & Sons.

Hornby, G., & Lafaele, R. (2011). Barriers to parental involvement in education: An explanatory model. *Educational Review, 63*(1), 37–52.

Huang, Y., & Liang, T. (2021). Effectiveness of Learning Management Systems in Face-to-Face Classroom Settings: A Systematic Review. *Journal of Educational Technology Development and Exchange, 14*(1), 1–19.

Inan, F. A., & Lowther, D. L. (2010). Factors affecting technology integration in K–12 classrooms: A path model. *Educational Technology Research and Development, 58*(2), 137–154. doi.org/10.1007/s11423-009-9132-y.

Individuals with Disabilities Education Act. (2019). Section 1400. Retrieved from sites. ed.gov/idea/statute-chapter-33/subchapter-i/1400.

International Society for Technology in Education. (2016). ISTE standards for students. Retrieved from www.iste.org/standards/for-students.

International Society for Technology in Education. (2017). *ISTE standards for educators.* Retrieved from www.iste.org/standards/standards/standards-for-teachers.

Johnson, N. (2019). An administrator's guide to online education. IGI Global. doi.org/10.4018/978-1-59140-555-9.

Jones, B., Toure, M., & Perez, J., Jr. (2023, August 23). Schools shrug off cheating concerns and embrace AI. *Politico*. Retrieved from www.politico.com/news/2023/08/23/chatgpt-ai-chatbots-in-classrooms-00111662.

Katzan, H., Jr. (2010). The education value of cloud computing. *Contemporary Issues in Education Research, 3*(7), 37.

Kirkpatrick, D. L., & Kirkpatrick, J. D. (2006). *Evaluating training programs: The four levels* (3rd ed.). Oakland, CA: Berrett-Koehler Publishers.

Klein, A. (2023, June 22). Schools Are 'Focusing on the Wrong Things' When It Comes to AI, Tech Leader Argues. *Education Week*. Retrieved August 16, 2023, from bit.ly/45yaYl9.

Knight, J. (2009). Coaching: The key to translating research into practice lies in continuous, job-embedded learning with ongoing support. *Journal of Staff Development, 30*(1), 18–20.

Kumar, P., Chetty, M., Clegg, T., & Vitak, J. (2019). Privacy and Security Considerations For Digital Technology Use in Elementary Schools. In Proceedings of the 37th Annual ACM Conference on Human Factors in Computing Systems.

Lane, D. (2023, August 21). *The Ethics of AI*. LinkedIn. Retrieved from bit.ly/3tIWaCM

Lesisko, L. (2005). *The K–12 technology coordinator*. Sarasota, FL: Paper presented at the annual meeting of the Eastern Educational Research Association, March 2–5, 2005. (ERIC No. ED490035)

Lesisko, L., & Wright, R. (2007). *School based leadership for instructional technology*. Chicago, IL: Paper presented at the Annual American Educational Research Association meeting, April 9–13, 2007. (ERIC No. ED497706)

Lewis, C., Perry, R., & Hurd, J. (2009). Improving mathematics instruction through lesson study: A theoretical model and North American case. *Journal of Mathematics Teacher Education, 12*(4), 285–304.

Li, L., & Pitts, J. P. (2020). Asynchronous online learning in K-12 education: A review of empirical literature. *Journal of Educational Technology Development and Exchange, 13*(1), 1–22. doi.org/10.18785/jetde.1301.01.

Manzo, K. (2010). Digital innovation outpaces E-Rate policies. *Education Week, 29*(20), 1, 16.

McGraw, P. (2019). *Are technology coordinators teaching teachers to teach with tech? A sequential explanatory mixed-methods study*. Doctoral dissertation, Rowan University. Retrieved from rdw.rowan.edu/etd/2685.

McLeod, S. (2003). *National district technology coordinators study. Technical report 1: Personal and professional characteristics.* Naperville, IL: North Central Regional Educational Laboratory, United States Department of Education.

Means, B., Padilla, C., & Gallagher, L. (2010). Use of education data at the local level. U.S. Department of Education.

Means, B., Toyama, Y., Murphy, R., & Baki, M. (2013). The effectiveness of online and blended learning: A meta-analysis of the empirical literature. *Teachers College Record, 115*(3), 1–47. doi.org/10.1017/CBO9781107415324.004.

Mertler, C. A. (2017). Action research: Improving schools and empowering educators (5th ed.). Thousand Oaks, CA: Sage Publications.

Microsoft. (2021). Make your Word documents accessible to people with disabilities. Retrieved from bit.ly/3tyg57J.

Mishra, P., & Koehler, M. J. (2006). Technological Pedagogical Content Knowledge: A Framework for Teacher Knowledge. *Teachers College Record, 108*(6), 1017–1054.

Moursund, D. (1985). The Computer Coordinator. Eugene, OR: International Council for Computers in Education. (ERIC No. ED256297)

Murray, M. (2015). Parent and family involvement in education, from the National Household Education Surveys Program of 2012. National Center for Education Statistics, U.S. Department of Education.

Nagel, D. (2008). *Education IT spending, fueled by telecom, to top $56 billion by 2012.* Retrieved from bit.ly/3LZSF1l.

Ngoma, S. (2009). *An exploration of the effectiveness of SIS in managing student performance.* (ERIC No. ED507625)

OpenDyslexic. (n.d.). *OpenDyslexic Free Font.* https://opendyslexic.org/

Pane, J. F., Steiner, E. D., Baird, M. D., & Hamilton, L. S. (2015). Continued progress: Promising evidence on personalized learning. RAND Corporation. www.rand.org/pubs/research_reports/RR1365.html.

Palloff, R. M., & Pratt, K. (2007). Building online learning communities: Effective strategies for the virtual classroom. Hoboken, NJ: John Wiley & Sons.

Picciano, A. G. (2017). The evolution of the LMS: From management to learning. *Journal of Educational Technology Development and Exchange, 10*(1), 1–14.

Reilly, P. (2023, March 17). Ohio district with 'work out' staff, students adopts 4-day school week. *New York Post.* nypost.com/2023/03/17/ohio-school-district-adopts-4-day-school-week.

Rogers-Whitehead, C., & Monterosa, V. (2023) *Deepening digital citizenship: A guide to systemwide policy and practice*. Portland, OR: International Society for Technology in Education.

Rose, D. H. (2014). Universal Design for Learning: Theory and practice. Lynnfield, MA: CAST Professional Publishing.

Rose, D. H., Harbour, W. S., Johnston, C. S., Daley, S. G., & Abarbanell, L. (2018). Universal design for learning in postsecondary education: Reflections on principles and their application. In S. E. Burgstahler (Ed.), *Universal design in higher education: From principles to practice* (pp. 17–47). Harvard Education Press.

Rovai, A. P. (2002). Building sense of community at a distance. *International Review of Research in Open and Distance Learning, 3*(1). doi.org/10.19173/irrodl.v3i1.79.

Section 504 of the Rehabilitation Act of 1973, Pub. L. No. 93-112, § 504, 87 Stat. 394 (1973).

Siko, J. P., & Hess, G. A. (2014). Implementing a one-to-one technology initiative in a rural K-12 school district. *Rural Educator, 36*(1), 20–29.

Song, L., & Singleton, E. S. (2018). Using Learning Management Systems to Facilitate Effective Instruction: A Case Study. *Journal of Educational Technology Development and Exchange, 11*(1), 1–14.

Solomon, G. (2001). Writing and winning grants. *Technology and Learning, 21*(11), 44–50.

Staihr, B., & Sheaff, K. (2001). *The success of the "E-Rate" in rural America*. Kansas City, MO: Federal Reserve Bank Center for the Study of Rural America. (ERIC No. ED455082)

Staker, H. (2011). *The rise of K–12 blended learning: Profiles of emerging models*. San Mateo, CA: Innosight Institute. (ERIC No. ED535181)

State Educational Technology Directors Association (SETDA). (2019). The broadband imperative III: Driving connectivity, access and student success. Retrieved from setda.org/setda_broadband-imperative-iii_110519.

Stone, A. (2023, July 21). AI in Education: New Guidance from the Department of Education. *EdTech Focus on K-12*. Retrieved from bit.ly/3FgITEi.

Strudler, N., & Hearrington, D. (2009). Quality support for ICT in schools. In J. Voogt and G. Knezek (eds.), *International handbook of information technology in primary and secondary education* (pp. 579–596). New York, NY: Springer.

Sugar, W., & Holloman, H. (2009). Technology leaders wanted: Acknowledging the leadership role of a technology coordinator. *TechTrends, 53*(6), 66–75.

Taie, S., & Lewis, L. (2022). *Characteristics of 2020–21 Public and Private K–12 Schools in the United States: Results from the National Teacher and Principal Survey First Look* (NCES 2022-111). U.S. Department of Education. Washington, DC: National Center for Education Statistics. Retrieved from nces.ed.gov/pubsearch/pubsinfo. asp?pubid=2022111.

The Associated Press. (2023, August 8). White House holds first-ever summit on the ransomware crisis plaguing the nation's public schools. www.pbs.com. Retrieved from bit.ly/48NxSaW.

Trust, T. (2020). Educators' perspectives on the impact of video chat technology on the development of productive online collaborations. *British Journal of Educational Technology, 51*(3), 802–819. doi.org/10.1111/bjet.12895.

Trust, T., Krutka, D. G., & Carpenter, J. P. (2016). "Together we are better": Professional learning networks for teachers. *Computers & Education, 102*, 15–34. doi.org/10.1016/j.compedu.2016.06.007.

Tucker, C. R. (2013). *Blended learning in grades 4–12: Leveraging the power of technology to create student-centered classrooms.* Thousand Oaks, CA: Corwin Press.

Tucker, C. (2020). *Balance with blended learning: Partner with your students to reimagine learning and reclaim your life.* Thousand Oaks, CA: Corwin Press.

Tucker, C. (2021). The top 15 ed tech products for virtual and hybrid learning. eSchool News. Retrieved from bit.ly/3Q1IKtm.

U.S. Department of Education. (2015a). *Family Educational Rights and Privacy Act (FERPA).* Retrieved from www2.ed.gov/policy/gen/guid/fpco/ferpa/index.html.

U.S. Department of Education. (2016). *Future ready learning—National Educational Technology Plan 2016.* Retrieved from tech.ed.gov/netp/.

U.S. Department of Education. (2015b). *Protection of Pupil Rights Amendment (PPRA).* Retrieved from studentprivacy.ed.gov/faq/ what-protection-pupil-rights-amendment-ppra/

U.S. Department of Justice. (2015). Information and technical assistance on the Americans with Disabilities Act. Retrieved from www.ada.gov.

United States Office of Personnel Management. (2008). Structured interviews: A practical guide. Retrieved from bit.ly/48ToDWN.

Van Laer, S., Elen, J., & Clarebout, G. (2017). Impact of learning analytics interventions on student academic outcomes: A systematic review. *Educational Research Review, 22,* 84–97. doi.org/10.1016/j.edurev.2017.08.001.

Virginia Department of Education. (2010). *Educational technology plan for Virginia: 2010–2015 executive summary.* Retrieved from www.doe.virginia.gov/support/technology/edtech_plan/index.shtml.

Walker, B. L. (2015). *Dimensions related to the role of a technology coordinator in schools that serve students with language-based learning differences* Doctoral dissertation, The George Washington University. Retrieved from tinyurl.com/yrjcds2k.

Webster, V.M.N. (2010). *An examination of the characteristics, duties, and training needs of district level technology coordinators in Mississippi school districts.* Doctoral dissertation, Mississippi State University. Retrieved from scholarsjunction.msstate.edu/td/539.

Watson, J., & Kalmon, S. (2018). *Keeping pace with K-12 digital learning.* Evergreen Education Group.

Watson, J., Watson, S. L., & Reigeluth, C. M. (2015). Education 3.0: Breaking the mold with technology. *Interactive Learning Environments, 23*(3), 332–343. doi.org/10.1080/10494820.2014.919184.

WebAIM. (2020). *Creating Accessible PDFs.* WebAIM. Retrieved from webaim.org/techniques/acrobat/.

WebAIM. (2021). Color contrast checker. Retrieved from webaim.org/resources/contrastchecker.

White House [@WhiteHouse]. (2023, August 8). *First Lady Jill Biden Hosts the Back to School Safely: Cybersecurity for K-12* [Video]. YouTube. Retrieved from www.youtube.com/watch?v=GaH9oJdbQZk.

Williamson, R. (2010). *Social media: Developing an Acceptable Use Policy.* The Principals' Partnership Research Brief. (ERIC No. ED538597)

W.K. Kellogg Foundation. (2004). *Logic model development guide.* Retrieved from wkkf.issuelab.org/resource/logic-model-development-guide.html.

World Wide Web Consortium (W3C). (2018). Web Content Accessibility Guidelines (WCAG) 2.1. Retrieved from w3.org/TR/WCAG21.

Wu, W. W., Wu, Y. W., & Huang, Y. M. (2020). A systematic review of research on the use of learning management systems in face-to-face classrooms. *Educational Research Review, 29,* 100304. doi.org/10.1016/j.edurev.2019.100304.

Zawacki-Richter, O., Tuncay, N., & Anderson, T. (2020). The impact of online teaching on teachers' roles, competences and professional development: A systematic review. *Educational Research Review, 30,* 100326.

Zepeda, S. J. (2015). Professional development: What works. New York: Routledge. doi:10.4324/9781315736894

Zimmerman, B. J. (2002). Becoming a self-regulated learner: An overview. *Theory into Practice, 41*(2), 64–70.

APPENDIX A

Tech Leader Job Description Examples

1. Ohio

TITLE

Executive Director of Instructional Technology and Innovation

REPORTS TO

Assistant Superintendent—Chief Academic Officer

SUMMARY

The Director of Instructional Technology has primary authority and accountability for the district's educational and administrative technology. He/she will lead strategic efforts to utilize technology in support of the district's mission and operations. He/she will articulate a compelling vision for technology and build the necessary support, both internally and externally, to realize the vision. He/she will evaluate, maintain, and enhance current systems and practices, while providing direction in all technology-related issues.

EDUCATION AND QUALIFICATIONS

- Master's degree in appropriate field
- Minimum of three (3) years' experience in leadership position directing technology initiatives in public school systems, private or corporate environments, or the armed forces
- Additional qualifications, training, or other credentials, as determined by the Board of Education

REQUIRED SKILLS AND ABILITIES

- Communication Skills: Must be able to read, analyze, and interpret information relevant to the position, including being able to speak effectively to small and large groups of people, and to communicate clearly and concisely both orally and in writing.
- Leadership Ability: Must be able to articulate a vision and mission for the district and provide the appropriate direction, guidance, and management skills to achieve them.
- Mathematics Skills: Must have the ability to work with basic mathematical and computational concepts.
- Reasoning Ability: Must be able to define problems, collect data, establish facts, and draw valid conclusions.

- Technology Skills: Able to effectively use, as it applies to your specific job function, typical office applications and computer programs such as word processing, spreadsheets, and presentations; must be able to use email.

PERSONAL QUALIFICATIONS

- Demonstrates enthusiasm and a sincere desire to aid and ensure the safety of all.
- Can accept constructive criticism/feedback.
- Demonstrates professional tact and diplomacy with administrators, staff, teachers, students, parents, and the diverse community.
- Is conscientious and assumes responsibility for one's own work performance.
- Anticipates problems and unforeseen events and deals with them in an appropriate manner.
- Demonstrates an ability to make proper decisions when required.
- Demonstrates loyalty to the administrative team.
- Possesses high moral character and a good attendance record.
- Promotes good social relationships as well as promoting good public relations by personal appearance, attitude, and conversation.
- Participates in appropriate professional organizations and their activities.
- Always maintains a calm attitude and sense of control.
- Maintains a high level of ethical behavior and confidentiality of information.
- Possesses the ability to be flexible and adaptable to changing situations.

WORK ENVIRONMENT CHARACTERISTICS AND CONDITIONS

The work environment characteristics described here are not listed in order of importance and are representative of those an employee encounters while completing the duties and responsibilities of this job. Reasonable accommodations may be made to enable individuals with disabilities to perform the duties and responsibilities. The information contained in this job description is for compliance with the American with Disabilities Act (A.D.A.) and is not an exhaustive list of the duties performed for this position.

- Frequent work that may extend beyond the normal workday
- Occasional exposure to blood, bodily fluids, and tissue
- Occasional operation of a vehicle under inclement weather conditions
- Occasional interaction among unruly children/adults
- Many situations that require hand motion, e.g., computer keyboard, typing, writing, etc.
- Consistent requirements to sit, stand, walk, hear, see, read, speak, reach, stretch with hands and arms, crouch, kneel, climb and stoop
- Consistent requirements to lift, carry, push, and pull various supplies and/or equipment up to a maximum of 50 pounds

DUTIES AND RESPONSIBILITIES

- Facilitate the process of priority setting and decision-making for meaningful and effective uses of technology in support of the district's strategic goals.

- Lead infusion of innovative technologies into all aspects of education and instruction.

- Develop and maintain an understanding of assessment, curriculum and instruction, including their interdependent relationship and how technology can support them.

- Work with key system leaders, people, networks, and departments to identify steps needed to meet strategic and instructional goals.

- Work with key system leaders, people, networks, and departments to identify budget and funding mechanisms needed to meet strategic and instructional goals.

- Know the current goals of the school district and align your team's work with those goals.

- Have strategic understanding and working knowledge of all district systems (e.g., instruction, assessment, finance, facilities, transportation, security, food service and others) to provide leadership regarding how technology can support them.

- Participate in the monitoring, reporting and evaluation efforts of the district's educational technology plan.

- Communicate to stakeholders appropriate ethical and professional behavior for technology use in the district.

- Demonstrate knowledge of vulnerabilities and issues pertaining to the safety of students and staff.

- Actively participate in the policy development process and ensure policy supports a high-performing learning environment.

- Facilitate equitable access to technology resources for all stakeholders.

- Plan for and coordinate on-going, purposeful professional development on technology integration in the classroom.

- Stay abreast of state and national standards, benchmarks, and frameworks for technology literacy.

- Promote the application of technology to address the diverse needs of students and maximize student learning, achievement, and growth.

- Analyze the structure and organizational chart of the technology department relative to its ability to address the district strategic plan.

- Deploy staff to best address the district strategic plan and meet its goals.

- Collaborate with stakeholders to create a vision for how technology will support the district's strategic goals.

- Build and leverage effective partnerships with technology organizations that benefit district stakeholders.

- Direct and coordinate use of email, district web sites, web tools, voicemail systems, social media, and other forms of communication.

- Have working knowledge of various communication tools and techniques.

- Be knowledgeable about emerging technologies to enhance learning, instruction and communication.

- Utilize knowledge of funding sources available to the district and appropriately leverage them to meet district and programmatic goals.

- Develop and manage budgets, both annually and long-range.

- Make effective purchasing decisions following relevant laws, policies, and guidelines.

- Direct, manage, and negotiate with vendors and business partners.

- Direct, coordinate, and ensure implementation of all tasks related to selection and purchasing (RFPs, purchasing guidelines, etc.).

- Holds all confidential information in which he/she has knowledge of in the truest confidence, as required by law and utilizes confidential information obtained only for the benefit of the employee or student or in performance of his/her job responsibilities.

- Collaborates and coordinates the design, planning, support, professional development, and implementation of technology use in teaching, learning, and district curriculum for the purpose of improving student learning in all subject areas.

- Lead strategic planning initiatives as designated by the superintendent.

- Directs, analyzes, and evaluates a variety of program related data (e.g., student assessments, teacher assessments, emerging technology trends, requested applications, systems, hardware, etc.) for the purpose of ensuring availability of technology resources needed to meet student, school site, and district objectives while adhering to budget limitations.

- Performs other duties as assigned.

TERMS OF EMPLOYMENT
260 contract days

2. Kansas

TITLE
District Technology Director

REPORTS TO
Superintendent

EDUCATION AND QUALIFICATIONS

- Master's degree from an accredited college/university

- Three years certified experience as a teacher with appropriate technology background

- Current Kansas State Administrator Certification on file

- Health and Inoculation Certificate on file
- Desire to continue career improvement
- Skills to effectively communicate, coordinate, and direct an outstanding educational program with students, staff, parents, patrons, other administrators, and the Board of Education

OVERSEE ALL ASPECTS OF THE TECHNOLOGY

- Oversee all undertakings of the district technology department.
- Submit and approve researched technology purchases within given budget.
- Work with a group to develop and follow a district technology plan as approved by the Board of Education and State Department.
- Serve on the Leadership Team and various committees where technology plays an integral part.
- Prepare and submit Universal Service Fund E-Rate application for needed district connectivity.
- Support district servers in set-up, maintenance, updates, and backups.
- Maintain district networks and internet bandwidth to a workable speed.
- Support, orient, and instruct users of personal computer systems and peripherals in both free standing and network environments.
- Respond to users' requests for help and provide troubleshooting and training.
- Provide technology in-services on an ongoing basis.
- Work with teachers in classrooms to incorporate technology with instruction.
- Review equipment records and equipment status report logs.
- Request and record service calls when necessary. Assist with maintaining a complete inventory of all computers, computer systems and peripherals.
- Provide resource analysis, maintenance, software installation, configuration, service requests, security, and monitoring.
- Ability to respond to information requests in a cooperative, courteous, and timely manner.
- Ability to keep student and personnel information and records confidential.

CONTRIBUTES TO SAFE AND ORDERLY WORK AREAS

- Ability to implement and follow all district health and safety policies, including all precautions of the Bloodborne Pathogens Exposure Control plan.
- Ensure compliance with all federal, state, and local safety regulations.

BUILDS POSITIVE EMPLOYEE AND COMMUNITY RELATIONS

- The application of systems analysis techniques and procedures, including consulting with users, to determine hardware, software, or system functional specifications.

- The design, development, documentation, analysis, creation, testing, or modification of computer systems or programs, including prototypes, based on and related to user or system design specifications.

- The design, documentation, testing, creation, or modification of computer programs related to machine operation systems; or a combination of these duties, the performance of which requires the same level of skills.

- Ability to orient and instruct staff and students in how to use and integrate technology.

- Ability to operate and support all technology equipment and networks.

- Ability to communicate and work effectively and cooperatively with members of the school district, students, and community.

- Ability to work to implement the vision and mission of the district.

- Ability to ensure all activities conform to District guidelines.

- Ability to react to change and frequent interruptions in a productive and positive manner, meeting deadlines as assigned.

MODELS POSITIVE PROFESSIONAL ATTRIBUTES

- Any other duties deemed appropriate as assigned by the Superintendent of Schools.

- Attend meetings as required and approved by the superintendent.

FOLLOWS DISTRICT POLICIES AND PROCEDURES
TO PROMOTE A PROFESSIONAL WORKPLACE

- Always observes and follows all district policies.

- Always observes, follows, and supports district sexual harassment policies.

- Always observes, follows, and supports district safety policies.

FOLLOWS DISTRICT ATTENDANCE REQUIREMENTS

- Always observes and follows all district attendance policies.

TERMS OF EMPLOYMENT

2-month employee at-will

3. Kansas

TITLE

Executive Director of Information and Communication Technologies

REPORTS TO

Deputy Superintendent

SUMMARY

Under the supervision of the Deputy Superintendent this position will establish and maintain culture and vision that guides and facilitates the department's development, deployment, and utilization of information and communication technologies.

EDUCATION AND QUALIFICATIONS

- 4-year college degree required. Master's preferred.
- 10+ years related experience at executive level; 15+ years total experience.

ESSENTIAL DUTIES AND RESPONSIBILITIES

- Oversees departmental responsibility in conformity with the policies and procedures of the Board of Education, federal, state, and local laws, regulations, and mandates.
- Leads development and implementation of plans to meet district short- and long-range goals regarding all departmental areas of responsibility.
- Supports department leaders in developing and supporting attainment of workgroup goals.
- Promotes and supports collaboration amongst all department staff members.
- Oversees the department budget.
- Enforces developed practices and procedures to safeguard the enterprise's technology environment.
- Follows the district employment process when selecting and assigning candidates to department positions in areas of responsibility.
- Establishes high expectations for staff performance and evaluates personnel in compliance with district policy and procedures.

QUALIFICATION REQUIREMENTS

- Knowledge of principles and practices of public-school education and related information and communication technologies and ability to apply them to the needs of the district.
- Ability to organize, coordinate, and execute programs in areas of responsibility.
- Ability to supervise others and develop effective working relationships with the senior management team, staff members at all levels, vendors, and community.
- Knowledge and ability to utilize appropriate technology to communicate and present information.
- Ability to collaborate and communicate effectively both verbally and in written language.
- Excellent people skills with ability to handle difficult situations.
- Excellent time management and organizational skills.
- Ability to multitask and prioritize.
- Strong troubleshooting capabilities evidenced by organized, analytical thinking.
- Ability to work with minimal supervision.

- Keen attention to detail, with a commitment to follow through and follow-up.
- Acquire and maintain current knowledge of relevant products, offering, and support policies to effectively collaborate with departmental leaders.
- Demonstrates ability to implement best practice and the motivation to set and achieve high performance levels.
- Desire to continue career improvement by enhancing skills and job performance.

LANGUAGE SKILLS

- Ability to read and interpret documents, including the analysis of district assessment data.
- Ability to write routine reports and correspondence.
- Ability to communicate well, both verbal and in writing, with parents, patrons, staff, and students.
- Ability to speak in front of large and/or small groups.
- Ability to communicate effectively with technical and non-technical audiences and interact with all types of technology users.

PHYSICAL DEMANDS

- Must have ability to travel in personal or school district vehicle.
- Must be flexible regarding scheduling, working conditions and location of work.
- May require some physical exertion.

WORK ENVIRONMENT

- Must be able to occasionally work in noisy and crowded environments, with numerous interruptions.

TERMS OF EMPLOYMENT

12-month contract

4. Tennessee

TITLE

Director, Field Support

REPORTS TO

Executive Director, Technology Services

SUMMARY

Responsible for all aspects of the technology support services in school sites which are provided through a field-based support services team. Serves as a key member of the Technology Services leadership team and closely collaborates with other sections of the department to streamline services to school personnel

EDUCATION AND QUALIFICATIONS

- Bachelor's and master's degree in field of Education and/or Management and Leadership
- 5 years prior management and leadership experience

ESSENTIAL DUTIES AND RESPONSIBILITIES

- Provides management and leadership to a field-based staff of Field Managers, technology leads, and technology specialists
- Develops and monitors Key Performance Indicators and Service Level Agreements. Works with Field Managers to continuously improve these services.
- Works closely with Director, Enterprise Services to support District Goals including remote technical support and written policies such as Service Level Agreements, the Service Catalog and Standard Operating Procedures. Works to collaborate in selection and support of classroom technology teaching devices such as interactive panels, iPads, and student computing devices. Works and collaborates with helpdesk staff and the hardware repair facility.
- Works and collaborates with the Enterprise Network Operations Department especially with troubleshooting and reliability of School Based Network Infrastructures.
- Assists in the development of policies and procedures regarding technology in the district
- Works with Project and Change Management to provide input and resources to District Projects and coordination with Change Management to achieve their goals.
- Stays current on new and emerging technologies and their uses in the field of education.
- Works with and develops relationships with technology hardware and software vendors.
- Interacts with district principals and executive leaders for technology support needs.
- Other duties and projects as assigned.

GENERAL SKILLS, RESPONSIBILITIES, REQUIREMENTS, AND IMPACTS

- Data Responsibility: Synthesizes or integrates analysis of data or information to discover facts or develop knowledge or interpretations; modifies policies, procedures, or methodologies based on findings.
- People Responsibility: Negotiates or exchanges ideas, information, and opinions with others to formulate policies and programs, or arrive jointly at decisions, conclusions, or solutions.
- Assets Responsibility: Requires responsibility and opportunity for achieving moderate economies and/or preventing moderate losses through the management or handling of supplies of high value or moderate amounts of money.
- Communications Requirements: Reads professional publications; composes complex reports and manuals; speaks formally to small groups within and outside the organization.

- Complexity of Work: Performs work involving the application of broad principles of professional management and leadership to solve new problems for which conventional solutions do not exist; requires sustained, intense concentration for accurate results.

- Impact of Decisions: Makes decisions with serious impact; affects most units in organization and may affect citizens.

- Equipment Usage: Leads or handles machines, tools, equipment, or work aids involving moderate latitude for judgment regarding attainment of standard or in selecting appropriate items.

- Safety of Others: Requires responsibility for the safety and health of others and for occasional enforcement of the laws and standards of public health and safety.

TERMS OF EMPLOYMENT
12-month contract

5. Tennessee

TITLE
Director of Instructional Technology

REPORTS TO
Executive Director, Technology Services / Digital Strategies and Implementation

SUMMARY
The essential function of the Director of Instructional Technology is to oversee the organization, development, implementation and outcomes of instructional technology across the district.

EDUCATION AND QUALIFICATIONS
- Master's in Education and/or Library and Information Sciences Preferred: Successful completion of 3 years in instructional technology and/or library media

- 3 years' experience as a school librarian

- Applicant must hold a valid teaching license with Librarian endorsement.

ESSENTIAL DUTIES AND RESPONSIBILITIES
- Responsible for leading a team consisting of instructional designers and learning technology specialists toward initiatives aligned to district strategic priorities.

- Oversees project timelines and coordinate team members with departmental members, subject matter experts, external vendors, and district personal to support all stakeholders.

- Oversees budget(s) to support school instructional technology goals and vision.

- Works with instructional coaches, administration, and department heads to implement technology best practices in support of the district's vision of student learning.

- Collaborates with Curriculum and Instruction, school leadership, and district and community stakeholders on the selection of instructional technology in support of student learning.

- Strategizes and implements project plans to increase instructional technology usage by students, educators, and district office personnel.

- Other duties as assigned by Executive Director of Technology Services

GENERAL SKILLS, RESPONSIBILITIES, REQUIREMENTS, AND IMPACTS

- Demonstrates the ability to work collaboratively with team, department, and stakeholders throughout the district.

- Excellent oral, written and presentation skills.

- Demonstrates the ability to evaluate the effectiveness and impact of materials, learning tools, and digital content.

- Data Responsibility: Collects, classifies, and formats data or information.

- People Responsibility: Speaks with or signals to people to convey or exchange information.

- Assets Responsibility: Requires some responsibility for achieving minor economies and/or preventing minor losses through the handling of or accounting for materials, supplies, or small amounts of money.

- Mathematical Requirements: Uses addition, subtraction, multiplication, and division; may compute ratios, rates, and percentages.

- Communications Requirements: Reads journals and manuals; composes specialized reports/analysis; speaks to large groups of coworkers and people outside the organization.

- Complexity of Work: Performs coordinating work involving guidelines and rules with constant problem solving; requires continuous, close attention for accurate results or frequent exposure to unusual pressure.

- Impact of Decisions: Makes decisions with moderate impact; affects those in work unit.

- Equipment Usage: Handles machines, tools, equipment, or work aids involving little or no latitude for judgment regarding attainment of standard or in selecting appropriate items.

TERMS OF EMPLOYMENT

12-month contract

6. Kansas

TITLE

Curriculum Technology Specialist

REPORTS TO

Assistant Superintendent for Teaching and Learning

SUMMARY

Improve learning and instruction through the efficient use of technology.

EDUCATION AND QUALIFICATIONS

- Master's degree with appropriate active teaching license
- Minimum 5 years teaching experience and some experience in a leadership position
- Substantial experience in instructional technology and professional development

REQUIRED KNOWLKEDGE, SKILLS, AND ABILITIES

- Knowledge of curriculum development, supervision, effective classroom practices, and development principles.
- Ability to demonstrate effective leadership skills in group settings.
- Effective written and oral communication skills.
- Knowledge and ability to use various forms of education technology.
- Ability to use effective public relation skills necessary for the successful implementation of new programs.
- Ability to plan, organize and deliver technology professional development for teachers, administrators, and other staff members.
- Ability to work with classroom teachers to develop specific strategies for integrating technology into instruction.
- Ability to assist with the implementation of technology in the classroom and existing lessons, grades K–12.
- Ability to work with curriculum directors to develop and evaluate curriculum based on needs as referenced through assessments.
- Ability to model the appropriate technology.
- Ability to promote the appropriate and ethical use of technology regarding copyright issues through the Acceptable Use Policy.
- Ability to work with information services to update and maintain the district's instructional technology plan.
- Must remain current in knowledge of technology, curriculum, and instruction.

PERFORMANCE RESPONSIBILITIES

- Assist the Assistant Superintendent for Teaching and Learning in curriculum evaluation and the implementation of technology into the instructional program.
- Serve as a technology liaison and coordinator of specific initiatives.
- Coordinate the instructional technology initiatives for all schools in the district which include school technology plans, internet resources sent to teachers for classroom use, and work with teachers to help students integrate technology.

- Coordinate the development and yearly updates of the instructional portion of the technology plan including administrative issues in each school's plan.

- Maintain current documentation on the status of individual school sites in the installation and use of instructional technology. Documentation should be collected through classroom visits, assessments, surveys, and observation of the modeling of effective practices.

- Maintain effective communication with all school representatives.

- Determine technology training needs through surveys and meetings with building- and district-level administrators and teachers.

- Coordinate the planning and implementation of training.

- Provide supervisors with periodic reports regarding recommendations for improvement, status of technology in schools, needs, and concerns.

- Attend meetings, conferences, and workshops as requested.

- Other duties as assigned.

PHYSICAL REQUIREMENTS AND ENVIRONMENTAL CONDITIONS

Physical and emotional ability and dexterity to perform required work and move about as needed in a fast-pace, high-intensive work environment.

TERMS OF EMPLOYMENT

Standard teacher contract of 192 days + 40 day extended contract

7. Wisconsin

TITLE

Instructional Technology Specialist

REPORTS TO

Director of Instruction

SUMMARY

The Instructional Technology Specialist is an innovator and experienced teacher leader who provides the expertise, information, and tools necessary to lead teachers to incorporate technology into their daily lessons and activities. Work includes designing and developing instructional materials, including scope and sequence, for computer based lessons, software, hardware, web sites and other online systems and delivery platforms for students and staff. Support is provided to staff through coaching, co-planning, collaboration, modeling, observing, and providing feedback on best practices for instructional technology. Provides school-wide leadership and guidance for all aspects of teaching and learning in a digital environment, including the selection and acquisition of instructional technology environments, programs, and projects.

EDUCATION AND QUALIFICATIONS

- Bachelor's degree
- Evidence of current certification by the Wisconsin Department of Public Instruction as a teacher preferred.
- Previous experience teaching technology to teachers and students in K4–8 environments preferred.
- Knowledge of and/or experience working with urban children and/or American Indian cultures, communities, and students preferred.

ESSENTIAL DUTIES AND RESPONSIBILITIES

- Provides project management and planning for one-to-one technology initiatives.
- Facilitates computer-based programming, platforms, assessments, the PowerSchool standards-based grading system, and serves as the technical administrator for student enrollment and troubleshooting.
- Coordinates the use of technology for all staff and students to enhance the efficiency and effectiveness of programs and services.
- Creates goals, action plans, deadlines, budget numbers and measurement tools to support the technology education of ICS students.
- Provides support and/or leadership in the implementation of the ICS Strategic Plan as it pertains to technology.
- Develops and implements short- and long-range plans for the use of present and emerging technology designed to improve the teaching and learning process.
- Assists in the development of policies and procedures regarding technology use.
- Develops and implements a procedure for evaluation of educational software.
- Coordinates the selection of technology equipment and software.
- Leads the Future Ready Committee and collaborates to improve student success and school improvement.
- Coaches teachers in using a variety of instructional strategies, to enhance, extend, and engage student learning within the curriculum for their assigned grade level(s) and subject(s).
- Supports classroom teachers with the integration of technology based on the Wisconsin state, national, and international standards.
- Responsible for organizing and providing technology related professional development for staff.
- Conducts classroom visits and provides formative feedback to teachers and administrators on the school's instructional technology program.
- Coordinates with members of the Instructional Support team during cycles of data review to develop measurable outcomes toward school goals and make recommendations for program development, under the direction of the Director of Instruction.

- Develops and reviews all instructional technology professional development offerings, procedures, and work practices to ensure they follow established legal, ethical, and security standards and are compliant.
- Supports classroom teachers with the integration of digital citizenship into their daily work with students for students to learn how to use technology appropriately and to prepare for the rapidly changing world of technology.
- Provides a variety of effective forms of communication for all aspects of instructional technology programs, digital citizenship, and technology use to families, including newsletter articles, handouts, letters, and the planning and facilitation of workshop sessions.
- Collaborates with staff to enhance the integration and use of technology across departments.
- Attends faculty meetings and leads/serves on appropriate academic committees as assigned.
- Incorporates American Indian culture, language, traditions and the Seven Sacred Gifts into the curriculum and educational programming.
- Actively participates in learning about American Indian culture, language, traditions, and the Seven Sacred Gifts.
- Participates in the school-wide student mentor program creating a community that embraces each one of its children with love, care and respect while teaching traditional values.
- Builds and maintains professional relationships with students, families, staff, and administration that are positive, constructive, and focused on team collaboration.
- Complies with State Laws in reporting suspected child abuse and neglect.
- Performs all other duties and responsibilities as assigned by the Director of Instruction.

MENTAL REQUIREMENTS
- Ability to define problems, collect data, establish facts, and draw valid conclusions. Ability to interpret an extensive variety of technical instructions in mathematical or diagram form and deal with several abstract and concrete variables.

WORK ENVIRONMENT
- Most work is performed in an indoor, climate-controlled environment. Noise levels may reach high volumes at times. Some work may be performed outside in weather and at various field trip locations.

PHYSICAL DEMANDS
- The physical demands described here are representative of those that must be met by an employee to successfully perform the essential functions of this job. Reasonable accommodations may be made to enable individuals with disabilities to perform the essential functions.

- While performing the duties of this Job, the employee is regularly required to talk or hear. The employee is frequently required to use hands to finger, handle, or feel and reach with hands and arms. The employee is occasionally required to stand; walk; sit; climb or balance and stoop, kneel, crouch, or crawl. The employee must frequently lift and/or move up to 10 pounds and occasionally lift and/or move up to 25 pounds. Specific vision abilities required by this job include close vision, distance vision, peripheral vision, depth perception and ability to adjust focus.

TERMS OF EMPLOYMENT
Full time, school year +10 days. Member of the Instructional Support team.

8. California

TITLE
Program Manager, Digital Learning and Computer Science Education

REPORTS TO
Assistant Superintendent of Education Support Services

SUMMARY
The Program Manager, Digital Learning and Computer Science Education is responsible for the management, development, and oversight of professional development, technical assistance, and program guidance for digital learning and computer science education programs and initiatives. This individual will be the lead administrator for the Digital Learning team that has the responsibility to support school districts in achieving county-wide technology and computer science education goals. The Program Manager is responsible for leading and developing projects, partnerships, and resources to improve access, equity, and outcomes in digital learning and computer science priorities. The Program Manager, coordinates, monitors, and facilitates various county committees, staff development and leadership activities to digital learning and computer science education.

EDUCATION AND QUALIFICATIONS

Minimum
- Possession of a valid California Clear Administrative Services Credential
- Master's degree in Education, Education Technology (EdTech), or a related field, from an accredited college or university
- Five (5) years of combined experience as an administrator at a school site, district, and/or county office
- Three (3) years of combined experience with the implementation of EdTech or Digital Learning programs at a school site or at the district/county level

Desired
- Doctorate degree in Education, or a related field from an accredited college or university

- Professional Certificate or Credential in EdTech, Computer Science education, or Online and Blended Learning
- Bilingual/Bi-literate (English/Spanish)

ESSENTIAL JOB FUNCTIONS

- Provides leadership/direction for the development, facilitation, and implementation of Digital Learning and Computer Science education projects, identified resources, and professional learning aligned to California Digital Learning Integration and Standards document with the team's vision and the organizational goals and objectives.
- Assists and supervises the implementation of state-wide computer science education standards.
- Directs, coordinates, organizes, prioritizes, and monitors the development and implementation of individual and team goals.
- Manages, monitors, and evaluates project operations, budgets and expenditures, and staff.
- Develops, maintains, and evaluates research-based, data-driven teaching and learning models that support digital learning and computer science education.
- Provides guidance and oversite in researching, developing, implementing, and monitoring local, state, and federal grant funded projects and services in digital learning and computer science education.
- Establishes and evaluates goals, priorities, processes, and systems for the effective digital learning and computer science education programs, systems, and tools.
- Collaborates with local, regional, and state representatives in the implementation and maintenance of digital learning and computer science education related programs.
- Coordinates pertinent county-wide networks and attends state, regional, and local meetings as a representative of digital learning and computer science education and/or an advocate of county offices.
- Promotes the use and integration of new/emerging technologies which support, accelerate, and sustain student learning and achievement.
- Performs related duties as assigned.

JOB REQUIREMENTS

- **Experience** managing large scale digital learning and computer science education projects and/or programs, in multiple districts, public schools, and county offices; securing and sustaining the implementation of the digital learning and computer science education initiatives; providing professional development; evaluating implementation stages, and providing appropriate coaching, technical assistance and interventions; identifying and incorporating innovative, promising, and best practices in creating and delivering project services; monitoring grant projects; conducting project reviews and evaluations; and analyzing and interpreting student/school/district project data including experience training and facilitating Multi-Tiered System of Support (MTSS) coaching and assessment process for the development, alignment, and improvement of digital learning and computer science education initiatives.

- **Skill** in establishing procedures and priorities; facilitating group processes; researching, interpreting, analyzing, reporting, and utilizing data; developing, marketing, and coordinating project activities and services; using student, school, and community data to monitor student improvement and school or district reform, facilitating school/district leadership teams.

- **Knowledge** of California academic standards and Digital Learning Integration Standards, regional project structures, pedagogical principals, and practices in teaching and learning for educators, parents, and all students; existing and emerging local, state and national resources related to the project focus, emerging technologies; federal, state, regional, and local account-ability systems; existing programs that have been instrumental in closing the achievement/access gaps and increasing college attendance rates; state and local laws, codes, regulations, and requirements pertaining to the specific project.

- **Ability** to establish program goals; train and supervise staff; prepare project presentations and publications, especially relating to digital learning and computer science education; work independently; establish and maintain project deadlines; work with a variety of individuals and groups; communicate orally and in writing; and travel to various locations.

- **Physical Abilities:** job requires extended periods of sitting, standing, and walking; stamina and agility to push, pull, lift, carry or move up to 40 pounds occasionally; climbing, balancing, squatting, twisting, turning, bending, kneeling, crawling, and stooping; and hearing, speaking, observing and significant fine finger dexterity. Specific vision abilities required by this job include close vision, distance vision, peripheral vision, depth perception, and the ability to adjust focus. The job is performed under minimal temperature variations, in a generally hazard-free environment, and in a clean atmosphere.

TERMS OF EMPLOYMENT
228 contract days

9. Kansas

TITLE
Director of Technology

REPORTS TO
Superintendent

SUMMARY
The Director of Technology will provide oversight over all technology resources, coordinate all technology-related activities, manage the technology budget, E-rate applications, prepare and execute technology grants, provide oversight over all technology expenditures and plan instructional (in-service) and administrative training. The Director of Technology will work closely with the Superintendent, Director of Teaching and Learning, principals, instructional coaches, and building technology coordinators to ensure the technology plan is being followed and that the technology is being integrated into the curricula.

EDUCATION AND QUALIFICATIONS

- Bachelor's degree
- Minimum three years successful experience in the development, installation, and maintenance of information systems
- Minimum three years successful experience with administrative and supervisory skills.
- Technology certifications or licenses preferred

KNOWLEDGE, SKILLS, AND ABILITIES REQUIRED

- Ability to work cooperatively and constructively with others, including the ability to communicate effectively with a broad number of audiences.
- Ability to manage job responsibilities and to meet the established district outcomes.
- Ability to use necessary district-identified computer hardware and software, and other district-provided technology.
- Ability to physically adapt to the compressed time schedule of a school day and year.

DUTIES AND REQUIREMENTS

- Communicate effectively with members of the school district and community.
- React to change productively and handle other tasks as assigned.
- Support the value of an education.
- Support the philosophy and mission of USD 469.
- Develop a long-range plan for the use of present and emerging technologies designed to improve the teaching/learning process.
- Manage day-to-day operations of technology department (including directing staff) to support instruction and district operations.
- Consult with department managers and district administrators to discuss technology program initiatives and changes.
- Establish and maintains strategic partnerships with service providers.
- Coordinate the use of technology by teachers, administrators, support staff, and students to enhance the efficiency and effectiveness of programs and services.
- Review, evaluate, and inform instructional staff of recently developed commercial software including recommendations to integrate it into the curriculum.
- Coordinate the purchase of technology equipment and materials to ensure that needs of the district are being met in the most cost-effective manner.
- Coordinate the distribution of technology equipment and materials in a manner that effectively implements the long-range technology plan.
- Maintain an inventory of technology equipment and materials.
- Oversee system automation and coordinate data uploads.

- Provide training for teachers, administrators, and support staff to ensure the appropriate application of technology.
- Provide consultation for teachers, administrators, and support staff to assist with the problems and concerns that arise daily.
- Coordinate the integration of district systems and online platforms.
- Consult with curriculum committees to ensure that technology applications are effectively integrated into all academic and vocational programs.
- Prepare grant proposals designed to secure additional technology funding for the district.
- Supervise and coordinate services available through utilization of LAN and WAN networks.
- Oversee the completion of technology work orders in a timely manner.
- Recommend employment and annually evaluate technology personnel.
- Meet with the superintendent yearly for an annual evaluation.
- Prepare monthly Director of Technology Report for BOE to be shared during each regular board meeting.
- Assist in developing the budget for purchase of technology hardware and materials.
- Perform other duties as assigned by the Superintendent.

TERMS OF EMPLOYMENT

12-month contract

GLOSSARY

1:1 computing. Providing every student, teacher, and staff member with a laptop, notebook, or tablet device for continuous use both in the classroom and at home. The intentions of such an initiative include improving the in-class educational experience, providing universal internet access to disadvantaged homes, and building stronger connections between teacher and parent, as well as better school and community relations.

Acceptable Use of Technology Policy (AUT). A document outlining expectation for and clearly defining appropriate use of technology resources for an organization. Many organizations require agreement with such a policy before using technology. Also sometimes referred to as an Acceptable Use Policy (AUP).

administrative computing. The computing done by an educational organization that includes such business tasks as budgeting, payroll, and purchasing. It also includes tasks such as management of human resources information and the processing of such student data as grades and other student records. These administrative tasks are usually carried out by professional office staff, and they are separate from the educational computing done by teachers and students.

adware. See *spyware*.

app. A software program with a specific purpose that is downloaded for use on a mobile device. An app is essentially a software application written to perform a certain task on a device such as shopping or banking.

archive. A backup set of computer files that have been grouped and usually compressed to make available more storage space on a hard disk.

asynchronous online learning. Asynchronous online learning is a mode of instruction where students access learning materials and complete assignments at their own pace, without real-time interaction with their teachers or peers.

backdoor. Access to a device or network that bypasses normal security. A backdoor is sometimes created by a programmer to provide easy access for solving problems, but these features often create security risks that allow hackers to exploit a vulnerability.

bid request. A formal or informal proceeding for obtaining the costs of specified goods or services. Formal bids are documents containing specifications detailing technical requirements for goods and services. Requests for bids are publicly advertised, and bids must be submitted in a sealed bid package or envelope. Formal bids are opened in public and read aloud.

blended learning. An educational process that combines digital and online learning with face-to-face instruction to create a hybrid taking advantage of the benefits of each.

broadband. A type of high-speed data transmission in which the bandwidth is shared by more than one simultaneous signal. Such a transmission might include web pages (HTTP), file transfer (FTP), and video all on the same transmission line. The transmission of data over a fiber optic cable at a speed of many million bits per second would be referred to as broadband, as compared to a telephone modem operating at a rate of tens of thousands of bits per second.

Bring Your Own Device (BYOD). A policy permitting students and staff to bring personally owned mobile devices such as tablets, phones, and laptops to school and use them to access the school network and internet for productivity.

cloud computing. A type of computing that relies on shared computing resources rather than local servers or devices to handle applications. This type of computing applies high-performance computing power to provide consumer-oriented applications such as financial portfolios or document creation and storage. Cloud computing networks rely on groups of servers, which spread data-processing chores across the server network. Cloud computing networks allow access to data and applications from any location with an internet connection.

computational thinking. A problem-solving process that makes use of methods and techniques based in computer science to think through a problem in a step-by-step fashion as is required when writing computer code.

cyberbullying. When students engage in bullying behavior using electronic means, it is often referred to as online social cruelty or electronic bullying. Examples of this type of behavior can involve sending mean, vulgar, or threatening messages or images; posting sensitive, private information about another person; pretending to be someone else in order to make that person look bad; or intentionally excluding someone from an online group.

cybersecurity. The process of protecting critical digital technology systems and information from outside threats and attacks intended to cause damage and interrupting regular processes.

CPU. The central processing unit, or "brain," of the computer. This main unit does all the work of the computer and controls all the various systems that make up the computer.

database. A collection of data organized in a standard format for easy access, management, and updating by a computer.

data processing. The conversion of raw data to a standard format that can be used by a computer and the subsequent processing—such as storing, updating, combining, rearranging, or printing—of this data by a computer.

digital citizenship. The norms of appropriate, responsible behavior with regard to technology use. Digital citizenship is a concept that helps teachers, technology leaders, and parents understand what students/children/technology users should know to use technology appropriately.

digital literacy. The ability to identify, evaluate, and make effective use of information through the use of digital tools and resources. With technology becoming an important part of daily life, digital literacy provides the skills necessary to succeed in the modern world.

disaster recovery plan/procedures. Describes how an organization will deal with potential disasters related to their technology infrastructure. A disaster recovery plan consists of the precautions taken so that the effects of a disaster will be minimized and the organization will be able to either maintain or quickly resume mission-critical functions.

document imaging. The conversion of paper-based documents into computerized electronic images. A scanner is used to input documents into the system. The document-imaging system is designed to store images on a hard drive or optical disc for easy access to documents by multiple users.

educational technology. A term widely used to describe the use of technology tools and resources in an educational setting. Instructional technology refers to the use of the technology for teaching and learning.

educational technology coaching (EdTech coaching). Technology staff members who work in conjunction with teachers and support staff to provide ongoing professional development and instructional support for using educational technology in the teaching and learning process to support district learning goals for students.

email archive. In 2006, the U.S. Supreme Court revised rules regarding federal lawsuits called the Federal Rules of Civil Procedure. These rules require companies, government agencies, school districts, and generally any organization that might be sued in federal court to have systems for retrieving electronic data, such as email correspondence, if it is needed as evidence in a federal case.

email client. A program running on a digital device that allows the user to send, receive, and organize electronic mail. An email client connects to a server-based mail account to check for new messages and send messages to others.

E-Rate. A government program that provides discounts to help most schools and libraries in the United States obtain affordable telecommunications and internet access. This program includes three service categories: telecommunications services, internet access, and internal connections of equipment. Discounts range from 20% to 90% of the costs of eligible services, depending on the level of financial need and the urban or rural status of the population served. Eligible schools, school districts, and libraries must apply for, and be awarded, the discounts on an annual basis, following the guidelines for the program.

e-waste. E-waste is a popular, informal name for electronic products nearing the end of their useful life. Certain components of some electronic products contain materials that render them hazardous, depending on their condition and density. For instance, nonfunctioning CRTs (cathode ray tubes) from televisions and monitors are considered to be hazardous waste and must be disposed of properly.

fiber-optic line. See *high-speed communications line.*

flipped learning. A learning experience where teachers create recorded lectures and other instructional materials that students study and learn from at home and then in class the teachers build upon what the students learned at home by implementing classroom activities requiring students to apply the concepts, or otherwise extend their knowledge in some way.

help desk. A person or persons in an organization who serve as the first point of contact for users needing assistance and information in order to solve technical problems. Help desks are normally established to provide information-technology support, but they may be designed to support other functions of an organization as well.

high-speed communications line. A T1, T3, or fiber-optic line used for carrying voice or data communications signals. A T1 line can carry 24 digitized voice channels, or it can carry data at a rate of 1.544 megabits per second. A T3 line is a superhigh-speed connection capable of transmitting data at a rate of 45 million bits per second. This represents a bandwidth equal to about 672 regular voice-grade telephone lines, which is wide enough to transmit full-motion real-time video, as well as very large databases, over a busy network. A T3 line is typically installed as a major networking artery for large corporations and universities with high-volume network traffic. Fiber-optic connections are essentially glass communications wire. Fiber-optic transmission lines can be used to support 30,000 times the traffic that can be carried on copper wires, which make up T1 or T3 lines.

hybrid learning. A learning experience where designated portions of a class are conducted online using a learning management system, and the rest of the class is conducted in a more traditional way in the classroom.

information management. Refers to the various stages of information processing—from creation and production to storage, retrieval, and dissemination—that is intended to improve the workflow of an organization. Before it enters the management system, this information can be from internal and external sources and in a variety of formats.

infrastructure. In information technology and on the internet, infrastructure is the physical hardware used to interconnect computers and users. Infrastructure includes the transmission media, including telephone lines, cable television lines, and satellites and antennas, and also the routers, aggregators, repeaters, and other devices that control transmission paths. Infrastructure also includes the software used to send, receive, and manage the signals that are transmitted.

instructional technology. Refers to hardware (such as personal computers, CDs, and multimedia, handheld learning devices) and software used in instructional programs. Also included are distance-learning activities, such as the internet, videos, television, satellite, radio, cable, fiber optics, shortwave, microwave, and other related technologies.

learning management system (LMS). A software system designed to provide a system for hosting, distributing, and tracking the learning process provided by an organization. An LMS may be used to provide an online learning experience or may be used to supplement a face-to-face program. These systems make it easy to distribute educational materials and track student progress and grades throughout the course.

maker spaces. A room that is equipped with all sorts of technologies and materials to enable teachers and students to build or create anything needed to support teaching and learning activities.

network. A series of points or nodes interconnected by communication paths. In the case of computer networks, it is a variety of different equipment resources, each having a unique identification and serving a particular purpose, such as server, printer, switch, or router.

online learning. A learning experience where teachers upload and create instructional content in a learning management system and students use these materials to learn, interact, and complete all or a portion of a class while online at home.

password. A sequence of characters typed during a connection sequence to verify that a computer user requesting access is authorized to use a system. In order to verify that someone accessing the system should be allowed to access it, the password, which is known only to that person and to the system itself, is entered by the user to gain access to the system.

phishing. The process of deceiving a user of an account and getting them to reveal private information including passwords and personal data, which allows malicious and often criminal access to online accounts for banking, credit, and other types of information.

podcast. This term originally referred to a digital recording of a radio-type broadcast or similar program, made available on the internet for downloading, but has expanded to include video as well as audio. The word was originally derived from a combination of *iPod* (a trademarked device sold by Apple Computer) and *broadcasting*. Despite the source of the name, it has never been necessary to use an iPod, or any other form of portable media player, to make use of podcasts; the content can be accessed using any computer capable of playing media files.

print server. A dedicated electronic server that connects a printer to a network. This device enables users to print independently of the file server or a dedicated PC.

professional development. Professional training to improve and advance the knowledge, skills, and effectiveness of teachers for their own benefit and the benefit of their students.

project based learning (PBL). A classroom approach in which students engage in developing solutions to real-world problems by working together to develop techniques and solutions of their own design.

repair ticket (trouble ticket). Keeping accurate records is vital to maintaining an organized, responsible IT support department. Help desks and computer technicians must sufficiently document the equipment they service and the work they perform. All help desks and support service offices should track the work done on every piece of hardware they service.

router. On the internet, a router is an electronic device that determines the next network point to which a packet should be sent on its way toward its destination. The router is connected to at least two networks and decides which way to send each information packet based on its current understanding of the state of the networks it's connected to. A router is located at any gateway (where one network meets another), including each internet point-of-presence. A router is often included as part of a network switch.

rubric. A scoring tool that lists the criteria for a piece of work, basically, "what counts." For example, purpose, organization, details, voice, and mechanics are often what count in a piece of writing. A rubric also articulates gradations of quality for each criterion, from excellent to poor. In essence, a rubric is an evaluation mechanism for rating the quality of a product based on particular criteria.

Science, Technology, Engineering, Arts, & Math (STEAM). An educational approach that incorporates the arts into the familiar STEM model, which includes science, technology, engineering and mathematics. Adding the arts allows educators to expand the benefits of hands-on education and collaboration in many different imaginative ways through creativity.

server. A specialized computer that is attached to a network and is used to provide the other computers in the network with such services as access to files or shared peripherals, or the routing of email.

site license. A license that gives permission to use a software package on more than one system. Site licenses are a means of providing a bulk rate to companies and schools that want to use software on many computers. Organizations are often able to negotiate special pricing when programs are used widely throughout the organization.

social media. A variety of web-based technologies and applications make up the social media that enable people to interact with one another online. Some examples of social media sites and applications include Facebook, YouTube, Instagram, X (formerly Twitter), blogs, wikis, and other sites that have content based on participation and user-generated contributions.

spyware. A technology that gathers information about a person or organization without their knowledge. Spyware usually refers to software that is covertly downloaded into someone's computer to secretly gather information about the user. It can be the relatively harmless gathering of generic information about websites visited, or it can be malicious, such as the collecting of passwords. A similar type of program is *adware*, a hidden software program that transmits user information to advertisers via the internet. Both types of programs use up computer resources and network bandwidth and often cause problems for the computers on which they are running. Considerable time is spent by technical support staff who must remove this software from users' machines.

student information system (SIS). A software application used by educational organizations to manage student data. Student information systems provide capabilities for entering student test and other assessment scores through an electronic grade book, developing student schedules, tracking student attendance, and managing many other student-related data for easy access, backup, and analysis.

Synchronous online learning. Synchronous online learning is a mode of instruction where students and teachers interact in real-time through video conferencing, chat rooms, or other online communication tools.

tablet. A computer with a touchscreen display that operates from a battery and does not require a mouse or keyboard for input. These computers normally connect to the school network and internet using wireless connectivity.

technology plan. A document that represents the very best thinking regarding technology use. In education, this thinking accumulates from a variety of stakeholders in a variety of environments—school buildings, school districts, communities, states, and so forth. Technology planning is used to determine ways in which the curriculum and the learning process can be strengthened through the use of technology, and the technology plan sets forth a detailed course to follow to achieve these goals.

Trojan horse. A program that does something that users would not approve of if they knew about it. A virus is a particular type of Trojan horse, namely one that is able to spread to other programs. It is often a destructive program that masquerades as a benign one. For example, the user runs such a program, believing it has a useful function, when in fact it is designed to erase a hard drive.

troubleshooting. The process of systematically locating, diagnosing, and fixing problems concerning machinery, technical equipment, and other resources.

virus. A program or piece of code that is loaded onto your computer without your knowledge and runs against your wishes. Most viruses can replicate themselves and spread to other computers. All computer viruses are human-made. Anti-virus programs periodically check your computer system for the best-known types of viruses.

videoconferencing tools. Tools that allow users to connect through both video and audio to conduct meetings or create a shared learning environment for class sessions. Many video conferencing tools include additional capabilities to share screens, provide break-out meeting rooms, share whiteboard capabilities, and to record meeting sessions.

VoIP. An acronym for Voice over Internet Protocol, a category of hardware and software that allows people to use the internet as the medium for telephone calls by sending voice data in packets using IP rather than by traditional circuit transmissions over the public telephone network. One advantage of VoIP is that the telephone calls over the internet do not incur a surcharge beyond what the user is paying for internet access.

Wi-Fi. This registered trademark term refers to a wireless networking technology that uses radio waves to provide wireless high-speed internet and network connections. Wi-Fi works with no physical wired connection between sender and receiver by using radio frequency (RF) technology. The cornerstone of any wireless network is an access point (AP). An access point broadcasts a wireless signal that computers can detect and connect to. To connect to an access point and join a wireless network, computers and devices must be equipped with special wireless network adapters.

worm. A self-contained computer program able to spread functional copies of itself to other computer systems, usually via network connections. Unlike viruses, worms do not need to attach themselves to a host program in order to do damage.

INDEX